LOW RISK PROFITS IN HIGH RISK TIMES

LOW RISK PROFITS IN HIGH RISK TIMES

Robert Kinsman
Kinsman Associates, Inc.

DOW JONES-IRWIN
Homewood, Illinois   60430

ISBN 0-87094-379-0

Library of Congress Catalog Card No. 84–71125

Printed in the United States of America

1 2 3 4 5 6 7 8 9 0 K 2 1 0 9 8 7 6 5

A
Quick
Guide

This book contains information that is directed at both inexperienced and experienced investors. It is organized so that the two levels don't collide. Those readers with greater-than-average investment experience who are looking for new ways to profit in the roller coaster markets of the 1980s should read the Introduction and may then skip directly to my discussion of cycles in Chapter 5 for background. Chapter 6 begins my specific method for creating low-risk profits. (Chapter 9 on insurance might be old hat for you, too.)

Those less-experienced investors are best advised to start at the beginning and continue straight through.

All readers should note that the final section of the book contains specific tips and ideas that can be utilized at any time, regardless of market trends or your experience.

I wish you all comfortable and successful investing!

Robert Kinsman

Acknowledgments

The writing of any nonfiction book is rarely the work of just one person, no matter how many authors are listed on the jacket. This work in particular simply could not have been created without the help of several fine professionals.

First and foremost is my longtime friend and business associate, Jack Padrick, a true expert in the area of real estate and the law, whose advice, counsel, and hard work have aided immeasurably in producing this volume. The chapter on real estate was originally written by Jack in the form of articles for my "Low Risk Advisory Letter," and I am indebted to him for its fine perspective.

I could not have accomplished the research necessary for this book without the hours of effort and wide knowledge of the securities markets given by Rhonda Gilbert. I am very grateful for her assistance and abiding patience during the more than two years that I've spent writing this volume. She was ably assisted by my associate and computer "whiz,"

Holly Newman, who has also devoted much time under pressure to this effort. This is all the more remarkable considering the fact that she had to learn the securities world from scratch. I'm most appreciative.

Special thanks for the lending of his knowledge of stock options goes to my associate, Vince Garone. His is true expertise, and his help in preparing the discussion on options as hedges has been an extremely worthwhile contribution.

To the many other persons who assisted in the gathering of information, offering ideas, or providing typing and office support—especially CPA and friend Ben Vernazza and colleague Ella Shore, plus editors Karen Liberatore and Kathy Ceraso—my appreciation is indeed great.

R. K.

Contents

Part Two: Formulating a Strategy

Part Three: Fitting the Pieces

Introduction: Why Aim for Low-Risk Profits Now?

Very few investors will argue with the idea that you'll never succeed with investments if you don't keep what you make. But there are a few corollaries to that which might stir debate. "You'll never make enough to keep if you don't make it carefully," is one. "Protect *and* profit is the name of the game," is another. And, "win big invariably means lose big," is a third. Those concepts are at the heart of low-risk investing.

This book is about how to make your money make money—possibly large amounts of money. It will show how to reduce the risks in making that money in order to sleep well while profiting. More importantly, this book will both establish the framework and set out the steps for protecting your assets before you profit on them. Not following that order is like diving into the ocean not knowing how to swim and without a life jacket.

From reading this book, you should be able to tell at any time by a glance at a chart exactly what the risk level is in the stock market, the gold market, and the bond and money markets. You'll know from that glance in which markets to place your investment funds. And you'll discover what type of securities to buy at each stage of the markets' cycles.

You'll also know which type tax shelter will best fit your circumstances, whether you need a formal financial plan, and even whether foreign investments will make sense for you. And you'll have at your fingertips more than a score of practical tips on taxes and real property investing, plus much more.

Why *Now?*

Why aim for low-risk profits now? Now is the entry window for the last sixth of the 20th century—the era of future shock, the third wave of civilization, and the information revolution.

It's easy to see that these are high-risk times when more than twice the net worth of America's nine largest banks is owed to them by nations that can't pay it back now and probably never will and when the real interest rate on borrowed money (the stated rate minus inflation) has recently been at the highest level this century. (The second highest rate occurred just before the Great Depression of the 1930s.)

These are clearly high-risk times for investments when several prime examples of "widows and orphans" stocks among the utilities are knocked down 40 to 50 percent in a few weeks because the public attitude toward funding nuclear power plants changed. Meanwhile, the major stock market averages were hitting record highs from June to November 1983, but the OTC Industrials were falling 30 percent at the same time and among Value Line's 1700 stocks, fully 4 percent of those traded on the NYSE, 10 percent listed on the Amex, and 15 percent traded OTC plunged a disastrous 50 percent. The commodity market was doing even worse. In short, there's little doubt that investing money these days entails a high degree of risk, whether it comes from the markets themselves or from outside.

Since the risks to our money today are so great and widespread, a pertinent question must be, Why add to them by also making investments that are inherently risky? One possible reason is expectation of much greater returns to compensate for the higher risk. The idea is valid in theory, but the problem lies in the reality of the marketplace.

Drawbacks of Volatility

In the investment world, the standard definition of risk is volatility. The more volatile a stock is, the more it will rise relative to the market in climbing markets and the deeper it will fall, relatively, in declining markets. It's the latter fact that causes problems for investors. It's fine to have a highly volatile stock while it's rising, but if you don't sell close to the top, it will eat you alive on the way down.

Therefore, aiming for the best gains means buying the most volatile issues, but it also means that timing is critical and must be continually successful to achieve good gains over time. One bad loss can wipe out a lot of wins. This win big, lose big strategy is great while you're winning, but what if you need the capital while losing or just plain don't like to lose money, even on paper?

The fact is that investing in high-volatility issues does not produce consistently superior results. At best, it produces above-average results only in rising markets. The evidence, and it is copious, confirms that "win big" eventually "loses big" (or at least underperforms) unless timing is constantly accurate. But the penalty for timing failure is very large. That's the markets' reality.

Another concern about this "big move" strategy is that Wall Street likes it. The Street spends a lot of money carefully promoting the idea of winning big without promising anything, e.g., "thank you, blank blank" and "you look like you just heard from XY." What is not stated is that if you invest in volatile issues with them, you'll want to trade out after having bought in. That means increased expenses, perhaps substantially so. Somehow, increasing expenses doesn't seem the shortest route to increasing your profits. Commissions are certain. Your profits are not.

Low-Risk Investing

The other side of the risk coin is low risk. As suggested above, the price paid for investment return is risk. The more return you expect on any investment, the more risk you usually must take to achieve it.

Does it follow that if you wish to obtain low-risk profits, you must be satisfied with low profits? Not at all. There's a great deal of difference between low-risk *investing* and low-risk *investments*. It's much more than a matter of semantics.

Low-risk investing is an approach to obtaining a good return on money that I've developed and refined since 1979. It's both a strategic and tactical investing method.

Strategically, it begins in recognizing that most investors don't achieve returns that they are satisfied with, nor should they be satisfied with them. This occurs primarily because of three factors: (1) our high-risk markets are so dynamic as to cause frequent changes of direction, (2) errors of timing are easily made even without direction reversals, and (3) selection of the right stock or bond or precious metal for a given market trend is often missed, even if direction and timing are good.

There's no surefire way of always overcoming these investment blunders, but low-risk investing has the best chance going because it begins by admitting a heresy: All advisors and investors do make errors for the above reasons. None are immune. Ask any investor who's been in the markets for more than a couple of years.

With that point clear, steps can be taken to increase profits and defend against major damage to total investment holdings. My program's steps include:

1. Assess the risk in each *market* in which you might invest with as much precision as possible. Then, and only then, quantify the individual issue's risk. Buying a good stock in a bad market won't do much for your profits.

2. In determining when a market is a sound buy or sale, use only thoroughly proven indicators that have stood time tests. And, cross-check those indicators against each other. I'll introduce you to the 30-year track record of my Money Cycle Index and its interaction with the stock market's own trend indicators.

3. Don't think that *any* indicators can regularly pick market tops and bottoms. Instead, they should tell you what level of real risk the market has at any time.

4. To guard against those potential timing, selection, and directional errors we all make, direct all your investments toward one goal, not a hodgepodge of purposes. Viewing all investments in the context of one single portfolio will help aim in one direction.

5. In high interest rate times, hold an extensive portion of your portfolio in high interest bearing cash equivalents. High, certain yields will improve consistency of returns. Manage those items as actively as your growth investments, balancing the percent in each on the basis of growth market risk.

6. The timing problem with individual securities' purchases and sales can be greatly aided by purchasing lower volatility issues. Volatilities of 65–85 percent of the overall market will reduce your need for exact timing. If you're caught with a loss before getting out, better that it's half of a 20 percent loss than half of a 40 percent dive. The only appropriate time to increase volatility of your holdings is just after a new bull market is confirmed.

7. Patience is an incredibly valuable virture in investing. When combined with sound, low-risk timing, it allows you to let profits run and stand clear of bear markets until they're ready to turn.

When these steps are followed, you will find that the pressure of making continually right calls is notably reduced. Ego can then be submerged, and that's a valuable investment act in its own right. What's more, the reduced pressure permits study of several different markets for investment opportunities. This can further reduce portfolio risk, assuming a truly attractive market is found as an alternative. For example, the U.S. stock market does well only a good fraction of the time. From 1946 through 1983 that market rose in 26 of the 38 years. That's a 68.4 percent batting average. Of the stock market's 12 declining years, however, long-term bonds rose in 5 of those years, gold in another 3, and short-term interest rates climbed in the remaining 4. By considering all those markets an investor need not have faced any down market years in nearly four decades. Put the other way, staying with the stock market meant down years over 30 percent of the time.

Another reason that lowering investment risk need not mean accepting poor performance is because it strives for *consistency* of returns as well as adequacy. This means smaller swings in your returns from year to year. As long as your gains remain above the risk-free rate (measured by 3-month Treasury bills) over time you'll have achieved a goal that's more difficult than it sounds: beating the money market return year in and year out *without* much more risk.

According to performance measurer Lipper Analytical Services Corporation, during a representative period of generally rising stock prices and rising short-term money yields, namely the five year period ending December 31, 1981, the average money fund showed a 64.9 percent return versus an 84.5 percent average return for all other taxable mutual funds—some 415 of them. So, the average mutual fund manager only topped the average money market fund by about four percentage points per year but by definition took much greater risk and certainly put in a lot more effort. And, money fund consistency handily outpaced the other funds: not one down year in the money funds but two out of five down for the average mutual fund.

Now, these statistics don't prove anything. But they suggest a point that is proved in other ways. The idea of low-risk investing, if taken to an extreme of investing in only money market funds, can still produce respectable returns and certainly achieves consistency. Therefore, doesn't it follow that a combination of money fund and growth investing should be able to take the best attributes from each, even with moderate success in timing? That's low-risk investing in a nutshell.

When low-risk investing advantages are added up, an apt analogy is that we aim to hit numerous singles and doubles in the investment ballgame and use several special disciplines to squeeze out extra results, instead of either waiting for just minimum-risk walks or constantly swinging for home runs. Home runs may be more spectacular, but singles and doubles win more games.

Our goal is to match or exceed the stock market averages' returns over time, but do so with about half the risk.

Low-Risk Specifics

Subsequent chapters will show why the *rental cost* of money has a pronounced affect on the stock market but why money's *value* is a different measure, and why it has a greater affect on gold and real estate prices. We'll then see that this translates into a definite cycle, the one I call the "money cycle," and see how to measure it in order to make stock purchases when the risk is low but the profit potential is high. I'll explain use of a value/price indicator to make the best buys in precious metals and other tangible investments, and how to measure such an indicator. Then we'll learn how to fit those timing considerations into a technique that balances investments with your goals and protects against the predictive or market errors that all investors (and their advisors) make. Most important, this low-risk approach will be shown to be sufficiently comprehensive to remove most of the daily emotions from investment decisions, to allow egos to relax in the high probability of making good profits, and to allow you to sleep better with them over time.

Of course, nothing is certain in the investment world. Investing remains an art, with some scientific principles applied. Recognizing that, the low-risk methodology will be a most satisfying one for any investors who are accumulating capital, and want to hold onto it while making it grow. It's certainly the best and broadest approach to investing that I've been able to put together in more than 20 years as an investment professional.

Part One of the book looks at the basics underlying sound investing, and gives us a common ground on which to proceed.

R. K.

PART ONE

A
Common
Ground

1

The Money-Management Problem

A government that robs Peter to pay Paul
can always depend on the support of Paul.

George Bernard Shaw

Suppose someone told you back in early 1975 that for the good of certain segments of the population, such as the jobless 9 percent of the work force, the suffering business community, and those otherwise economically or socially disadvantaged, the value of all your dollars would have to be cut dramatically over the following few years. Would that have been all right with you? Impossible, you say? Who is that altruistic?

Yet that's almost exactly what government officials suggested they were going to do during those dark days a decade ago. Unfortunately, the facts weren't spelled out quite that precisely, and your permission certainly wasn't asked. There is also doubt that all the officials knew what was afoot.

In his State of the Union address in January 1975, President Ford said, "The State of the Union is not good. Millions of Americans are out of work. Recession and inflation are eroding the money of millions more. Prices are too high and sales are too low." He then proposed a two-

3

pronged plan to cut taxes while increasing energy-conservation measures. The ideas were taken up by the key government mandarins.

Federal Reserve Board Chairman Arthur Burns said in early February 1975 that the Federal Reserve System would continue "to expand at a *moderate* rate the supply of money and bank credit" [emphasis added].

House Ways and Means Committee Chairman, Democrat Al Ulman, outdid the president more than a third on taxes by proposing an $18 billion tax cut to stimulate the economy. In March President Ford said in response, "There's room for flexibility."

Recognizing an anticipated federal spending level of about $350 billion in fiscal 1975 to be capable of pushing the federal deficit the following year to $45 to $50 billion, Treasury Secretary William Simon said simply, "It's horrifying."

It all sounds familiar, doesn't it? All those suggested economic stimulations—the money growth, the tax cuts, and the deficit financing—came to pass, and then some. And amid those nicely chosen words and conservatively delineated phrases, all seemingly appropriate to the economic situation and certainly innocuous in sound, the systematic destruction of our money's buying power began anew.

The destruction wasn't recognized for awhile, and whether or not there was intent to wreck such havoc is debatable, at least in the case of some of the provocateurs. Certainly, it was the Federal Reserve Board that provided the fuel for the fire. The Carter administration gave both the real driving force and the coup de grace to the process.

The fact remains that the domestic buying power of the dollar was cut almost exactly *in half* between the end of 1974 and year-end 1982, as measured by the consumer price index (CPI). The country's greatest inflation in a century was accomplished by more than a 90 percent increase in the broad money supply, while the nation's output of goods and services rose less than 24 percent in real terms. It will come as no surprise to those seeking a doorstep at which to lay the blame to know that money is not created in Keokuk, Iowa. Figure 1–1 shows what was happening to money as the administration, Congress, and the Fed spoke in early 1975 and what has happened since.

Timing Inflation and Deflation

Still, as far as investors were concerned, this was only the tip of the iceberg. The era of 1975 to the present has been the first period in a half

FIGURE 1–1
M2 MONEY SUPPLY (percent growth year-on-year)

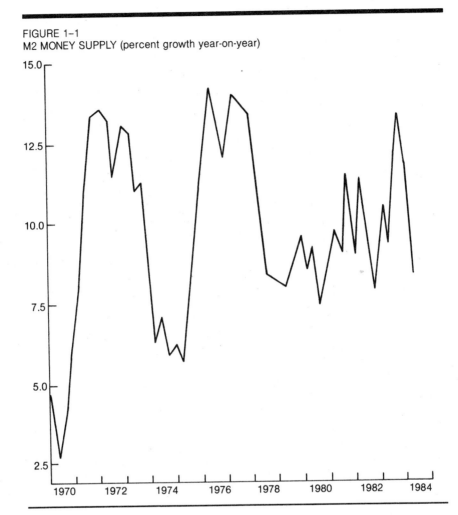

century in which both inflation *and* deflation have been *critical* to investment success.[1] What has been seen in this era is nothing less than a future shock surge of inflation followed by just as dramatic a slashing of it.

To see the sort of problem this climate creates for investors, imagine
that you were prescient enough to realize that the seeds of a 15 percent

---

[1] The previous inflation/deflation cycle, 1966–72, saw CPI inflation reach a peak just
over 6 percent in early 1970 and a bottom just under half that level in 1972. This pales in
comparison with the subsequent quadrupling of the rate by 1974, a cut to less than one
third of that peak by 1977, and the current era's 15.5 percent high in 1980 and plunge to one
quarter of that rate by mid-1983. With each cycle lasting five to six years, it was the magnitude of the changes that most affected investments.

inflation rate were being planted in those early days of 1975, as they were. What would you have invested in?

Gold, that prime inflation hedge, was 20 months—and about a 40 percent decline—away from its bear market *low*. Silver, another great inflation hedge, was not to make a significant move above its January 1975 level for 3½ years. Treasury bill yields were plunging like a rock and were 23 months away from their lows, thereby making money market investors less than ecstatic.

On the other hand, long-term bond prices were enjoying a spell that showed that even a stopped clock is still correct twice a day. Of course, one would have had to ignore the fact that inflation is the nemesis of bonds in order to participate in the next 2½ years of bond market profits.

The inveterate stock market watcher, who had survived two years of the worst punishment that market could offer and who, like the bond buyer, could ignore the worries about inflation, had the opportunity in 1975–76 to ride an enormous surge in stock prices for nearly two years.

All told, knowing about the incipient inflation in early 1975 could have been dangerous to your wealth for a nerve-rattling period. The investments that benefit from *deflationary* strategies were the ones to hold for the next two to three years. Winning in this economic cycle meant riding first the downswing in inflation, then an upturn that became an explosion. Finally, it was critical to catch the next downswing—all this in just seven years.

The heart of the investment matter, it seems, is not in knowing whether inflation or deflation will take place, but rather to be prepared for when and how and to what degree *either one* will occur. One year's inflation causes an inflation hedge to become a winner, and the next year's price rise causes disaster in that hedge: but the currency buys less each year.

That's the conundrum this volume addresses. It treats inflation and deflation as *equally critical* investment problems. Identifying the correct timing between them is the key objective. This is what permits winning in the new "swing" era, in which losing is a financial disaster.

It Comes Down to Debt

Naturally, there's more to this investment game than just timing investment moves between inflationary and deflationary environments.

Federal government officials and Congress, however well intended, have been principal destroyers of your money, but they have not done this by allowing inflation to soar and then lopping it off like a piece of salami. The government has also grabbed your money by going into debt, which has encouraged consumers, state and local governments, and corporations, to do the same. The result is that as a nation we have a staggering mountain of debt saddling our bloated money.

In March 1981 the aggregate debt in the United States, composed of all public, private sector, and personal debt, was estimated at about $4.3 trillion. A number of that magnitude, which then included only about $960 billion of U.S. federal debt, is almost impossible to imagine. It's so big that $4.3 trillion as a stack of $1,000 bills would be more than 325 miles high. But that's not the staggering part, nor am I even addressing foreign debt. At year-end 1983, conservative estimates put total debt in the United States in excess of $5.8 trillion. The interest on it, assuming it is as low as the average rate on U.S. government debt, 10.7 percent, amounts to the truly mind-wrenching number of $620 billion per year. I say *wrenching* because, although repayment of the total debt itself can be put off, repayment of interest cannot. As the old saw goes, "When you can't borrow the interest, you're broke." We're still borrowing all right, but much of that new debt is going to pay interest alone. For example, the estimated *interest* on the federal debt in fiscal 1983, $108 billion, was almost equal to the whole federal deficit the year before.

This is the latest and ultimately greatest money management problem: The interest bill on our total debt is now unmanageable. In 1983 alone the amount of aggregate debt interest paid (or borrowed to pay) was estimated at $100 billion *more than* the average M1 money supply! That's more than *four times* all the *currency* available in the country, and it's still growing.

There's an even more disturbing angle to this. Using the broadest definition of money calculated by the Federal Reserve Board, measure L, at year-end 1983, the interest on the nation's aggregate debt was taking about $1 in every $5 in existence![2] That truly sobering fact, coming from an estimate as rough as one of this magnitude must be, means that our financial situation is caught in a vice.

---

[2]This measure, "L," includes all short-term money instruments and deposits in the United States, plus marketable short-term Treasury obligations and Euro-dollar deposits held by U.S. residents.

If nothing changes, the steely reality of compound interest will bring our economy to its knees. Why must this be so? If the aggregate debt does not increase at all, and if the interest rate on it averages the same as its present level for only about 6½ years, we'll be paying nearly $1 of every $2.50 in existence (using measure L) for interest alone. Recalling the problems in funding the debt right now, you know that somewhere between here and there such a burden must become too great for the U.S. financial system.

One way of dealing with the problem would be to depreciate the currency at a rate greater than the rise in the interest cost. Unfortunately, that's just what the Washington visionaries did beginning in 1975. What about cutting the rate of debt formation way down or reducing interest rates? These steps are theoretically feasible, but to do that, we'd all first have to operate on a balanced budget, including the federal government. What's the chance of that? Of course, a flat reduction in outstanding debt would solve the repayment problem, but that can only be accomplished by surplus budget or debt collapse. The latter is usually described as an economic depression.

Interest rate reductions have marvelous potential, but the numbers work mightily against even a sizable interest rate cut being useful. Leaving out state, local, and corporate debt, even a modestly feasible one-year federal budget deficit of $150 billion equals about *one quarter* of our total debt's *annual* interest payments. So the average interest rate on the total debt would have to fall by more than one quarter from its present level to offset that one federal deficit. But if only *current* interest rates fell that far, they would affect only the rate on new or refinanced debt, not remaining outstanding debt. Current rates would have to fall by one quarter for a period longer than the average debt maturity. That's around four years for the federal government. If that happened, we would have offset that *one year's* federal deficit.

Finally, borrowing to pay the interest on our debt won't work as a real solution either, because it adds to total debt. Thus, all the methods for debt reduction are unacceptable in the long run. *They'll all work temporarily,* though, because they postpone the final day of reckoning. And that's the name of the 1980s economic game.

Therefore, the investor's critical money-management problem of the 1980s decade is recognizing this: Increasing debt and continued shrinking value of the dollar are the two greatest money destroyers. The ways in which the government alternately causes them and reacts to what it has wrought are the worst money-keeping problems to beat.

The New Real World

In a nutshell, winning at this game requires an investment approach that can handle both inflation and deflation turns, while keeping a watchful eye on the mushrooming debt interest cost. That's not a small order.

Finally, winning means doing it yourself in this game, too. Yet, that's where the rules have taken a nasty turn. During 1981 it was reliably reported that more than half the population was either directly or indirectly receiving an income check from the same government that was the prime mover in the money-destruction process. In the truest sense of the word, we've been co-opted.

It takes true individualism to win investment battles under these conditions, and that's what must be asserted. You're willing to advance that independence, or you wouldn't be reading this book.

To tackle the seemingly tough odds against investment success requires looking more closely at the commodity used to measure financial gains, investment results and, probably too often, some personal achievements: money itself. It may be surprising, but although most people know what money is, they don't really understand it.

Summary

In promoting money growth and deficit financing, the federal government has systematically destroyed the buying power of our currency. Everyone knows that. What is less well known is that the same government has reacted to that destruction process by periodically reversing it just as dramatically. This double-barreled strategy has caused the economic roller coaster of the past 15 years. It will continue to roll, due in part to the mountain of debt growing amidst us, the interest on which must be paid at an annual rate greater than the whole M1 money supply.

To win in the investment climate arising from the careening economy, you must be able correctly to anticipate the swings of both inflation and deflation, exercise strong independence of thought, and adopt an investment approach that keeps at bay the high risks to your capital. I call this simply low risk investing.

So You've Got Money?

2

Most things in life—autos, mistresses, cancer—
are (most) important to those who have them.
Money, in contrast, is equally important
to those who have it and those who don't.

John Kenneth Galbraith

Although everyone "knows" what money is, either instinctively or as a result of experience with it, coming up with a concise description of money is tricky because money is much more than cash. Consider the efforts of the Federal Reserve Board, the U.S. banks' central bank, which has been trying for years to come up with a precise definition of money so that it could tell how much is around and perhaps exercise some control over it.

Money Defined

Since 1978, the Fed has found it necessary to use three different definitions of the *basic* money supply, which it has lately called M1. Each definition (M1A, M1B, M1) included all the currency in circulation plus demand deposits at banking institutions. Each also had some variation on the amounts that should be included from checking, savings, NOW accounts, money market deposit accounts at banks/savings and loans, super-NOW accounts, ad infinitum. At one time the broader money supply had definitions of M1 through M5. Now, as noted in the Chapter 1, the Fed uses M1 through M3 plus L for its definitions of money.[1]

Perhaps for our purposes, as long as everyone understands money's basic nature, there's no need to define it further. Economist John Kenneth Galbraith offered that conclusion when he observed that the average person should consider money "nothing more or less than that he or she always thought it was—what is commonly offered or received for the purchase or sale of goods, services or other things."[2]

Unfortunately, that definition doesn't address investment of money, a point Galbraith might have thought of when he added to the above, "The forms of money and what determines its purchasing power are something else again."Indeed. Arcane definitions are one thing. How money is created and what money can do and how, are paramount matters.

To get to those points, we should first recognize that there are many aspects of money that are in nearly constant debate within the economics profession, including its best definition, the appropriateness of various rates of money growth, and how to effectively control it. We can leave those fights to the profession without fear of missing anything profound.

However, we must note three practical points of agreement. First, there is broad concurrence among economists that as the quantity of money increases relative to the output of goods and services it supports, conditions become increasingly ripe for prices to rise. In modern economies a price inflation inevitably occurs under these conditions, and this inflation is measured by several methods, the most popular of which is the Consumer Price Index. The converse is also true: As the quantity of money decreases, a deflation in the rate of growth of prices is probable.

Second, the way in which one defines or measures money does not seem to matter empirically in regard to the above broad rules. It does seem to matter some in the timing of events to follow. Finally, there is no disagreement about how money is created, a matter worth looking into in more detail.

---

[1]The exact current definitions of money supply are available in a Federal Reserve booklet, "What's All This about the Ms?" Federal Reserve Bank of New York, July 1983.

[2]John K. Galbraith, *Money: Whence It Came, Where It Went* (Boston: Houghton-Mifflin, 1975).

"Making" Money

Theory says that money is created by placing into public use the current medium of exchange at one or more financial-system entry levels. In the United States in the 1980s, this translates into placing of new dollars in bookkeeping form into the reserve accounts of the nation's banks.

The actual creation process is begun by the Federal Reserve Board's Federal Open Market Committee, which consists of the president of the New York Federal Reserve Bank, 4 of the other 11 Federal Reserve district bank presidents, and seven governors of the Federal Reserve Board. This Committee's job is carrying out the broad policy guidelines of the board itself, and this group decides at regular meetings (by phone when necessary) a bottom-line question: Should bank credit be expanded, reduced, or left alone? Money is created when the answer is to expand.

Creation is accomplished most directly when the Federal Open Market Committee directs its staff to enter the open market for federal obligations (the "money market" in Treasury bills, notes and bonds) to buy those obligations. This action can take a number of forms, including arrangement of customer and system repurchase agreements and direct purchases of Treasury coupon-bearing notes and bonds. The transaction form and size control the duration and magnitude of the Federal Reserve's impact on the money-creation process.

This impact actually occurs immediately after the Fed has bought these obligations, when it credits the sellers' bank accounts from its own credit balances. The recipient banks, which maintain reserve accounts with the Federal Reserve System, then find those accounts increased as a result of the Fed's transactions. The money-creation egg has at that point been fertilized, but no new money has yet been born. The banks must first loan the money out. When they do, new money appears in the system. Money has been created.

From this process came the name of our so-called fractional banking system. Banks are required to keep a specified fraction of their capital in those Federal Reserve accounts. When those accounts are increased in total, the banks' capital available for loans is automatically expanded.

At the beginning of 1984, the nation's banks were required to keep one eighth of their demand deposits in their reserve accounts with the Fed. For example, if the Fed then paid $1 billion of its credit for instruments in the money market and credited the same amount to the reserve accounts of a group of banks, $8 billion worth of new money could be created by loans within the banking system.

The moment this loan credit appears in a borrower's checking account, money has been created. That's how money is most readily placed into the system and how it begins to work.

Money and credit are also created by two other means that are implicit in the one just described:

1. The Fed constantly offers to loan money to member financial institutions at its prevailing discount rate. When utilized by the banking system, this borrowing creates reserves upon which the banks can build their loan pyramid. The Fed controls this credit source through changes in the discount rate itself.

2. The Fed also has the power to change the fraction of bank deposits that must be held as reserves, the so-called reserve requirement. Clearly, each time this rate is changed it provides more (or less) leverage behind each dollar of reserves. A 12 percent reserve requirement permits loans of eight + times the reserves.

Since the Monetary De-Control Act of 1980, reserve requirements have been cut from a maximum of 16¼ percent to a 1983 top of 12 percent, depending on type and amount of deposit. Final reductions were made in April 1984 for member banks. The act lowered requirements for member banks and imposed new requirements for nonmember institutions. So, even without buying one security in the open market or loaning $1 at the discount window, the Fed has increased money growth *potential* enormously over recent years.

Notice that no mention has yet been made of cash or currency, and the words *money* and *credit* have been used interchangeably. *Cash* and *currency*, the actual dollar bills and coins used in daily transactions, are synonymous, and they represent only one form of money—a rather minor one at that. Currency composes only about 30 percent of what the Fed now defines as M1 money supply and less than 5 percent of the L money definition. In fact, the cash/currency form of money comes into use only in person-to-person transactions. By far the greatest amount of money being transmitted around the country (and out of it) moves in credit form, and all money created shows up in bank accounts as bookkeeping entries, not as cash or currency.

Although *money* and *credit* are synonymous for the above discussion purposes, the terms have different meanings later in the money-use process, as when someone opens a credit account at a store. However, at the money genesis point, money first appears as a credit in a bank account, and that credit is counted as money by the Fed that moment.

These mechanical points clarify one of the common confusions about money: the printing of it as a cause of inflation. The actual printing of currency takes place at the National Bureau of Printing and Engraving in Washington, D.C., but the money-creation process, as described above, has nothing to do with printing. The difference is between money and currency. Only the modest part of money called currency is printed. The rest of it exists without ever touching a printing press.

What's more, currency is printed only when enough of it wears out, transaction levels require it, a denomination falls into short supply, or a new one is authorized. It is not *printed* just because the Fed buys some securities in the market and needs to hand money over to the seller. Accordingly, the idea that "printing too much money causes inflation" is just a shorthand way of saying that creating too much money causes inflation. Actual printing affects only 30 percent or so of the idea.

Money creation in our financial system begins with expansion of bank credit, extends through bank loans to a certain amount of currency printing, and results in our buying things with all money forms, including cash, checks, and credit cards.

The "Who Dunnit" Problem

The identification of the Federal Reserve Board and its Open Market Committee as the actual initiators of the U.S. money-creation process still leaves out one critical detail. Do these folks act alone in creating money?

As far as that question extends to the actual creation of money through bank credit expansion, the answer is yes. However, the Fed in no way operates in a vacuum, turning the money spigot on and off with abandon. Clearly, the Fed Board and its market operations people function in a real world of economic conditions, statistics and their interpretations, and political pressures. In short, they see, hear, and feel the socioeconomic circumstances around them and then act, not the other way around.

Because of this real-world interplay, Fed actions are often more reactionary than initiating, and it is accordingly often wrong to blame the Fed *alone* for taking monetary expansion or contraction steps. The Fed may rightfully be criticized for many things—such as carrying a given expansion or contraction process too far or misinterpreting certain economic conditions—but it rarely acts without an outside stimulus, usually one that has been shoved its way by a vacillating Congress or a criticizing administration.

This distinction in responsibility gives rise to the difference between monetary policy, which is clearly in the Fed's purview, and fiscal policy, which is the territory of Congress and the Administration. The former deals with credit expansion or contraction, and the latter is a matter of federal income and outgo. Since Congress and the administration have so often abdicated their fiscal responsibilities, Fed action in the monetary area has frequently been the only way to tackle the fiscal problem. Nowhere is this clearer than in the recent years' battles over the burgeoning federal deficits. Inability of Congress to come to grips with the spending-versus-tax increase problem has left the brunt of the matter in the Fed's hands. As a result, the Fed's choices have been far less than ideal.

This is by no means an attempt to absolve the Fed of blame for many of our economic problems, but realization of the circumstances under which it operates helps to lay the ultimate blame at the correct doorstep.

Money Destruction

If money is created by the relatively simple process of expanding bank credit, and if the act is directed by a handful of individuals irrespective of how they are driven to their decisions, how is money destroyed? Does the foregoing discussion imply that the same people who create it also destroy it? These are key questions for the 1980s because not in a half century was the monetary expansion process so dramatically reversed for as extended a period as it was from 1979 to 1982.

In the U.S. form of banking system, the money creators must also be the money destroyers because money is credit, and credit production must be a monopoly. Can you imagine the chaos if every bank, or even a group of banks, created its own money and credit? Under their defined duties as central bankers to both defend the currency and act as lenders of last resort, the Federal Reserve governors and operating units have the power to manufacture and eliminate money as they see necessary in any given economic climate.

However, it is doubtful that the money stewards, monopolistic as they may be, truly think of their efforts to control bank credit as actually causing money destruction. Still, the effect of their actions when they attempt to reduce credit outstanding is exactly that of destroying money. More precisely in this case, the opposite of money creation takes place. When the Federal Open Market Committee directs its staff to *sell* government securities in the market, the purchasing dealers and banks pay for them with reductions in their reserve accounts in the Federal Reserve System. Each dollar reduction in the respective banks' reserve accounts recently equated with an $8 reduction in allowable loans. Money is actually cut back in quantity.

The result of this destruction shows up in the same statistics as money growth. For example, the process negatively impacts such items as total Federal Reserve credit and nonborrowed bank reserves, just as money creation affects them positively. The difference is that the cutbacks show up in the *public spotlight* differently from the expansions. Money destruction is seen most clearly in *its result*—as personal and corporate loan defaults, bankruptcies, and lost jobs. In the banking crises of 1982–84, it was also seen as threatened sovereign (national) loan defaults and rescheduling demands. This involved more than a U.S. money problem, although much of the difficulty revolved around the dollars residing outside the United States known as Eurodollars.

Thus, in broad-brush terms, money expansion can be correctly seen as causing economic expansion, which at some excess level and under specific conditions becomes inflationary. Money contraction or destruction is seen as causing economic slowdowns, which, when carried further, cause the pain of job losses and bankruptcies. Small wonder that most people prefer money creation as long as it doesn't get out of hand. Unfortunately, in this era it has.

Monetary Seesaw

So, the Fed must frequently deal with the two resulting extremes of its credit policies—inflationary periods on one hand, wherein people and corporations rid themselves of rapidly depreciating money, and economic pain on the other hand, as debts are rapidly liquidated.

As the Fed pursues first one policy and then the other, the economy eventually (usually with a notable lag effect) responds. As either the inflationary or deflationary public pain thresholds are reached, the monetary policies are inevitably reversed. It's true that there are often smaller temporary policy reversals, but these are usually not much more than hesitations in longer-wave policies. Figure 2–1 shows the trend of money

FIGURE 2-1
M1 MONEY SUPPLY GROWTH VERSUS INFLATION TWO-YEAR LAGGED, 1960–84

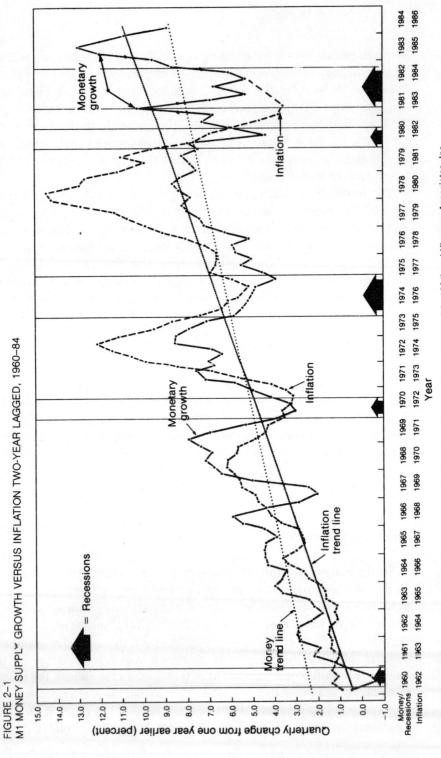

Source: Milton and Rose Friedman, *Tyranny of the Status Quo* (New York: Harcourt Brace Jovanovich, 1984) and Kinsman Associates, Inc.

growth and contraction along with a two-year lagged inflation rate and recessions since 1960. Notice first how recessions have followed sharp declines in money growth. Then notice that the frequency with which the up/down reversals occur has increased greatly in recent years. This provides a clear picture of the money management obstacle to be overcome.

Summary

Exact definitions of money might please economic purists but are unnecessary for developing the right basis for a workable investment approach. We do need to know, however, that growth in a quantity of money creates conditions in which the general level of prices in the economy increases, and vice versa. We know this is caused by actions of the Federal Reserve Board, not by any other governmental body, although Congress and the administration can create conditions that push the Fed in one direction or another. These directional changes emanating from the Fed are the pinpointed causes of our economic roller coaster.

Now we're prepared to look at how the true value of money is determined and, most important, what that means to investments.

3

Making Money Worth Something

Never invest your money in anything that eats or needs repairing.

Billy Rose

Consider this proposition: The true value of any money is measured only in terms of the goods and services it will purchase. Hardly revolutionary, is it? Yet, from this modest fact spring direct explanations for several important uses of money. For example, compare buying goods with investing during inflationary periods.

How Much Money Buys

As one unit of paper currency buys fewer things during inflation, most people notice two points: The money buys less, and the things it buys are going up in terms of the unit price of the paper currency. Most often the recognition is in terms of the prices of the goods or services increasing; but the true other side of the coin is that the value of the money is falling, which is more significant to investors than to consumers.

If $100 bought four quality tires one year, three tires the next year, two the following, and one the fourth, the price of each tire would have gone from $25 to $100. That's the consumer's way of seeing it, but the price of the money would have dropped from $100 = 4 (tires) to $100 = 1, a fall of three units in four. The money would have lost 75 percent of its value over those four years in terms of tires. At the same time, it would have lost a considerable (but probably unequal) percentage of its rail ticket, rhubarb, and Hershey Bar value, too.

Therefore, a useful definition of *money value* is the number of units of goods and services money buys. The *inflation rate* is the other side of the coin; it is the rate at which the prices of goods and services are rising.

This falling value of money has an instant effect on investors. It spurs them to rid themselves of a losing investment and to acquire something that holds value at a minimum and increases in value if at all possible. This is not the same as buying to consume something before it goes up in price, although the effect is the same in decreasing the amount of currency held. The investor looks first at loss avoidance, then profitability. The consumer looks at buying for the best value before prices increase.

These seemingly insignificant, but greatly disparate differences in views of inflation cause knowledgeable investors to realize a key fact: Short of a German-style hyperinflation, wherein even the appreciation from an inflation hedge is not worth having if it's paid in currency, *any investment vehicle that provides a total return that exceeds the investor's own currency price loss rate is worth having, no matter how it is paid to the investor.* A definition of *total return* is income produced plus any price appreciation.

Total Return

Intelligent investors know that inflationary periods don't require commitment of all their capital, or necessarily even a good percentage of it, to so-called inflation-hedge assets. They also know that their total investment capital should be committed to production of total returns exceeding that of inflation. The difference between these two ideas is a fine, but important, line. The former rejects selection of only appreciating assets. The latter correctly suggests that the asset need not appreciate in itself but rather that the total return on it must exceed the inflation rate.

That's a very important distinction, and one that far too many amateur investors overlook during inflationary surges. Amateurs believed that property—gold, silver, diamonds, antiques, and so on—were the true inflation hedges but that Treasury bills and notes or bank CDs were not. That's essentially the consumer's approach to inflation: Buy something ahead of the rise in price. In these cases, investors just planned to hold the asset for later resale rather than to consume it. The approach is the same—a price hedge.

However, the focus should not be on price alone. It should be on *total return*. Price hedges achieve only the commitment of large sums to essentially illiquid or very volatile assets or "things," which if not properly disposed of before a disinflationary period sets in, will wipe out the whole inflation hedge advantage and create real capital losses. Thousands of first-time inflation hedgers discoverd this with disastrous effects in the 1979–1981 period. In fact, it's quite probable that more money was lost trying to beat inflation during that period than was lost to inflation itself.

Instead, had investors realized that *total return* is what matters, not just price, they would have been able to sleep better during the violent price swings of their hedge assets. Furthermore, they would actually have been increasing their cash flow as the hedge assets declined in price during the disinflation. The reason is that they could also have extensively used short-term money market and fixed-income assets to provide a balance with standard inflation hedges in an investment portfolio.

As Figure 3–1 clearly shows, 91-day Treasury bill average yields matched the inflation rate over this decade remarkably well. They proved to be excellent inflation hedges as well as highly liquid investments. Similar performances were shown by money market funds and even Treasury notes with maturities up to two years. In short, these cash equivalents can accomplish much during inflationary periods, and they have the enormous advantage of not having to be sold when disinflation sets in.

Accordingly, an important money concept is thinking about inflation not as a consumer trying only to beat price but rather as an investor fighting currency depreciation by insisting that your capital's total return exceed inflation. Further, once the advantage of inflation protection via total return on assets is recognized, other benefits accrue.

Suppose you had $100,000 total capital available for investment and were satisfied that your currency depreciation rate would be approxi-

FIGURE 3–1
SHORT-TERM INTEREST RATES AND THE CPI

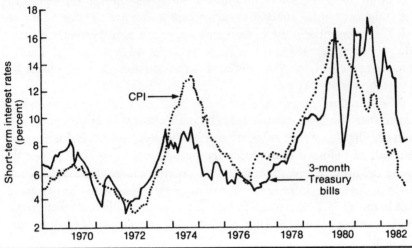

mately 10 percent in the next year. Your capital would be worth—in the price of goods and services it could buy after 12 months—only $90,000, unless you did something about it. Assume that your practical action choices to beat that loss were:

1. To speculate in commodity futures.
2. To buy a so-called appreciating asset, such as gold.
3. To buy a Treasury bill that would have a net return of 9 percent in 12 months.
4. To use the money for a down payment on a piece of income property that was anticipated to appreciate 12 percent to 14 percent in price in the next year but had a negative cash flow.

With tax-free funds, your choices would be nicely laid out.

Although your temperament and understanding of the various markets represented would and should influence your choice, despite the previous discussion, your *least*-likely choice would probably be the 9 percent T bill, since the T bill guarantees a return of less than your assumed 10 percent currency loss. Your real return (nominal return minus inflation) would be − 1 percent.

In fact, the T bill might well be an excellent choice for a sizable segment of your capital. First, it would fulfill a very large (9/10) part of your currency value loss requirement over the following 12 months, and it would do so on a guaranteed basis. Second, even if your total capital were invested in the T bill, the 1 percent loss in currency value remaining could be ignored in practical terms. If a 1 percent currency price loss were taken every year and compounded, it would require 72 years for the money to depreciate by one half.[1] Then too, if the T bill were purchased with a significant portion of available capital, you would be taking relatively low average risk on investment of the total capital. All other things being equal, this is desirable.

On the negative side of the ledger is the increased percentage of return on the balance not invested in the T bill necessary to fully beat the currency depreciation. After investing a large amount of the capital, say 80 percent, in the T bill at 9 percent, you would need to achieve a 14 percent return on the balance to equal the overall 10 percent currency loss. In numbers: $80,000 × 9% = $7,200. The $10,00 buying power loss minus $7,200 = $2,800 needed. What return on the remaining $20,000 to be invested equals $2,800? The answer is 14 percent. Achieving this return could be difficult or could require more risk than one might wish to take on even the $20,000 segment.

A better approach is to survey the markets to determine what other investments can earn *without great risk* over the next year in a 9 percent T bill world. Assume you located an acceptable investment that carried some moderate risk, had a fixed reutrn of 12 perent, and also matured in one year. A pair of simultaneous equations shows the balance between the two investments needed to achieve a 10 percent *average* return:

$$0.09x + 0.12y = 10,000$$

where

$$y = 100,000 - x$$

Substituting

$$0.09x + 12,000 - 0.12x = 10,000$$
$$0.03x = 2,000$$
$$x = 66,666$$

---

[1]To determine an "acceptable" loss in capital buying power, I use the following formula: During periods when I expect inflation to exceed 5 percent per year, I strive for a minimum 3 percent per year *real* return after inflation (the real total return) and after taxes. However, recognizing that this isn't always possible, for planning purposes I assume that persons will live to be 85 years old, and I subtract the investor's present age from 85 and divide the result into 72. This determines the maximum annually compounded postinflation *loss* that's acceptable if the capital's purchasing power is not to decline below half its current value by age 85. Naturally, I attempt to exceed that as much as practicable under acceptable risk parameters. See Chapter 4 for further details.

So, two thirds of the capital could be invested in the T bill and one third in the 12 percent item to offset the 10 percent currency depreciation in one year. If that 12 percent yield vehicle were relatively low in risk, you'd have matched inflation with almost no market concerns at all.

The investment decision process is virtually never this simple, and taxes have been left out of the equation; but the numbers have worked on a total-return basis versus our inflation requirement. No attempt has been made to beat inflation, but so far only to tie. Some growth is also required, a point we'll get to shortly.

More benefits are gained by this approach. Focusing on an asset's total return as a means of matching inflation and seeing that such returns can be calculated quite precisely give us more to deal with than just hoping for a good gain. It shows that investment selection should include a real consideration of risk. Or, put another way, this approach forces one to look at the matter of risk because it starts with the lowest risk item (T bills) and works higher. Finally, it combines the considerations of total return with risk management in such a way as to actually be an elementary exercise in true portfolio management. That's quite a lot to get out of the simple idea that investors should look at money differently from consumers during inflationary periods. This fact is an important base upon which a sound approach to the markets and portfolio-management success can grow.

Notice, however, that the foregoing has focused on the interest income return on such assets as T bills, whereas price was dealt with earlier as a separate function. Yet, the concept of total return requires that both price and income be combined.

To win in the inflation battle at something less than hyperinflation rates, it doesn't matter which component provides the bulk of total return, as long as one isn't pressed into taking inordinate risks by expecting either component to make up all the return and losing capital as a result. There's one investment that offers practical proof of the two interchangeable aspects of total return.

The high interest rates of 1980–82 spawned an important variant on fixed-income securities, the "zero coupon" note or bond. "Zeros" are nothing more than bonds or notes that have had their interest coupons removed, thereby eliminating fixed-interest payments. In this process, the interest is converted to capital appreciation potential through a cut in the offered price to investors. Like Treasury bills, zeros are priced by the offering companies and their underwriters by reducing the price to the current market's level for the appropriate quality of issuer and the maturity of the issue. The difference between the issue price and the maturity price of par (100) is the discount. It is the equivalent of the interest due at current rates over the life of the note or bond.

Thus interest payments are converted into potential price appreciation through the simple device of a price discount, a fact making it absolutely clear that the price of a security and the interest return on it are interchangeable functions of its total return.

Now let's put aside the total return idea for a bit and look more closely at the concept of a portfolio and its balance. In my experience, the whole idea of achieving portfolio balance is too often ignored instead of being used to obtain an extra measure from the investments. Rather than arranging their investments in a portfolio to achieve a given goal, most investors just try to make money and forget about the methodology. To a degree, that's understandable. Working with multiple facets of a portfolio requires more effort and knowledge than just acquiring assets for either gains or income and ignoring how well they're pulling together or what risks go along with them. It's true that if you make *enough* money, most financial problems can be sorted out later; but it's just as true that very few investors will ever make that much, and they usually stack the odds against themselves in trying.

Setting up the proper investment portfolio allows you to shift the money-making odds as far in your favor as possible. That's largely achieved through making *all* your investments work toward your goal(s) while assuming the overall risk level that's most comfortable for you.

Why Consider a Proper Portfolio?

It's easy to think of a portfolio as *any* list of securities belonging to one person or legal entity. That's precisely what most investors do think of, if indeed they ever get around to thinking about that list as a portfolio at all, and the list usually includes only stocks and bonds. Yet, such items as three-year CDs, tax-deferred annuities, and a bag of silver coins must fit somewhere. These items are part of a total investment picture (portfolio) whether or not you think about them in that way. Not organizing all of them to point in one direction usually causes them to work partially against each other. That creates something of an "investment stew"—a brewing conglomeration of items that can't financially blend well unless it has a robust central theme.

A proper portfolio has three qualities: organization/direction, risk control, and manageability.

1. A proper portfolio takes into account all your liquid financial assets and organizes them toward one or more compatible goals.

2. A sound investment portfolio should do what the investor wishes with regard to the risk in its components. It's one thing to organize a diverse group of investments toward a goal and quite another matter to be comfortable with the risk taken with them. That risk is usually evidenced by the volatility of the individual investments and that of the overall portfolio. Much can be done to tame this risk while still pointing the portfolio toward the right goal. Ignoring overall portfolio risk often leads to a high level of personal discomfort and worry, which is unnecessary when a portfolio is properly designed.

3. So obvious that it is often overlooked is the quality of manageability. The portfolio must be changeable as investment or personal conditions change. It should not be so deeply locked into long-term commitments that its sails can't be trimmed in times of tight money or high inflation or adjusted to a booming stock market. It must also allow for personal need or goal changes, such as approaching retirement or loss of the family breadwinner.

All of these portfolio qualities are obvious needs when one stops to consider them, but many people fail to do so. I've seen numerous investment failures and goal shortfalls that were traceable to a failure to address these simple qualities. Lack of attention to these points is one of the greatest destroyers of wealth, albeit a most insipid one. Some of the money lost in this way isn't lost in the tax-deductible sense; it's just never made. Since it's not there when it should be, that's virtually the same thing as having been lost in the market.

Setting Up a Proper Portfolio

To set up a proper portfolio, first divide the portfolio into functional segments. Three segments are sufficient: cash equivalents, growth, and protection.

1. Cash equivalents are, in the strictest terms, securities that produce income and have maturities from one day up to a year's time. They include Treasury bills, commercial paper, bankers' acceptances, money market funds, money market deposit accounts, and all other short-term, financial institution paper.

A subcategory of this segment is fixed-income financial paper, which has maturities from one to three or four years and is properly called a

note. This intermediate-term paper, if it is of high grade, can serve a most useful function in the interest rate cycle and is not usually acquired for growth of capital invested in it (although it can be). It can quickly be turned into cash, and has only moderate risk as to price. The U.S. Treasury note is the most useful form of this paper.

2. The growth segment is composed of any asset that is purchased for growth of capital. The usual types are common stocks and some tangible assets with varying degrees of liquidity, ranging from platinum to gold at pertinent points in their cycle. However, longer-term notes and bonds (over about five years' maturity) should properly be included here also. Inflation has made long-term fixed income paper a trading vehicle since its price and buying power is constantly eroded. Bond purchases should be timed for capital growth and then sold, not held for income.

3. The protection category includes precious metals for asset hedging during times of rising secular financial liquidity. (The most recent period dates from about the mid-1960s on, although it can be argued that this era began in the mid-1940s.) Also included are long-term bonds, but only in eras of *declining* system liquidity (e.g., the 1930s). Life insurance can be included here in the broadest sense of the protection concept. Since it doesn't have the usual portfolio-inclusion attribute of a regular market in which to buy or sell identical units, life insurance is excluded from the balancing discussion below (it will be addressed in the chapter on protection).

Viewing an investment portfolio in terms of the above broad segments can make it possible to assign duties to each segment for achieving any one or more of the wealth-accumulation goals noted in the next chapter. For example, those concentrating on growth of net worth will give greatest attention to the growth portfolio segment. Some of these growth vehicles should stress maximum *after tax* returns because the wealth stages that we'll identify and which prioritize net worth growth also stress tax-related investments. In many cases these portfolios' cash equivalents should also be paying tax-deferred (or exempt) returns insofar as possible.

The same kinds of considerations apply to investors seeking maximum income after retirement. The three portfolio segments can readily adapt to a weighting in that direction without eliminating any category.

In other words, this portfolio-division concept dovetails with my upcoming wealth-accumulation ideas and permits varying degrees of investment concentration as individual circumstances require. It will meet the first test of any fresh idea: It's adaptable without requiring numerous exceptions.

The proper portfolio concept is discussed in greater detail in Chapter 7. Before that, we must develop a personal strategic foundation.

Summary

Keep in mind these important definitions about money in general:

Money value is the number of units of goods/services money buys at a given time.

Inflation rate is the rate at which prices of goods/services are rising.

About investments:

Total return is the interest rate on a security plus any price change.

Real interest rate is the interest rate minus the inflation rate.

Real total return is the interest rate plus any price change minus the inflation rate.

The first two definitions are measures of money that affect how investments perform. The second group consists of direct measures of the performance itself.

Achieving a good *total return* should be the first investment objective. A satisfactory *real total return* is the ultimate objective, even though it is difficult to achieve at relatively high rates of inflation. This is especially true on an aftertax basis.

The simple idea of beating inflation with investments gives rise not only to the concept of total return but also to the concept of the portfolio, where more than one investment is combined to achieve that which one cannot do alone. The portfolio is critical to investment success in the 80s: the high risk times and plethora of investment vehicles demand risk-controlled organization and manageability.

PART TWO

Formulating
a Strategy

Planning Is a Pain

4

I never think of the future.
It comes soon enough.

Albert Einstein

I know very few people who like to plan for the future, and many who will go to great lengths to avoid it. In our one-day-at-a-time era, whole lifetimes that are unplanned aren't uncommon. In the financial world this usually spells disaster because making correct investments requires frequent estimates of the future. For those whose basic attitude is summed up by "planning is a pain," this chapter addresses a basic need.

Here's the problem. A person who is serious about financial planning must at least take into account (1) the bulk of the 5,100-plus page Internal Revenue Code; (2) the key legal matters concerning wills, estates, and trusts; and (3) the pros and cons of scores of financial vehicles ranging from stocks to investment property and from insurance to tax shelters.

33

With this in mind, the person must subject his or her current finances to extensive number crunching, probably with the aid of a computer, and apply several years' experience in markets to the result. All this in order to create a sound, long-range financial plan.

Given this scope of the problem, two steps must be taken to deal with it. We must identify those readers whose financial affairs are sufficiently complex as to clearly require outside professional assistance. Also, we must provide an investment framework that is useful to investors who don't need that help as well as those who do. Let's determine your true needs first.

Do You Need a Full Financial Plan?

The following list of questions focuses on several key aspects of financial planning and is designed to help you determine your financial planning needs. If you answer *no* to more than half of the questions, you probably *do need* a formal financial plan. Positive answers are normal for the average investor of moderate means who does *not need* a full plan. For those queries marked with an asterisk, negative answers are especially indicative of the person or family who should contact a financial planner soon. On question 21, the answer for the person who should seriously consider a formal plan will be "appropriate." Yes answers to questions 2, 3, and 7–11 provide the first cut: A formal plan is probably *not* required.

All answers should also be used to identify specific financial areas that might need greater attention. For example, negative answers on insurance with a majority of positive answers elsewhere might mean you should just consult an insurance specialist. Many negative answers on the estate points covered in questions 22 through 26 could mean that an estate planner would be an appropriate contact for you, without suggesting that you need a more formal plan.[1]

In any case, results on the questions won't affect the importance of the balance of this chapter, which addresses the proper fit of investments into your total financial picture and is designed to improve your financial success probability either with or without a formal plan.

---

[1]Further reading on the subject of financial planning could well be appropriate if your answers approach an even yes-no split. A comprehensive book in this field is Hallman & Rosenbloom's *Personal Financial Planning*, 3d ed. (New York: McGraw Hill, 1983).

FINANCIAL PLAN NEEDS

**(More negative than positive answers suggest the need
for a formal financial plan. Asterisked questions
are most important.)**

General

*1. Have you set out your financial objectives for the years up to your retirement in specific terms (other than to make as much money as possible)?

*2. Is your current family income under $50,000 annually?

*3. Is your present net worth, excluding your home, less than $200,000?

Insurance

*4. Do you know whether you have enough or too much life insurance?

5. Do you have only term life insurance, or if you have loan value (cash value) life insurance, have you made plans to invest the cash available?

6. Do you have disability insurance, and is it adequate for total and permanent disability?

Investments

*7. Are the size and variety of your investments too small for them to be treated as a portfolio?

*8. Are your liquid investments worth less than $150,000?

*9. Do your liquid investments consist of fewer than five different types of investments (e.g., stocks, bonds, precious metals, CDs, tax shelters)?

10. Are your investments prepared for economic (a) prosperity, (b) recession, (c) depression?

11. If you own common stocks or stock mutual funds, are they meeting the objectives for which you bought them?

Retirement

*12. Do you know how much after tax income you'll want after retirement

a. While both you and your spouse are alive?

b. For a surviving spouse?

*13. Do you know how you'll achieve that income?

*14. If you are nearing retirement and will have pension or profit sharing funds available at that time, have you determined how you'll receive those funds (in a lump sum or as an annuity)?

*15. Do you know what the tax consequences of that form of retirement plan receipt are and what to do to minimize them?

*16. Will you be *free from* special funding requirements in the next 10 years, such as children's education, extensive travel, elderly parent care?

*17. If you do have such requirements, have you developed a funding plan for them?

Tax and Estate Matters

*18. Do you know into what top state and federal tax brackets you and your spouse fall?

*19. If your combined tax bracket is over 40 percent, are you investing for tax-free or tax-deferred income?

*20. Have you invested in tax shelters and, if so, has there been a coordinated plan for doing so?

*21. Would it be appropriate or inappropriate for you to consider most of the following tax-planning strategies:

    a. Buying municipal bonds?
    b. Making added tax-sheltered investments?
    c. Giving long-term capital gain property to charity?
    d. Making gifts of income-producing investments?
    e. Using charitable remainder trusts or "Clifford"-type trusts?

*22. Do you and your spouse have wills?

23. Do you know how large your estate is in the following forms:

    a. Gross, for federal estate tax purposes?
    b. Probate estate?
    c. "Net" estate going to heirs?

24. Can your estate meet its liquidity needs?

25. Are you and/or your spouse employed in work *other than* your own closely held business?

26. If not, have you let plans go unformulated for continuance or disposal of the business after death?

With your planning needs now broadly identified by answers to the above queries, we are ready to develop an asset-use strategy—a financial deployment plan—that can accomplish your financial goals throughout life. If a formal financial plan was indicated in your answers to the foregoing questions, the following strategy will act as the framework for it. If no plan is now required, this approach to asset deployment will substitute for one until your situation develops more precise questions and problems that require outside help.

Investment Framework

Our investment framework is comprised of three interrelated notions. The first is the wealth-accumulation stage, one of four financial goals to which I've rather arbitrarily attached certain age categories (See Table 4–1.)

Since the ages matter less than the concept embodied in the titles of the stages, age specifications may well be violated by individual circumstances. The successful entrepreneur who makes a million dollars before age 40 may suddenly find that preretirement money-handling methods are more appropriate than any further accumulation, even though retirement is not expected soon.

The average retired family in high-inflation periods may find that some preretirement ideas will continue to be important because financial ends just won't meet any other way. In fact, there are some accumulation concepts in all stages because of inflation, thus, the stages are not precise demarcation points. Note also that the retirement stage does not require *complete* dependence on capital. It may include any amount of employment short of principal reliance on work.

Next, in broad brush, there are five comprehensive categories of asset use that are important *in each* of these wealth stages. They also overlap, but are the most useful general phylums with which to work. They are

TABLE 4–1
WEALTH STAGES

Stage	Name	Appropriate Age
I	Early acquisition	30–45
II	Prime accumulation	45–55
III	Preretirement	55–60/65
IV	Retirement	Any age during which one's principal reliance is on capital rather than employment.

TABLE 4-2
INVESTMENT VEHICLES BY USE CATEGORY

Use Category	Investment Vehicle
Cash accumulation	Money market funds, savings accounts, and CDs.
Net worth growth	Employee-deferred compensation (including stock options and personal retirement plans) plus common stocks, real property, and other nondepreciating assets held long term.
Protection	Life insurance. Precious metals.
Tax-related investments	Municipal securities, tax-deferred insurance, real estate limited partnerships, at-risk tax shelters.
Income production	Money market funds and related bank accounts; bills, notes, and bonds; income programs in real estate, oil, and gas.

shown in the left column of Table 4-2. Think of these as the types of jobs a given asset might be asked to perform. In the right column are the investment vehicles that are typical of each.

The above list is not intended to be comprehensive as to all investment vehicles that fall within each category, but rather stresses the most important in each. The list should be read in the sense that when your wealth stage calls for emphasis on a given use category, the investment vehicles listed for it should be those on which you will concentrate.

The term *cash equivalents* will appear throughout the later sections of this volume, and this term is used somewhat differently from the selective emphasis on cash accumulation above. Cash equivalents constitute a *portfolio segment* of liquid investments in the money market, such as money market funds, Treasury bills and notes, and commercial paper. Cash accumulation is the process of acquiring cash items for eventual redeployment. So, holding cash equivalents as part of a portfolio strategy in dealing with certain market conditions is quite a different idea from emphasizing cash accumulation in early wealth-building years. The temporary result of utilizing either of the two may be the same—a relatively high proportion of total investment assets in cash-equivalent items—but the reasons for doing so are different.

Now we can combine Tables 4-1 and 4-2 to prioritize investments in each wealth stage.The numerical rank 1 through 3 that precedes each category in Table 4-3 suggests the relative importance that should be attached to it at each stage. The absence of a category in a stage does not mean it's unimportant, but rather that it's not usually a prime objective in that stage. Emphasis means investing should be concentrated in that type of vehicle, not just in holding previously acquired items.

TABLE 4–3
ASSET USE EMPHASIS BY WEALTH STAGE

Stage	Use Emphasis
Early acquisition (age 30–45 years)	1—Cash accumulation 1—Protection 1—Net worth growth 2—Tax related
Prime accumulation (age 45–55)	1—Net worth growth 1—Tax related 2—Protection 3—Cash accumulation
Preretirement (age 55–65)	1—Net worth growth 1—Tax related 2—Protection
Retirement	1—Income production 2—Tax related 2—Net worth growth

Of the stages, the first is the most flexible, and the latter two are the most susceptible to special personal circumstances. The first stage should also vary somewhat between its early years and the 40-plus era, in that accumulating cash is undertaken only when one is lacking it to make investments with adequate diversification or size, as in a portfolio of stocks or a down payment on property. Cash accumulation could be omitted altogether from the emphasis list because it's obvious, but is included as a reminder that it's necessary. By the second wealth stage, cash accumulation should never be an end in its own right but always a way station to a better use objective.

In Table 4–3, protection is listed in the first two wealth stages because these are the times such items as life insurance and precious metals as ultimate disaster hedges can be acquired most cheaply. Life insurance is there because it's often aged-priced, and precious metals because the acquisition can be done at leisure in weak markets (presumably) rather than in the midst of a crisis. Persons lacking adequate coverage in later years may simply have to use other assets to buy this protection at higher costs.

Probably the key point that the table makes is that producing growth of net worth is a most important aspect of all stages, but it is a top priority in the prime and preretirement periods. This is simply another way of saying that if you are to rely on your capital later, you had better accumulate as much of it as soon as possible, both through directing investments toward its growth and through combatting the taxes that take it away from you.

Of course, in a very real sense, this entire book is about how to increase net worth/capital. But it is in the two middle-wealth stages that special emphasis must be placed on it if one is to avoid capital adequacy problems later.

A second aspect to the capital growth matter is often overlooked or minimized: From the standpoint of maximizing capital, it is clearly more beneficial not to filter it through the IRS in the process. Consequently, earning taxable income as a means of generating capital is the worst way to go about it. Letting your capital be taxed while it's in the growth mode is also undesirable. Tax concerns lead to placing capital growth-planning emphasis on the many forms of *deferred compensation and retirement plans* while you are employed and on long-term capital gains for capital growth outside the plans. The tax-related category is important in all stages, even the first.

There is no magic in this formulation of investment emphasis by wealth-accumulation stage, any more than there is in the accumulation stages themselves. The table's purpose is simply to point out which asset-use categories should be emphasized in each stage of wealth accumulation. For example, it should be clear that income production *as a goal* is probably a misuse of assets prior to retirement years. The portfolio chapter will explain some exceptions to this guide, but they will be made with tax considerations in mind.

Net worth growth and tax-related categories should be considered together: They're given equal weight in each stage. Indeed, only three actual investment vehicles are suggested under net worth growth. The others listed are actually forms of tax-deferred capital accumulation.

At this point see where you personally fall in the wealth stages and which types of investment vehicles/concepts you should be emphasizing. Then look at your own investment picture and see whether or not it matches. Where it doesn't match, earmark those investments for reconsideration. Are you emphasizing income too early? Are you giving enough consideration to tax-deferral vehicles? Do you have protection of your assets against both death and inflation? Are you ignoring capital growth in your early retirement years?

If the answers to these questions reveal that your broad investment emphasis is out of line with that suggested (assuming you don't have good reasons for being atypical), some serious thought should be given to restructuring. A financial planner, CPA, investment advisor, or broker may still need to be consulted in reshaping your plans.

Investment Suitability

Investors vary temperamentally, sometimes dramatically so. Nowhere does this difference show up more than in the type of investments with which they are comfortable. Some investors can deal with almost any type, from high-flyer stocks with unknown names to obscure oil and gas drilling partnerships. Others find that just knowing that the price of an investment might change tomorrow is enough to make them nervous.

The best advice on this point is the simplest: Know yourself. There is no substitute for understanding exactly how comfortable you feel with certain types of investments, be they common stocks or real estate or long-term bonds or R&D limited partnerships. Once you know your comfort levels, don't violate them. If common stocks bother you, don't invest in them just because they're the new darlings of the cocktail circuit or fit in your wealth stage and asset-use category. Someday something or somebody (usually the Fed) is going to remove that particular punch bowl from the party. Guess who'll be caught with the bag. Since there are always investment alternatives, stick with the ones that suit you and your circumstances best.

The above concepts and tables are intended to give any investor a good framework for investment emphasis throughout life. They can be used by those investors who need a formal financial plan and those who don't. They are the simplest alternatives I can find for investors for whom planning is a pain. For most people, this framework will be the only financial planning needed until their assets become sizable and complex or they approach retirement. However, there are probably almost as many exceptions to those general rules as there are investors who fit them. If you believe you are such an exception, don't hesitate to invest according to your own temperament and needs.

What Return Should I Achieve?

Few investment questions are subject to more individual considerations and uncontrollable forces than the query of what rate of return you should pursue. Such considerations as the date (and whether) you are planning to retire, how much income you can expect to live on comfortably in today's dollars, what the future rate of inflation will be, how much capital and/or earning power is available, and the like all affect the answer to that question. The question needs to be asked—and answered. Nevertheless, because of these variations the answer must be generalized.

Footnote 1 in Chapter 3 presented a method for determining how much *net real capital loss* per year one can afford if investment assets are not to lose more than half their purchasing power over a given time. A loss parameter was used because in inflationary times (even at the relatively low rates of 1982–84) and with the high tax levels most successful investors encounter now, it is difficult to project net positive real returns. For example, an investor expecting to be in a minimum 40 percent top tax bracket for several years cannot obtain less than a 10 percent compounded annual return while inflation averages more than 6 percent per year, or else the investor's net real return will be negative. I don't believe that inflation can realistically be projected to average less than 6 percent annually over the long term.

A relatively simple estimating method to determine capital/income adequacy is based on these assumptions. Given the magnitude in the estimate of the unknowables, a simple method is best. There's little point in going through a detailed exercise when an item like the inflation rate is virtually impossible to forecast several years ahead, and yet its weight in the estimate is great.

Examples

Assume that an investor and spouse are planning to retire in the next year or so at age 64 and that they believe about $30,000 per year in taxable income from capital will be sufficient to live on, as long as it *holds its purchasing power.* Also assume that income tax rates will remain at 1984 levels (the first big and shaky assumption), which for a couple at this income level means a marginal or top tax rate of 28 percent, after tax deductions. Also assume that inflation will *average* 8 percent per year for the estimable future.

Query: What *net real* rate of return is necessary to hold the buying power of that income at a level that will lose no more than *half* its buying power by the time the investors reach age 85?

The arithmetic works this way in my quick estimate method. Subtract current age 64 from 85, equaling 21 years. The number 72 is used to determine how long a period is required for a given interest rate to double money if the rate is positive and compounded. It also gives the time required for money to fall to half its value if the rate is negative. In this example, divide 72 by 21 years to obtain the *annual* compounded rate at which the real return can *decline* to equal one half of the purchasing power at age 85. The answer is 3.4 percent per year. (For the moment don't worry about aiming for a *negative* return.)

If the couple had a *net real loss* of 3.4 percent before taxes every year for 21 years, the buying power of their $30,000 taxable income would be cut to one half.

Now the questions are these: What pretax return on investments, before adjusting for inflation, will provide that annual minimum − 3.4 percent? What amount of capital will be needed to have that return equal $30,000 in the first year? The couple's top tax bracket is used to project the rate at which the next dollar of income will be taxed. (Technically, if the $30,000 were their entire income, a lower *average rate* would apply.)

Assuming that at the $30,000 taxable income level the couple's deductions don't increase to reduce taxable income below the next lower bracket amount at $29,900, the 28 percent top rate would reduce a gross investment return by that same 28 percent. Any income return would then be after tax 72 percent of gross return under our assumptions. Thus, the formula:

$$\text{After tax return } \times \text{ Percent investment return} - \text{ Inflation rate} = -3.4 \text{ percent}$$

Solving for investment return, x, $0.72x - 0.08 = -0.034$; and $x = 6.4$ percent. That is the minimum *gross return* the couple can earn *pretax* per year in an 8 percent average-inflation world for 21 years if their income's buying power is not to fall below one half of its present level by age 85. This should be their absolute minimum goal. Setting 6.4 percent as the return on initial capital needed to equal $30,000 income, the capital required is about $469,000. (To be more accurate in this capital calculation, the $30,000 taxable income should be increased to allow for the amount of the couple's deductions.)

This minimum estimate is probably unrealistic because it doesn't relate to any current market rates of interest and because it assumes that an annual loss is a satisfactory goal, which it should not be. Nevertheless, it does represent a minimum return under the assumptions.

Adjusting the figures will relate it better to the real world. Take a 3 percent *positive* return on capital as the minimum goal for a *net real* return, and see where that leaves the couple in comparison with recent market rates of return.

Substituting, x now equals 15.3 percent gross return. That was reachable in the high-rate era of 1980–81 and again in 1984 in some long-term bonds. But it was not readily achievable without high capital risk. This example shows why it is difficult to project anything but very modest rates of positive net real return these days. To do so, one must lower the inflation-rate assumption. Here, your guess is as good as mine.

To complete the exercise in the recent real world, reduce the gross investment return goal to 12.5 percent per year, a rate that has been available on Treasury notes or bonds for some time and therefore is a reasonable goal. (But it is not a recommendation to buy the bonds!) Under the 8 percent inflation assumption, the net real return requirement will drop to + 1.0 percent annually. That's hardly a great goal, but it provides a workable assumption. As long as the net real return remains positive and is reinvested, the income's buying power will not be reduced at all at an average 8 percent inflation rate. Then with that 12.5 percent gross investment return, the $30,000 gross income level requires a more modest $240,000 initial capital.

Building Net Worth

Taking this exercise a step further, we can also estimate in another way the amount of capital an investor should attempt to accumulate prior to a distant future retirement in order to have a reasonable income after that retirement date. Here the importance of developing tax-sheltered capital growth becomes clear.

If an investor's capital and income goals are the same as those above but (s)he is 10 years away from retirement and in a 40 percent top tax bracket, the after tax real return on the 12.5 percent gross return assumption becomes a negative 0.5 percent per year at an 8 percent inflation average. That's no way to build capital buying power. True, the capital pile itself will grow after tax at a 7.5 percent annual rate, and if reinvested at that rate it will still double in about 9½ years. However its purchasing power will have been slipping, albeit at a modest 0.5 percent annual rate.

So, if one had $100,000 in capital 10 years prior to retirement under the above conditions, not only would the 7.5 percent after tax capital growth rate be too low to sufficiently increase capital to earn the $30,000 income at a 12.5 percent gross rate on retirement day, but its buying power would be lower than needed, as well.

It is clear that the most desirable choice is to have the capital earn its return on either a tax-free or tax-deferred basis. That means utilizing the tax-related builders of capital for the $100,000 original capital and a retirement plan for additional contributions. Tax-exempt notes/bonds, very conservative limited-partnership income investments, long-term

capital gain-achieving assets, and single premium life insurance are other choices. Each would have to be selected on the basis that its after tax
or tax-deferred annual return must *exceed* the inflation-rate assumption.

The goal should be achieving the highest tax-deferred *real* return
available consistent with safety. Remember that even a 5 percent annually
compounded tax-sheltered return will require more than 14 years to
double one's capital buying power.

Figure 4–1 is a useful extension of the above discussion.[2] To use the
chart in the above examples, assume that you wished total capital
buying power to last 28 years and to approach zero on that date. If its

FIGURE 4–1
HOW LONG WILL MY CAPITAL LAST?* (curves represent the annual compound earnings
growth rate of the capital remaining after each withdrawal.)

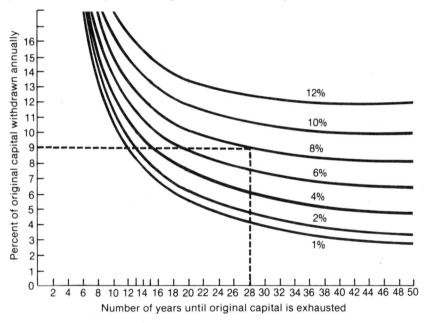

*Lawrence Rosen, *The Dow Jones-Irwin Guide to Interest* (Homewood, Ill.: Dow Jones-Irwin, 1974).

[2]The mathematical formula from which Figure 4–1 is derived is:

$$x = \frac{i}{1 - (1 + i)^{-n}}$$

where

x = Percentage of capital withdrawn and/or inflation rate annually.
i = Annual compound earnings rate of remaining capital.
n = Number of years before capital is exhausted.

after tax return were 8 percent, you would move up the vertical line from 28 years to the 8 percent curve and left, which would meet 9 percent. The latter number represents the percentage of capital *and inflation* that can be taken away each year to exhaust the capital's buying power in 28 years. If inflation made up 8 percent of the 9 percent, you could only withdraw 1 percent cash per year to exhaust the capital's buying power in 28 years. (The actual capital would be declining by by only 1 percent per year, and thus the inflation "withdrawal" would not actually reduce buying power to zero in 28 years but rather to a small percentage of the original amount.)

Summary

To summarize, check yourself in following these steps.

1. Take the quick financial plan need test at the beginning of this chapter. Heed its advice to consult a financial planner if warranted.
2. From Table 4–1 locate your capital accumulation stage, and note any personal circumstances that might make you an exception to it.
3. From Tables 4–2 and 4–3 you'll know which types of investments you should be concentrating on now as a typical investor in your accumulation stage. Note if you'll need to rearrange these because you're atypical.
4. Now match the tables' appropriate asset use and investments with your actual investments to see if you're placing your capital in (and holding) the right type. If not, it's time seriously to redirect your investment emphasis.
5. Before taking a new investment departure, reconsider your retirement and other financial goals. In doing this, the capital and income adequacy tests described will be informative. (For another aspect of future-value determinations see Chapter 6, pp. 66–67.)

Using this capital-accumulation framework, typical investment vehicles, and a method for roughly estimating capital and income adequacy, the average investor can do the most important basic jobs of financial planning. With this information in hand, plus the additional knowledge provided in later chapters on specific investment vehicles, you should be in a position to structure your actual investments with a broker or advisor. Many individual differences from the "average investor" will turn up, so don't hesitate to discuss plans with a competent professional.

5

Using Cycles

A study of economics usually reveals that the best time to buy anything is last year.

MARTY ALLEN

Stepping up from the necessary, if arguably mundane, matter of discussing what money is and how to plan its strategic placement, we can now deal with tactics in the real investment world in which that money must operate. It is a world of constantly gyrating cyclical forces interwoven with the mists of political rhetoric and economic jargon. In it we need the clearest signposts and best road maps available.

This chapter probes the first of two big-picture navigational aids through the rugged investment terrain and suggests ways of best using it. Chapter 6 focuses on the second. With the two, and our risk control guidelines in the succeeding chapter, you'll be prepared to chart a direct path toward low-risk financial independence.

Types of Market Cycles

As is well documented, many cyclical forces are at work in the investment world, and virtually none that affect securities or commodities

47

price or yield trends are scientifically replicable. In other words, a lot of apparent cyclical happenings relate to investment prices or yields, but none of them is certain to happen exactly the same way next time. The investment world is simply too dynamic for that.

Even so, investment practitioners are constantly looking for provable cyclical trends, and occasionally they claim to have found them. A catalogue published two decades ago listed more than 200 "apparent" stock market cycles, ranging from 20 hours to 89½ *years* in length. Stock market author Burton Crane recalled a man who years earlier had operated an advisory service allegedly based on events in the comic strips of the *Chicago Sun*.[1] Some present-day advisors base predictions on astrology or astronomy, notably advisory letter author Arch Crawford. Sunspots, phases of the moon, and the planets' Jupiter effect have been cited by market gurus as reasons for expecting a given market event.

These authors *know* (at least I think they do) that if someone could cause a cycle to repeat tomorrow, the effect on the markets would probably be different from that of the previous cycle. We certainly could not assume it would be exactly the same. However, cycles, defined by Webster's dictionary as "regularly recurring successions of events or phenomena," don't have to be scientifically provable or replicable to be of use. Probability is the basis for the reputations of many cycles. In fact, most of these would probably be better termed *cyclical tendencies*, but in verbal shorthand, the word *cycles* is handier.

A few widely recognized investment cycles appear to fit this description. The monthly stock market cycle is based on the tendency of the Standard & Poor's 500 Index to rise from the last day of one month through the fourth day of the next. Preholiday seasonality in stocks covers two trading days prior to each of nine public holidays and has a remarkable record.[2]

The full-moon cycle, although far weaker, is said to impart to the Dow Jones Industrial Average a tendency to fall in the period from the day before through the third day after a full moon. There's also a countervailing new-moon cycle of five days on both sides of its appearances.[3]

The so-called Super Bowl Predictor is one of the more bizarre cycles. It claims that the annual Super Bowl winner, based solely on the original

---

[1]Burton Crane, *The Sophisticated Investor*, rev. ed. (Hamden, CT: Fireside Press, 1964).

[2]Norman G. Fosback, *Stock Market Logic* (Fort Lauderdale, Fla.: Institute for Econometric Research, 1981).

[3]Ian McAvity, *Full Moon and the Market* (Toronto, Canada: Deliberations Research, 1982).

conference of the winning team, can predict the stock market trend for the year. NFC teams are bullish. Through 1983 this cycle had predicted 17 out of 17 correctly using the New York Stock Exchange Index. (It missed one using the S & P 500 Index.)

Gold appears to have roughly a six-year trough-to-trough cycle dating back to the 1950s for Canadian gold-mining stocks, despite a pair of year-plus gaps. Many other cycles relate to seasonality in commodity prices.

However, these apparent investment cycles and dozens of others like them are not truly rhythmic. They operate not with an exact predictability, but rather with only some degree of probability. Therefore, it makes sense to be wary of them for market forecasting.

Improving Reliability

One way of improving cyclical reliability is to find overlapping or re-inforcing cycles. Even then we must be careful. For example, *if* the stock market had a tendency to rise around a new moon *and* at the turn of the month (as two cycles arguably say it does), presumably a new moon at the beginning of a new month would offer even better probabilities for profit. Alas, it doesn't work. No sound economic or financial theory says that the moon and the early days of the month ought to be good for equities, and the pairing has not been verifiably better than random predictions, at least in recent years. One can only guess the reason, but it probably has to do with the mismatched days of the 5-day new month's cycle and the 10-day new-moon period. So much for a promising cycle pairing-to-be.

The Kondratieff Wave

A Russian name has become prominently associated with cycles, especially in doom-and-gloom crowds wherein fatalism seems to prevail. Nikolai Kondratieff was a man who attempted to prove, through papers published in 1922 and 1926 in the Soviet Union, that capitalist economies behave cyclically in conjunction with a so-called long wave of 45- to 60-years duration, centering on 54 years. Specifically, he said that this wave applies to prices, interest rates, and economic production in major industrial nations.

Many economists and economic soothsayers have taken up his cudgel since the 1920s, and whenever a serious recession strikes the Western industrialized world, they trot out his theory in an attempt to pinpoint that slump's location on the wave. It seems that the worse the economic slump, the closer these people believe the world is to the next major downleg in Kondratieff's wave.

Because of the worldwide attention given to it, the Kondratieff wave is an intriguing cycle to examine. Extensive attempts have been made to prove or disprove the theory.[4] The most optimistic conclusion I can draw from these efforts is that the theory is not provable. Following are three of its most important discrepancies.

Inaccurate Prices

The first problem with the Kondratieff wave, commonly seen in an idealized form compared with a chart of U.S. wholesale prices, is that somebody has been fiddling with the prices that made up a key element in the wave theory.

To see this problem, compare the wave with a chart used by Kondratieff himself in 1935, which is shown in Figure 5–1.[5] Notice first the magnitude of the U.S. wholesale price change on the "idealized" wave chart from about 1870 to just before 1900: It falls from approximately 80 to 30 on the scale, about 63 percent. On Kondratieff's 1935 chart, the U.S. figure drops from about 70 to under 25, clearly a greater percentage decline of over 78 percent. Perhaps one of the charts just got the numbers wrong or the magnitude doesn't count.

There's more. Note that the idealized wave itself completely lacks a secondary and flatter downleg around 1940 similar to the ones from about 1825 to 1840 and from 1880 to 1900. If it had such a leg, the low would be out near 1955, quite a distance from the low in wholesale prices that the chart and real-world facts show to be in 1933.

Both the actual and idealized graph lines agree that a peak in U.S. prices occurred about 1920, so how could the real low in 1933 have happened so soon? That would make the last cycle stretch only from the 1896 low (where Kondratieff stated it occurred) to 1933, a period of only

---

[4] C. Van Ewujk, "The Long Wave—A Real Phenomenon?" *The Economist* (The Netherlands), no. 3., 1981; and John A. Pugsley, "The Long Wave: Should We Praise or Bury Kondratieff?" *Common Sense Viewpoint*, November 1982.

[5] N. D. Kondratieff, "Long Waves in Economic Life," *The Review of Economic Statistics* 17, (1935).

FIGURE 5–1
THE KONDRATIEFF WAVE

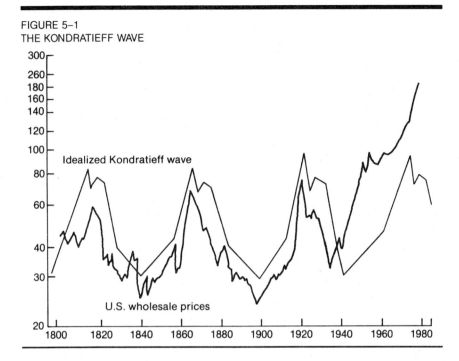

37 years, not Kondratieff's expected 45 to 60 years. Was it sort of a "short, long wave"?

Another problem with the chart is that only two trough-to-trough wholesale price cycles exist, and one of them (as just noted) is suspect. Is the wave to be a "long" wave of about 50 years followed by a "short, long" wave of under 40 years? Possible of course, but that fact cannot be determined by a chart of this short a duration (in number of cycles).

Period Studied

The matter of cycle duration causes another problem. Drawing sound conclusions about the validity of a cycle based on finding physical evidence requires a significant number of cycles. What number is appropriate is disputed. Pugsley notes that one expert requires the period studied to be 10 times the length of one apparent cycle. There is general agreement that a minimum of a half dozen apparent cycles need to be compared. Yet, in Kondratieff's case the maximum number of cycles observed in all of the statistical series he measured was 2½! Moreover, that many cycles were found in only 4 of some 36 sets (series) of data he used. The rest had fewer cycles, and 11 sets covered only *one cycle*.

If all this weren't enough, the individual contributions of each of those 36 series are a bit unusual. They cover a wide range of variables, from prices to interest rates and production levels to consumption rates, but the eight that were of the maximum 2 or 2½ cycles in length were all *monetary* series (i.e., related to prices and interest rates). Of the remaining 28, 7 of which were also monetary, fully *10 showed no cyclical action at all*, and 18 revealed no more than 1½ cycles.[6]

In sum, the Kondratieff wave theory is based on drawing correlations (and not statistical ones at that) where less than one fourth of the data series studied covered even two full cycles, which is about one third the widely accepted minimum for valid comparisons, and all of these were monetary indicators, not production or consumption series.

One could argue that some sort of long-wave cycle might exist in monetary measures, but Kondratieff's evidence didn't prove it, let alone extend it to whole economies, as his proponents claim. Kondratieff himself stated in his paper *Long Cycles in Economic Conditions* delivered in 1926, "Although the period that was studied, covering a maximum of 140 years, *is too short to permit of definitive conclusions*, the existence of long cycles would appear to be, at the very least, extremely likely."[7] (Italics mine.)

I believe a more accurate statement would be that over the period studied, some data suggest the existence of a "long cycle" in financial matters in a few capitalist countries studied (England, Germany, France, and the United States). Such a cycle can be neither proved nor disproved from the data. Its demonstrated variability in length and form, plus the changes in the world economy since the 1930s, make forecasting any future reoccurrence absolutely unreliable. But, it's an interesting idea.

By the way, finding cycles that "work" doesn't mean you can make money from them. Cycle researchers Fosback and McAvity each stress that despite the apparent strong degree of predictability of some cycles, basing actual transactions in the marketplace on them may not be profitable. The real world raises such defeating problems as finding the right vehicle, the cost of broker commissions, effective market executions, and exact timing of the trades. It's the real world in which we must deal.

---

[6]Pugsley, "Long Wave."

[7]Nickolai Kondratieff, *The Long Wave Cycle*, new translation by Guy Daniels (New York: Richardson & Snyder, 1984).

General Cycle Inadequacies

Some flaws are very common in the use of cycles to forecast markets. Consider these:

20/20 Hindsight

If a researcher looks at a reasonably large set of historic market data, it is very likely that (s)he will locate one or a few patterns that actually did exist over the period involved. Since market players are creatures of habit, some patterns invariably had to develop over a large enough data sample. Then if some particular event is located which seemed to precede most rising markets, for example, participants would look for that event again to "cause" a similar market rise in the future. This cause will appear to work until other circumstances change the significance of the event, but before this happens the apparent cycles that are still operative are termed *valid cycles*.

Unfortunately, this sort of hindsight is usually based either on the use of statistics with a lack of sound supporting theory (e.g., the Super Bowl Predictor or full-moon cycles for the stock market) or on a changeable set of assumptions.

The January Barometer is a good example of the latter. This predictor says that the stock market trend in January (up or down) will be matched by the rest of the year. Simple as that sounds, there are problems. First, the predictor is usually used by taking the January trend and then forecasting the whole year, January through December, from it. That creates a statistical difficulty: If January was up, say, 10 percent and the whole year rose 5 percent, how can one say the predictor (January) was useful? February through December would have had to *decline* 5 percent. Besides, there's nothing like getting a running start with $1/12$ of your measurement.

On the other hand, using January to forecast the rest of the year, February through December, could be on more solid ground. In fact, in the 35 years from 1948 through 1982, January correctly called the balance of the year's trend 27 times, or 77.1 percent. This sounds good, except that this period covered one of the great bull markets in history. A logical question would then be, what if you simply predicted that *every year would be up* over this 35 years? You'd have been right 25 times, or 71 percent!

It gets worse. Going back to 1925, January forecast the trend correctly *less than half* of the years through 1948. If you'd predicted an up year every year during this period, you'd have done better! As you can see, hindsight isn't all it's cracked up to be.

Tiny Sample (The Kondratieff Fallacy)

Often, cycle followers will use a small data base and short time frame to project future results. The gold and silver markets are good examples of this practice because free-market trading in them has existed only since the late 1960s. Since the observable cycle for gold has run five to six years during that period, there are only two past cycles from which to draw data. That is patently an inadequate base from which to predict future trends as to either direction or price.

The Toronto gold-mining stock index gives a stronger statistical base, having five full cycles during its bullish trend from 1950. However, its bear market from the mid-1930s had only two cycles—one of 10 years, the other of 22 years. As a result, the statistical data alone were useless in forecasting the switch from bear to bull in Canada.

Thus drawing useful conclusions from small data samples is risky at best, unless they're connected with other cycles and have a sound theory behind them.

"Something Fits"

The "something fits" method of cyclical analysis uses 20/20 hindsight to find historical patterns and then to locate those around which a whole series of different cycles apparently fits. Often, these are called primary and secondary cycles. By then identifying several overlapping trends— say, a 5-week, 12½-week, 3-month, and 4¼-month period—the researcher is almost assured that one of the trends will appear to fit all situations. If the alleged five-week pattern doesn't appear this time, the three month will, etc. So, the whole series is said to work and the given market is stated to have four cycles at work in it. When even that misses, less-than-perfect circumstances can be blamed and the next cycle focused upon. This flawed method is widely found in commodity trend analysis.

From the preceding analysis of cyclical flaws and extensive mathematical work done by researchers with cycles in the investment world, we can adopt a conclusion about cycles and periodicity. Any apparent cyclical trend in the investment markets should be considered only when it meets at least these four criteria:

1. It is supported by a sound economic or financial theory that says it should exist.
2. It is verifiable over a sufficient number of cycles to establish a good probability for repetition, preferably a minimum of six.
3. Its principal strength does not arise because it is one of the multiple cycles with varying lengths arising from the same data.
4. One can actually profit from the use of it alone, or preferably in conjunction with other cycles.

It is also possible to productively utilize multiple sets of separate data, none of which is valid alone, but when used together confirms a cycle in a similar way each time.

If such data support cannot be found, all is not lost. This happens frequently. Instead investors must recognize the flaws and adjust their thinking by not relying totally on that cycle. The following two examples of cyclical tendencies are useful in predicting market actions. These cycles are partially flawed, but are still useful in limited degrees. The first tells which way the economic wind is blowing.

The Political or Weather-Vane Cycle

Figure 5–2 combines short-term interest rates, stock prices, and inflation with elections and recessions for the 15-year inflation-deflation era 1968–82. This chart gives the strongest graphic evidence behind the claim that Washington is the principal creator of our economic roller coaster. Let's see how good its support is.

The evidence suggests a distinct four-year influence is at work on both stock prices and interest rates. Studies of the stock market averages going back to 1917 have found a pronounced tendency toward a four-year cycle. Of 15 full cycles since then, 10 have been four years, only 2 were three years, and 3 were five years long.

During the most recent inflation era shown in the chart, the stock market cycle clearly tended to peak in presidential election years and to bottom in congressional election years. Since 1968 four market tops have occurred at or within a few months following the four presidential elections. The four succeeding congressional election years saw bot-

FIGURE 5–2
S&P 500, CPI, SHORT-TERM INTEREST RATES, AND RECESSIONS

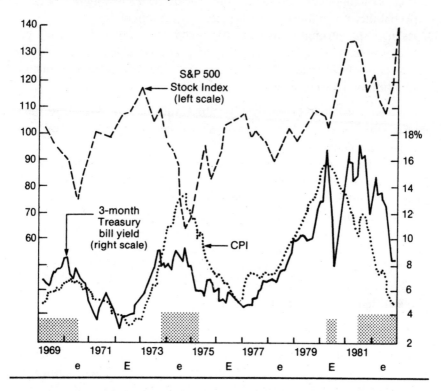

toms or interim lows in the stock averages within three months of the election—except when the low preceded ballot day by just over four months in 1970. In fact, since 1947 there has been a significant series of nine consecutive bear market lows in stocks reached within 12 months of midterm congressional elections. That's one of the better cyclical records around.

Also interesting during this era was the tendency for price inflation as shown by the CPI to be at or approaching its *lows* in presidential election years (1968, 1972, and 1976), and highs or proximities to them were seen in midterm years of 1970, 1974, and 1978. Short-term interest rates tracked the inflation pattern closely, except for an added cyclical low in 1980.

Finally, as might be expected from the foregoing, three of the four recessions of the past dozen years began after presidential elections and were over before the next; but they were in full swing or ending as Congress went before the voters in 1970, 1974, and 1982. The exception was the Carter blunder of 1980.

Thus empirical evidence suggests that an election cycle is working within our economic framework, and it is certainly based on a compelling theory: the need for politicians to put a best financial face forward when appealing to voters. It is not surprising that each presidential administration swings the greatest weight in this cycle, not Congress. These facts make the political cycle useful in dealing with markets, but it must be used with care. Remember 1980.

As a weather vane, such a broad pattern as the political cycle should tell us in which direction to look but *not what to do*. This is especially so because the cycle has a high potential for being disrupted if the economy doesn't respond properly or on time to the politician's exhortations. The "what to do and when" part is properly identified through other, more sensitive market-oriented indicators.

When to Look Up

The political cycle can thus be used to *prepare* for investments that will ride with the cycle, both up and down. A good example of how to do this with upward signals was revealed around the 1974 congressional elections.

The economy was deepening its slump during the worst recession since the 1930s as Congress went to the voters in the fall of 1974. The OPEC oil embargo and price explosion were nearly a year past, but the world economic gloom had gotten very deep. *The Wall Street Journal* reported on September 4:

> A bewildering combination of frightening economic developments is tumbling out; soaring prices and eroding wages; topless interest rates and a bottomless stock market; a mortgage-money crunch and a home building crash . . . . A Washington authority confides, "I've never lived through as gloomy a period as now, with so many people calling me to ask if we're going to have a depression."

U.S. industry was operating at just 77 percent of capacity in the third quarter and was on its way to a 68 percent low, although the jobless rate had not risen too far. In September 5.4 percent of the labor force was out of work, but the percentage grew to more than 9 percent the following spring. Inflation hit a 23-year record just above +11 percent on a 12-month basis in the CPI during September. Reflecting all this, the stock market (S&P 500) had plunged 50 percent from its 1973 high and lost nearly one third in just the six months through September 1974.

By October 18 *The Journal* also reported: "The economy sagged further in the third quarter, but the administration again insisted that the nation isn't in a recession. Real GNP fell a seasonally adjusted 2.9 percent after two previous quarterly declines."

The economic-political situation was clear. An economic slump was underway, but it was being flatly denied by the Ford Administration, quite probably because of its so-recent (August) assumption of office at the end of Watergate. To be sure, Ford and his people had held economic summits with key economists, and modest proposals to aid the nation's economic plight were made, but none were considered more than contingency plans.

Under that set of conditions and knowing only that previous recessionary congressional years saw the *beginnings* of economic stimulus, what should investors logically have looked for that summer and fall? Obviously, proof of an effort to stimulate would have been a sensible object of search. Stock market investment cycles *should* bottom around midterm congressional elections, as we've seen.

The indication was found at both of the usual sources of such stimulation—the Federal Reserve Board and comments by key administration aides.

FRB actions clearly began to turn in the summer from their earlier restrictiveness. In August Chairman Arthur Burns proposed a $4 billion program to provide 800,000 new jobs to be activated if the jobless total reached 6 percent. The administration concurred in a watered-down form over the Labor Day weekend.

In early September the Fed eased credit conditions by cutting the reserve requirements on large CDs a whopping 37.5 percent and by October was regularly injecting funds into the banking system. The first of a series of discount-rate cuts came in December.

On October 23 Treasury consultant (and former chief White House economic advisor) Paul McCracken was quoted by *The Wall Street Journal* as saying that the nation was in a recession that would be "sharp," if not necessarily "deep." He observed that the president was "ill advised not to call a spade a spade" and label the nine-month downturn a recession. The next day in the same paper, Treasury Secretary Simon was

Keep It Fresh!

A good way to keep LOW RISK PROFITS IN HIGH RISK TIMES fresh in the future is to subscribe to Robert Kinsman's *Low-Risk Growth Letter.* (It outperformed the S & P 500 Index for 6 months, 1 year and 3 years through June 30, 1984, at **less than half** the risk of the Index.)

For a FREE copy of the Letter and a Special Discount subscription rate, without obligation, just fill out this postpaid card.

(Please print or type.)

Name _____

Address _____

City _____ State/Zip _____

(Offer expires March 31, 1985.)

said to have "voiced fears that inflation [might] be losing out to recession as the targeted public enemy No. 1" and noted that the White House was under rising pressure to abandon the inflation fight in favor of a fight against recession. (He added that the pressure should be resisted.) The priority shift to economic ease and recession-tackling was starting.

A modestly well-informed investor, therefore, who should have been looking through the gloom of fall 1974 for initial signs of economic stimulus because of the election cycle, would have seen their first glimmers. To be sure, those glimmers would have produced few market results by the 1974 election and no turnaround in the economy for six months.

So far, so good, but what concrete evidence should investors have been looking for besides administration words and Fed deeds? A key object of search should be the beginning of a decline in interest rates, according to my research.

As Table 5–1 shows, short-term interest rates have generally peaked 3 to 14 months before midterm elections since 1966, and the stock market bottomed within 9 months. This frame would also have caught stock market lows as measured by the S&P 500 in every midterm election year since 1948. Thus, looking for an interest rate decline and stock market upturn would have been wise in all those midterm election years.

A final element of testing for the "look upward" approach must be its profitability. Here the stock market is very instructive. *If investors could have bought the S&P 500 Index, or stocks that performed equally to it, and done so just at the average level of the index in congressional election years and sold at the index average of presidential years, some very nice gains would have resulted. There would have been not one losing sequence, since 1958–60. See Table 5–2.*

TABLE 5–1
SHORT-TERM INTEREST PEAKS VERSUS MIDTERM ELECTIONS

Election Year	Interest Rate Peak	Major Stock Market Low
1966	Within 3 months	October 1966
1970	Within 11 months	May 1970
1974	Within 3 months	October 1974
1978	None	March 1978
1982	Within 14 months; a secondary peak within 9 months	August 1982

TABLE 5–2
ELECTION CYCLE STOCK MARKET GAINS USING S&P 500 INDEX AVERAGE LEVELS

Year	S&P 500 Average Level	Percentage Gain
1962	62.38 ⎱	
1964	81.37 ⎰	30.44%
1966	85.26 ⎱	
1968	98.70 ⎰	15.76
1970	83.22 ⎱	
1972	109.20 ⎰	31.20
1974	82.55 ⎱	
1976	102.01 ⎰	23.57
1978	96.02 ⎱	
1980	118.59 ⎰	23.48
Average gain		24.89%

Of course, it was not easy to buy the S&P 500 itself prior to 1975, but it could be done with an index fund since then, and more recently with an index futures contract. Picking the average level for the year would have been more difficult, but through the use of other indicators, picking a lower-than-average buying point and higher-than-average selling point should not be too much to ask.

Interim Summary

This upward election cycle has both a strong theory supporting it and a demonstrated, verifiable pattern of repetition over many cycles. It is *not* successful just because it has overlapping subcycles supporting it. As Table 5–2 shows, it has also been very profitable. Thus it specifically appears to be a most useful cycle.

There is a *caveat* in our use of this cycle: Remember that nothing *requires* events to occur according to the cycle. Having politicians working to make the cycle happen doesn't ensure results. Both political and economic events can and have intervened to disrupt the cycle, as happened in the cycle ending in 1980. This shows that even the upward election cycle doesn't always beat Washington's inflation-deflation roller coaster. This exception is instructive.

The 1978–1980 Exception

Given the above election-cycle logic and facts, the topping of the long economic expansion of the 1970s during the presidential election year of 1980 seems surprising. Yet, it is less surprising when one recalls that there was no recession in midstream (1978) and that the boom had reached disastrous inflationary proportions by late 1979.

The beginning of the end of the boom came when Paul Volcker took over as chairman of the Federal Reserve Board in August 1979 from an in-house job as president of the Federal Reserve Bank of New York. He instituted a monetarist policy in FRB actions to regain control of the money supply and to slow its growth in October that year, thereby initiating an exception to the election cycle. Its ultimate effects were not readily discernible then, however.

Targeting monetary growth rates in FRB open-market actions instead of targeting interest rates, as was prior policy, had the desired effect. Money growth slowed abruptly. However, the side effect was that interest rates were free to react to market forces, and they accordingly swung wildly higher as those forces demanded more money as less was being made available. The combination pushed business into a severe slump, accelerated by the March 1980 credit controls, only to have business rescued by a dramatic resurgence in monetary growth. The net effect was a recession and recovery in 1980 and another recession in 1981–82. Thus 1978–80 provided a fine exception to the election-cycle theory and great confusion in the financial markets.

Interestingly, had investors still blindly followed the election cycle by purchasing the S&P 500 by proxy at its average level in 1978 and remaining invested through the tough markets of 1979 and 1980, they would have earned substantial profits by the November 1980 election. This may suggest that dogged adherence to the upward election cycle, no matter whether recessions and countervailing stimulation occur, is a fine idea. Certainly, some statistics suggest it. However, this exception to the "look up" in midterm election years rule must remind us that it should not be used in lieu of better market timing. Despite the investment results shown from this cycle, it is still only a weather vane.

Looking Down

Regarding economic tops in relation to elections, theory says an economic slowdown should follow presidential elections. The expectation

TABLE 5–3
ELECTION-CYCLE BUSINESS PEAKS

Election Year	Business-Cycle Peak
1948	November 1948
1952	July 1953
1956	August 1957
1960	April 1960
1964	None
1968	December 1969
1972	November 1973
1976	None
1980	January 1980
	July 1981

is partly based on the logic that if the economy was stimulated preceding the election, it might require dampening by the year afterward. A second basis is that the next election is far enough away for voters to take some bitter medicine and forget its taste by the next polling day. Table 5–3 shows the presidential election years since World War II and the subsequent peak of economic activity. Only three were not followed by recessions: 1960, 1964, and 1976.

Predicting downward pressure on the economy after each presidential election would have been correct six of nine times, a reasonable batting average, and the business cycle peaked at times *other than* postpresidential years in only two of nine cycles.

Profiting from this knowledge is more problematic. The stock market, having a tendency toward peaks in presidential election years and lows in congressional election years, is bound to be far less cooperative in post-presidential election years. It rose in only two of nine postwar post-presidential election years. Each of those years also had rapidly rising short-term interest rates and either a bottom or a steady rise in long-term rates, which also made the bond market a poor place to be invested.

Gold did somewhat better, having had bull markets in the 1973 and 1977 postpresidential election years (and modest gains from some gold mining stocks in 1961 and 1965), but trouble abounded in the 1969 and 1981 editions of the cycle.

Looking for a cyclical investment trend in post-presidential years seems to be a highly uncertain exercise. However, recognizing the change of economic wind at the tops of business cycles is more valuable than its 67 percent recession rate implies. It permits investors to be ready for profit-taking in the stocks that were bought 2 years earlier and to redeploy those assets in the increasingly profitable money market funds, whose yields rise in this part of the cycle. That makes it an extremely important period to watch for.

Specifically, savvy investors look for sound indications that Washington is starting to take away what was made during the two preceding years. The actions of the Federal Reserve Board must be watched for signs of increasing restriction on money and credit. Keeping an eye on the politicians' publicly announced worries over what may then be a surging inflation will also be useful if it can be caught at the time the mood has first shifted from "fight joblessness" to "stop inflation."

Looking in the anticipated downward direction prepares investors for the correct action most often. However, they must take that action only after other confirming signals are observed because the down cycle is more aberrant than the upward one.

Thus, we have in the election cycle a series of useful probabilities arising from sound theory. But they vary considerably in observed results. Accordingly, the election cycle is a fine orientation series, but a poor director of actions.

We turn now to a second critical cycle to watch. This is the one to follow after the election cycle points the way in which the economic wind is blowing and during times of shifting financial breezes.

Summary

Investors are constantly looking for replicable cycles to use in predicting market behavior. There are many apparent cycles to be found—including astrological cycles and the Super Bowl predictor. The Kondratieff Wave is one cycle that has earned worldwide attention since the 1920s. But most cycles have serious flaws, including 20/20 hindsight, too small a sample, and fitting the data into reinforcing cycles.

Still, cycles can be tamed. Sound statistical methodology is the best discipline, but even flawed cycles can be most helpful when used for limited purposes. The American political cycle is the premier example of this, offering investors excellent profit potential when carefully reinforced by additional observations.

The Money Cycle

6

*It is almost impossible to pinpont cyclical turning points
in the interest rate cycle with any degree of accuracy
or reliability based on the mechanical action
of any one indicator.*

Martin Pring

If the election cycle is aptly described as a weather vane for the economic climate, then the cyclical trend in interest rates is the barometer. Interest rates, both long- and short-term, measure the pressure in the financial atmosphere under which the various markets must operate.

This meterological parallel has its limits, but a general rule about markets is that the easing of interest rates reduces the pressure on them, providing a more favorable operating climate, whereas rising rates put the markets under greater negative pressure.

Since, as with most rules, there are exceptions, be wary of flatly predicting economic storms as a result of rising interest rates and vice versa. Nevertheless, the rising and falling pressure of rates is sufficiently useful to provide an important second cyclical tool in the investment workshop.

What's more, this tool has flaws that can be allowed for, albeit carefully.

Rates and Prices

Theory says that changes in the fixed return on money (also called its rental cost, to differentiate it from money's price in goods and services) should affect investment performance. If the rental rate on any item rises, it will make that item less affordable and will tend to dampen demand for it, and vice versa. In this sense, the rental rate and the actual price perform a similar function. There is no reason to expect that this function should be any different with money than with an automobile or an apartment. In fact, the close adherence of short-term interest rates to inflation rates presented in Figure 3–1 shows the connection between money rental rates and the price of money in goods and services.

What's more, fixed interest-bearing (and zero-coupon) securities actually prove one aspect of this rate-versus-price relationship. When the market rate of return or interest rate rises, those securities with fixed-interest returns must decline in price. Simple mathematics demands it and the reverse as well.[1]

Another way of seeing the effect of interest rates on investments is by determining what a sum of money (or a bond or stock) that has an exact expected *future* value is worth today.

Assume that you are promised the sum of $100,000 will be paid to you in 20 years and that the payment is certain; that is, there's no risk of nonpayment. The person or entity that made that promise must now fulfill it. (S)he is faced with a simple question: How much must be deposited now and at what rate of interest in order to grow to $100,000 to pay out in 20 years? Or, it might be alternatively asked: How much must be deposited *periodically* at a given interest rate to meet the obligation? The answers to those questions are mathematically certain. Pick a rate of in-

---

[1]For example, suppose that several years ago the U.S. government issued a bond to mature in 2001 and that the prevailing rate for such a bond at the time was 8 percent. Assuming the bond was issued at par or face value of $1,000, the interest rate coupon would have been fixed at $80 per year to obtain the 8 percent yield. Now, what would happen to the bond's price if interest rates for that type of bond rose to, say, 12 percent? The price would have to fall to give it a comparable 12 percent yield. A price of $667 equals 11.99 percent yield with an $80 annual interest payment. In fact, there is such a bond, the Treasury 8 percent of 2001, and it sold at this price at the end of the third quarters of 1982 and 1984.

terest, and tables that specify the future value of $1 now (or $1 periodically paid in) will provide the answer. The results arise from the process of compounding interest.

The answer to the first question, if a compound interest rate of 10 percent is selected, is that $14,864 must be deposited and left to compound at that rate for 20 years to equal $100,000. Now, notice the reverse of that: The 20-year future sum of $100,000 is "worth" only a bit ($136) less than $15,000 now, assuming the 10 percent interest rate. A table showing the future value of 1 shows that if the interest rate were cut in half, to 5 percent, the *current* value of that 20-year future $100,000 would be well more than double the previous current value: $37,689. The difference is the effect of compounding at work.

The important point is that the interest rate, called the discount rate in such present value calculations, and the time period have precisely determined the present value of some future amount. From this it must be true that not only does the interest rate dictate the current value of an assumed future sum, but that somehow this sort of calculation must go into rational market expectations for current values of bonds and stocks. To see how this works, take a Treasury note example.

Remember the second parameter above: The amount of money periodically paid for a specified time at a given rate has both a future and current discounted value. Since notes and bonds have such specified periodic payments based on their interest coupons and since they have fixed maturity dates, a present value for a note's principal and interest payoff must be calculable.

To calculate the present value of a $1,000-face-value Treasury note with interest paid at the rate of $100 per year that matures in five years, first select a discount rate, that is, the interest rate expected to prevail on *average* in the market for this note over the years until maturity. Using 8 percent, add the *present* value of the $100 interest paid in the first year at 8 percent discount to the present value of that interest in the second, third, fourth, and fifth years. To this add the present value at 8 percent of the $1,000 principal payment in the fifth year. This sum will be what the present value of that note should be in the market if rate expectations are 8 percent for that period. If such a note existed and it was selling in the market for less than your calculated amount, the market would be expecting rates higher than 8 percent over that period. A higher comparative price would mean market expectations of lower rates. This is a relatively simple method for determining market comparisons for interest rates on fixed-income securities.

Stock Valuations

A less precise result of the effect of interest rates on investments is shown when rate movements are compared with the value of equities. This result is to be expected, since there are several determinants of stock price changes, the most direct of which is the outlook for corporate earnings and dividends. However, interest rates and the outlook for them play an important part in key corporate decisions, including the financing of inventories, borrowing for new equipment, and the balance between companies' short- and long-term debt.

Thus the outlook for and realization of a significant change in interest rates should have a flow-through bearing on corporate profits, although this would certainly not be the only factor involved. Therefore, if stock prices anticipate changes in corporate profits, interest rates should also have a bearing on stock prices.

With stock there is a flow-through of ideal value to actual price through the perceived trend in short-term interest rates, but first one must determine an ideal value. Here's how it works. (Readers who prefer to skip math and theory may move on to "The Chart Evidence," p. 70.)

For dividend-paying stocks, a simple formula discovered about a century ago relates the present value of future dividend expectations to current stock price:

$$P = \frac{D_1}{k - g}$$

where

D = The dividend amount.
P = Present value of an infinite stream of dividend income.
g = The rate of annual growth of that income.
k = A discount rate for that income in the market.

Suppose a stock pays a dividend of $1 per share. If that dividend is expected to be increased 5 percent annually because of the company's growth rate, and if it is assumed that this growth should be discounted 8 percent per year on a future-value basis similar to the way note and bond present values have been calculated, then the estimated value for the stock is:

$$\frac{1}{0.08 - 0.05} = 33.33$$

Naturally, things aren't that simple in the real world. All stocks with this growth rate and dividend don't sell at $33 per share. The critical part of this formula is in the denominator factors of k and g, but how can one estimate these accurately? Estimating growth for established dividend-paying companies requires no more than a sound consensus of estimates made by analysts and company officers of earnings growth for several years ahead. Although those figures are not easy for them to arrive at, they are easy to find in brokerage firm-published estimates.

Calculating k involves using historical data about the relationship between bond and stock returns. Research shows that from 1926 to 1978 the average stock on the NYSE had a total average annual return of 7.6 percent above the long-term government bond yield.[2] (The latter, by the way, averaged 1.2 percent above the inflation rate over the 50-year period studied.) From this research has been developed a formula known as the Capital Asset Pricing Model, which determines the discount rate (k) that brings future equity returns down to present values. It also equals the cost of equity capital to a firm selling stock to investors:

$$k = \text{LBR} + 0.076 \times \text{beta}$$

where

LBR = Long-term government bond rate.

beta = The stock's volatility compared with a market volatility of 1.0 (see also Chapter 7).

Thus the k used in the first formula is figured by adding the government bond rate, say 0.10, to 0.076, multiplied by 1.2 for a stock that is estimated to be 20 percent more volatile than the overall market. In this case the result is 0.211.

Inserting the value for k into the previous formula gives:

$$\frac{1}{0.21 - 0.05} = 6.25$$

and that result gives us some real food for thought.

First, notice that in using a 10 percent government bond rate, historically the inflation rate should be a relatively high 8.8 percent (1.2 percent less than the bond rate). Under that condition, k becomes a much larger number than the one used to estimate the company's earnings growth

---

[2]Roger G. Ibbotson and Rex A. Singuefield, *Stocks, Bonds, Bills and Inflation: Historical Returns 1926–1978* (Financial Analysts Research Foundation, 1982).

rate (5 percent). Thus the equation's denominator was also much higher than previously estimated, and the resulting stock price for a $1 dividend was only about one fifth of the earlier estimate.

This means that under historical terms a high level of inflation and related high bond rates require companies to grow at higher rates in order to keep their stock prices up. In other words, *stock values will decline with rising inflation unless company growth rates also increase a similar amount.* What's more, since bond rates rise with inflation, it's also clear that rising bond interest rates tend to lower stock prices. That's exactly what we find true in the marketplace.

Since these calculations provide a theoretical or ideal value for a given stock, they are useful in determining whether a stock is over- or under valued in historical terms. However, in looking at how the stock price relates to the current market, one must examine evidence that the market's assumptions about either the discount or growth rates are changing. This brings in such nonemperical factors as psychology and perceptions.

The Chart Evidence

Figure 6–1 combines graphs of the S&P 500 Index, long-term bond yields, Treasury bill yields, the London gold price, and the consumer price index, all for the period 1969 to 1983.

There is an observable correlation between three of these data plots up to about 1978: T bill yields and the CPI moved together and generally opposite to stock prices during that period. Even long-term bond yields tracked reasonably well but inversely to stock prices until 1977–78. In fact, the relationships shown from 1969 to 1978 were largely the same as those that existed from World War II until 1969.

However, it is quite obvious that something dramatic occurred in 1977–78 that affected the correlations, and again in 1980 something sharply disturbed the relationship of interest rates to stock prices. The facts are: (1) The rise in interest rates from mid-1977 had little effect on the broad stock price trend and even accompanied a rally from early 1978 into 1980, although interruptions are clear. (2) The fall in the inflation and interest rates in Spring 1980 was accompanied by falling stock prices. (3) As interest rates again rose in mid–late 1980, so did stock prices. But inflation was falling. (4) Interest rates began falling by mid-1981 and so were stock prices and inflation.

FIGURE 6–1
FIFTEEN YEARS OF PRICES, INTEREST RATES, GOLD, AND STOCKS

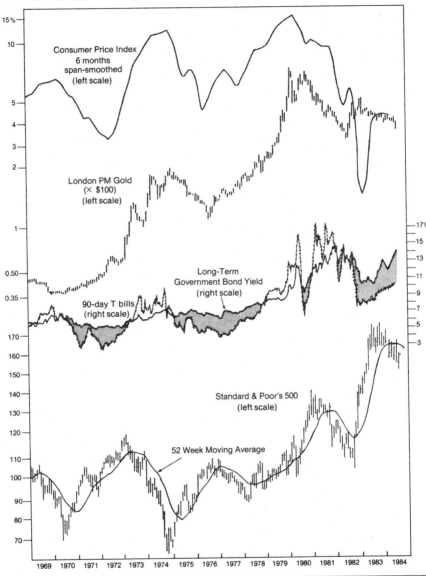

Conclusion: The best correlation during this period 1977–81 is not the historic inverse one between short-term interest rates and stock prices. It is the direct one between inflation and stock prices. More important, the traditional relationships reasserted themselves as both rates and inflation declined in 1982.

These observations strongly suggest that interest rates have a notable impact on stock prices but that it is not necessarily the same effect at the highest inflation levels recently seen as it is at "more normal" levels.

Can we be more precise about this? A few years ago, while researching this idea by comparing the trend in short-term interest rates with the movement in stock prices, I verified that for a period of 30 years (1954 to 1983) there was a distinct interest rate-related trigger to rising stock trends. Table 6–1 shows each occasion over this quarter century when short-term interest rates began a downtrend as measured by either a downward *reversal* of the Federal Reserve Boad discount rate or a three-month downward reversal of Treasury bill yields and federal fund rates. (Federal fund rates are those obtained on overnight borrowings among bank members of the Federal Reserve system.) The "sell" points were determined by an upward reversal in either or both of those same two indicators.

As indicated, each falling rate period was followed by a subsequent gain in stock prices as measured by the S&P 500 Index, except for that in mid-1981. Now, it's worth noting that in 1962, 1981, and 1982, the stock average was sharply lower for a period of several months following a rate reversal before recovering. However, the interest rate rule still held and ultimately produced good investment results.

Had you just bought and sold a list of stocks according to the above "trigger" (by using an indexed stock fund after 1975), and had these stocks performed as the S&P 500 did, you would have showed a gain of 228.7 percent or 20.8 percent per year invested *plus dividends*. That compares with a gain of 17.8 percent per year invested from a buy-and-hold strategy with the same S&P 500 over the same period.

Thus a little math, some theory, and a good deal of empirical evidence tell us that there is much value in forecasting interest rates because of their observed impact on the value of both fixed-income and equity securities. However, the foregoing has proved that at *any given moment* there is not always an inverse reaction between stocks and interest rates—exceptions have arisen. Yet, changes in rate trends provide valuable insight into *probable* market behavior over time.

TABLE 6-1
INTEREST RATE—TRIGGERED STOCK MARKET RECORD FROM 1954 TO 1981

Date	Action	S&P 500 Price	Gain	
			Percent	Number of Months
February 1954	Buy	26.23		
April 1955	Sell	38.27	45.9%	14
November 1957	Buy	40.04		
September 1958	Sell	48.96	22.2	10
April 1960	Buy	55.43		
May 1962	Sell	65.70	18.5	25
March 1967	Buy	87.68		
October 1967	Sell	96.32	9.8	8
September 1968	Buy	99.32		
December 1968	Sell	106.97	7.7	3.5
August 1970	Buy	77.02		
July 1971	Sell	98.93	28.4	11.5
November 1971	Buy	90.79		
June 1972	Sell	109.69	20.8	6
December 1974	Buy	67.38		
September 1975	Sell	85.48	27.0	9
January 1976	Buy	90.90		
August 1977	Sell	99.12	9.0	19
May 1980	Buy	111.35		
September 1980	Sell	126.12	13.2	4
April 1981	Buy	136.57		
July 1981	Sell	129.77	(4.9)	3
December 1981	Buy	126.10		
July 1983	Sell	168.40	33.5	19
Total gain			228.7%	132
Average per month			1.73%	

There is also a case for precious metals moving in the same direction as short-term rates, but its derivation is different. Gold and silver are inflation bugs. They move up in anticipation of an increase in the inflation level and down with prospects for the reverse. They also react upward to world financial frights, but only for as long as the scare lasts. Fortunately, these scares have not usually been long, except for the Great Depression. Thus, insofar as interest rates move in anticipation of the inflation level, gold should be expected to do likewise. Unfortunately, the pattern hasn't turned out to be quite that simple.

Fluctuating interest rates also cause the carrying cost of owning precious metals to change, both physically for storage and insurance and as a function of lost opportunity for interest return on invested funds. This change causes these metals to have a factor in their price movement that works contrary to the expected ones of rising and falling in parallel with inflation and interest rates. However, this factor does not lend itself to direct analysis on the basis of the evidence. It seems to exert a force only over very short periods and at times when price movements could also be ascribed to other factors such as the value of the U.S. dollar abroad.

Figure 6–1 also shows the gold price compared with the CPI and 90-day T bill rates. From it we see that the inflation parallel-movement theory has ample evidential support. Gold did rise from mid-1977 to 1980 along with rising rates when rates were predicting greater inflation, and it fell in 1981–82 with declining rates that accompanied prospects for decelerating inflation. Thus the rule appears to be that gold rises and falls most directly with evidence of inflationary acceleration or deceleration, but gold moves *inversely* to rates in the absence of strong inflation evidence, e.g., parts of 1981 and 1983.

The Money Cycle Index

We have come a good distance in exposing the relationship of short-term interest rates to price movements in three key markets. It has a mathematically inverse one in the bond/money markets. It has an inverse probability in the stock market, and has a direct long-term relationship in precious metals when they are anticipating changes in inflation, and an inverse relationship to the metals at other times. What is needed now is a good forecaster of the changes in these rates.

The problem, of course, lies in having to make an assumption that interest rate movements *cause* equities and precious metals prices to react *uniformly* over time. They clearly don't. What's more, finding a good forecaster can hardly be a snap. As with the election-cycle weather vane, not trying to force interest rates into becoming all things to all investors and being content with the barometer concept (useful but not infallible) will bring us closer to the mark.

Recall that the U.S. Federal Reserve Board most loudly calls the tune in the money markets. So, development of an index that shows *what the market thinks the Fed intends to do* with short-term rates should give a useful measure of how the interest rate climate is developing. Smoothing that index to avoid being tripped up by market misinterpretations and short-term ambivalences, should make the picture clearer.

The Money Cycle Index in Figure 6–2 is my answer to these needs, especially when used with the smoothing techniques of moving averages and momentum. *This Money Cycle Index is composed of equally weighted short-term interest rates, including the federal funds and 90-day Treasury bill rates, and a single heavier weighting for the Fed's most significant monetary weapon, the discount rate.* The component rates are then combined into a numerical index. It is a fundamentally simple index, but one with weighting done to induce the greatest changes when the Fed dictates a change in the discount rate and when it alters direction from a previous course. Accordingly, this index tracks short-term interest rates quite closely as to direction and it exaggerates their magnitude when the Fed swings its discount weapon.

Since Treasury securities and federal funds are the prime movers of the index and since the markets for these securities are those in which the Fed carries out its monetary policies, the index would be expected to reflect Fed intentions adequately in guiding the economy. What's more, since the Fed adopts the monetary policies that fundamentally move toward either expansion or contraction and then usually maintains that policy for more than just a few months, a good filtering system to eliminate short-run, nonpolicy movements in the index is both necessary and rewarding in catching broad policy changes. Thus, the use of moving averages and momentum.

I have used a measure of short-term rather than long-term rates, not only because the Fed executes its policies in the short-term market, but also because a more homogeneous mix of short-term rates is available. Also, at least at the major interest rate turning points, both long and short rates change direction at approximately (within a few months at most) the same time. However, they both make numerous false starts. Nevertheless, I suspect that a long-term rate index would be useful.

Money Cycle Use

Of course, the goal in using the Money Cycle Index is to develop a profitable investment strategy, but a couple of points need to be made before any specific strategy is suggested.

First, the Money Cycle itself, or interest rate cycle if you prefer, as contrasted to the index of it, is a graphic measure of how often investors should expect to change strategies to avoid the Fed-initiated capture of their money. Measuring the cycle peaks to troughs and vice versa over

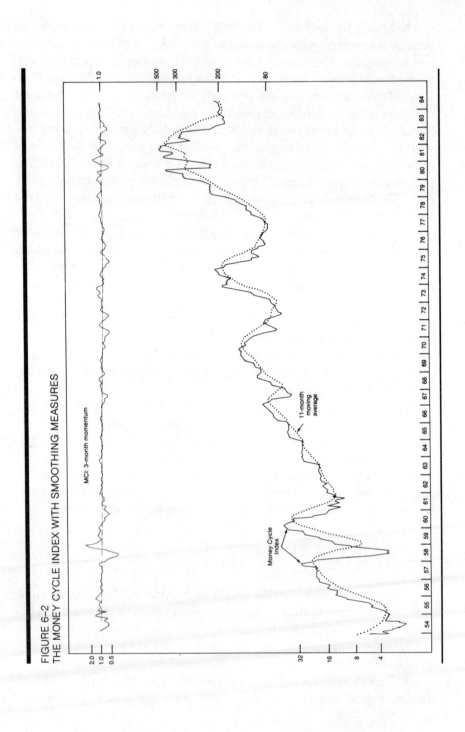

FIGURE 6–2
THE MONEY CYCLE INDEX WITH SMOOTHING MEASURES

the most recent era shows that reversals occurred about every 2½ years, give or take six months, with the exception of the sharp V change in 1980. It is not certain that the time frame in this pattern will continue in the future, but it is true that investors should be prepared for a change in investment strategy roughly every couple of years until there is clear evidence that the Fed has mastered the art of gradualism in monetary policy action. No such evidence is currently available.

A second point about the Money Cycle requires a quick refresher course in fixed-income securities. A bond or note of some years' maturity is favorably impacted by falling interest rates (since its price will climb) and adversely affected by rising rates (because of its opposite price reaction). If one could determine about when the cyclical reversals were due to occur, fixed-income security losses could be avoided on the rate upturns, and nice profits could be captured on the downdrafts. The Money Cycle giveth and taketh away.

In the short-term money market, too, the same process takes place, but with money market instruments maturing by definition in less than a year, price changes are not the critical factor for the average investor. Instead, it is a matter of how much income is generated: in rising-rate markets, there's more, and with lowering rates, less.

Thus an important distinction arises for fixed-income securities between results in rising interest rate markets and those in falling interest rate markets. With rising rates, longer fixed-income securities both fall in price—thus losing part of the capital invested in them—and lose the income that lost capital might later produce. (If not sold, they often cause "lock ins" for periods up to 20 or 30 years.) Shorter-term maturities show only a reduction in current income produced in the rising-rate environment. Longer-term notes and bonds are, therefore, highly risky in an inflationary climate and are certainly doubly disadvantaged when compared with money market maturities.

Of course, the reverse is also true. Bonds appreciate in falling-rate eras, thereby providing more capital on which to earn future income, and money market instruments lose current income but keep the capital intact.

In sum, longer term note and bond purchases must be timed in the Money Cycle because of market-risk changes, whereas money market vehicles have virtually no market risk and can be constantly held. (This latter point is clearly seen when the inflation-beating qualities of these vehicles, even in low-rate periods, is recalled.)

The investor not wishing to be forced to trade in and out of the bond market (at least every couple of years) does well to avoid bonds and concentrate that capital in the short-term money market. This condition of the inflationary era is diametrically opposed to the rules of the deflation era from the early 1920s to the mid-1940s (and during the cyclical downdrafts of the past three decades). However, an inflationary bias is still in operation in the 1980s. Inflation may have been sharply reduced in the 1981–84 periods, but it was not eliminated.

In short, the Money Cycle in an inflationary era is biased to take money away from long-term fixed-income investors rather than to make it for them. The money-making opportunities when rates go favorably downward are the rare exceptions to the bias. This is a key lesson that the Money Cycle teaches.

The Index Itself

The first quality of the MCI is that, since it's based on interest rates themselves, it will move *with* those rates, not ahead of them. As such, it is subject to all the short-term fluctuations and market foibles of the money market. Taken by itself, the index can't predict anything. It can only measure what is happening, and that can be misleading. But don't throw in the towel yet. A couple of measurement techniques that have proven value in recognizing changes in trends are the moving averages and momentum measurements referred to above. These charting procedures, shown in Figure 6–2, have become quite useful with the MCI. (The 6-month MA referred to below is not plotted.)

A moving average (MA) is exactly what its name implies, a numerical average that moves relative to a basic chart plot. For example, a 6-month MA of the MCI shows where the actual plot would be on a chart if any week's plotted point were numerically equal to the average of its past six months' levels. It is calculated by adding the past six monthly MCI values and dividing by six. The following month's value is then added, and the 6th prior month's value is removed to arrive at the next month's moving average level. The same process is used with the 11-month MA shown.

A moving average can tell two important things: (1) whether the current index level is above or below its recent average and (2) whether that fact has been important historically. Adding to this information a charting rule of thumb that says a trend in being remains in being until clearly reversed, allows one to draw some useful conclusions about current index data with the aid of MAs.

Incidentally, there is nothing magical about the length of 6-month or 11-month MAs. MAs of any length can be calculated and used *if they reveal meaningful information.* The two MAs discussed have proved useful with the MCI because the 6-month measure has acted primarily as a line about which the trend in being has oscillated for many years. It seems to be a type of moving anchor to which the broad trend of short-term rates is tied. The index itself seems to return to this MA periodically, but it is only on significant movements through and then away from this MA when important interest rate-trend changes have occurred. As such, it provides an excellent alert signal.

The 11-month MA is far more important. It is a line that has been broached by the index during the past three decades only when a significant rate change took place. In fact, all the index movements through this line in the period since 1955 have signified major alterations of Fed policy, with the exception of summer 1971. (Its timing was a bit slow for the 1980 flip-flop though.)

In 1971 a valid rate change was aborted by President Nixon's removal of all gold backing to the dollar and a wage-price freeze. The case stands as an excellent reminder that no index or charting technique can be blindly relied upon to predict future events. Still, this fact does not greatly reduce the value of the MCI or its MAs as a cross-check on one another and the economic fundamentals. The truth remains that any valid change in interest rate trend must appear in these data. The art is in determining whether a given movement is a major change or not.

An excellent additional aid is the *momentum* of the MCI. A 3-month measurement is most useful because it's short enough to catch quick reversals (such as the one in 1980) and with trend lines is able to visualize long-term pressures, such as that of 1975–79. Momentum is simply a proportion of a current index reading compared with its level of a given time past, in this case three months. By plotting the decimal proportion as a moving line of consecutive readings around an unchanged or "even" line, we can often determine several characteristics of a given rate movement.

In 1971, for example, MCI momentum bottomed a month before the index itself did and later reversed to a new downtrend with the same advance warning. What's more, the momentum upturn was unsustainably steep, and so was the downswing, suggesting that neither should have great duration. In addition, the momentum *level,* a second criterion, topped at + 32 percent, not a particularly strong level (+ 50 percent to + 70 percent is a historically important range). These measurements alone would not have been sufficient to override the clear trend indicated by MCI's breaking of its MAs in 1971, but they would have suggested wariness for reversals, which is exactly what occurred.

A similar situation happened in 1980 when rates bottomed in the June-August period, but the MA crossovers were still 30 to 60 days away for the 6- and 11-month lines, respectively. Momentum, however, turned up the second week in June and was headed sharply higher by the first week of August. Again, there was no certainty, but the momentum gauge gave clear warning to check declining-rate assumptions because all was not as it appeared from rates, the MCI itself, or its MAs.

In sum, these plots achieve three goals:

1. Movement of the actual MCI away from its 6-month MA in either direction or a change in the MA slope gives an early warning that a change in interest-rate direction may be in the offing. Agreement by the economic fundamentals that this change is feasible, even without confirmation from the other plots or MAs, forewarns us to be prepared for the change and not to take investment steps that would be detrimental if a complete change in trend actually did occur.

2. This same 6-month MA aids considerably in determining whether a quick change in interest rates that often occurs week to week has any true significance. If the MCI does not penetrate well through its 6-month MA and is not accompanied by a parallel change in momentum, it is likely to be a false move or to require further confirmation. In other words, this early warning system also acts as a noise inhibitor, helping to filter out the minor squiggles and keep attention focused on the critical broad trends.

3. Movement of the MCI past its 6-month MA and through its 11-month MA, when accompanied by a parallel momentum movement, has been a highly reliable signal for a major directional change in short-term interest rates. It has allowed us quite sufficient time to profit from the largest market changes of the past 30 years. I know of no other measures that have been more timely and that are as statistically sound.

Table 6–2 shows the major signals from MCI and its chart assistants from 1969 to 1983. Since it is based largely on hindsight (MCI was developed in 1978 and has since been refined), we can't be certain all the "calls" to buy/sell in a given market could have been made at the times indicated, under the stress of the day. We can be certain that the signals were given.

In any case, the table is instructive in that it shows that significant profit potential exists in market participation based on accurate predictions about the way in which the Fed directs the major trend in short-

TABLE 6–2
MCI SIGNALS 1969–1984

Date	11-Month MA Break	MCI Level	Subsequent High-Low
March 1970	Down	87.60	35.85 Low March 1971
July 1971	Up	54.30	54.30 High July 1971
November 1971	Down	43.84	29.52 Low February 1972
July 1972	Up	38.84	170.40 High August 1974
October 1974	Down	142.16	49.09 Low January 1977
May 1977	Up	54.81	432.97 High April 1980
May 1980	Down	273.34	185.34 Low August 1980
November 1980	Up	340.17	494.13 High June 1981
October 1981	Down	424.23	141.49 Low January 1983
July 1983	Up	158.53	190.41 and rising June 1984

term interest rates. It also creates a simple guide to the best market prospects for a given trend in rates. At this point, it shouldn't be surprising that they are:

Rate Trend	Best Market Prospect
Rising	Short-term money market Gold market*
Falling	Bond market Stock market

*As noted earlier, this market has exceptions to the rule.

Summary

There is ample evidence, both statistical and theoretical, that the prices of fixed income securities and stocks attempt to discount future expectations of interest rates. This is empirically confirmed by a 30-year record of the stock market's S&P 500 Index in relation to important turning points in the short term money market, and by simple math—with bonds. Thus, the use of short term interest rates as a signal device for buying and selling in both the stock market and bond market is soundly based. However, it is far less legitimate in the gold market.

The Money Cycle Index is a numerical measure of key short term interest rates weighted to depict intentions of the Federal Reserve Board as it operates in the money market. By utilizing the charting techniques of two different duration moving averages and a momentum measure with MCI we've been able to separate the random market movements from true directional changes intended by the Fed. When the actual directional changes have been located by MCI, the stock and bond markets have responded as expected.

Accordingly, we now have two cyclical measurement tools, the political cycle and the money cycle, which can act as cross-checks on each other to forecast favorable investment periods in selected markets. The temptation is to rush after more precise timing refinements in them now and plunge into those markets. This would destroy our goal of building low risk profits and merely focus on the "hot" market of the moment. Instead, it's time to get to the heart of the matter of risk control: building a proper portfolio. The cyclical indicator refinements follow shortly.

7

Portfolio Control of Risk

There are some men who, in a fifty-fifty proposition, insist on getting the hyphen.

Laurence Peter

Here's a worthwhile investment goal: Try to get the very most out of investment risk, even to the point of Mr. Peter's hyphen. That may seem like an unusual objective for low-risk investing, or even for the average investor. But in fact it is risk acceptance that creates profit opportunities as well as losses. We know that risk is volatility, and volatility has both up and down components. Therefore, both profits and losses accrue from volatility/risk.

Knowing these simple facts is one thing. Knowing how to use them to your investment advantage is another. They can be used, most definitely, but to do so we must look deeper into risk and its management.

Types of Risk

Overall market risk in any market is known as *systematic* risk. This is the risk to holding an investment issue when the market of which it is a part moves against the issue. Owning a stock during a broad market decline that was caused by factors other than those indigenous to an individual stock. For example, when Fed Chairman Volcker threatens higher interest rates are ahead due to the federal deficit, and the stock market falls carrying your General Motors shares with it, that's systematic risk.[1] The degree of systematic risk found in a given stock is measured numerically as its *beta*. More on it in a moment.

What must be known about this form of risk is that you can't diversify away from it. Owning more stocks, even the whole NYSE list, won't get you away from the market's decline that day, even though some stocks will rise against the trend. However, you can still take two actions to prevent systematic risk from affecting your portfolio too greatly. You can increase your cash position and thereby dampen the effect of the market fall (and a future rise). Or you can switch to another market such as gold, that might go against the stock market's drop and likewise cushion the stocks' decline in your portfolio. Other than not owning stocks at all, those two actions are an investor's only methods for dealing with systematic risk.

The second form of investment risk is called *specific* risk, and it's just what you'd expect it to be: that risk associated with an individual issue, and only that issue. Taking our example above a step further, let's suppose that General Motors issued a poor earnings report on the day in question. The stock probably reacted negatively to Chairman Volcker's statements, and undoubtedly to its corporate earnings report as well. It got something of a double push downward. The earnings report provided the *specific* risk.

This risk form can be eliminated by not owning GM stock on that particular day, or it can be reduced drastically by diversification into other stocks. If you owned the whole NYSE list, you might not have avoided the general market drop, but you would have significantly reduced any portfolio damage done by the GM news. The key fact to remember here is that the more widely diversified your investment portfolio is, the closer its results will approach that of the market, and vice versa.

A third form of risk is *extramarket* risk. This is simply risk arising from an issue's belonging to a group. In stock groups, for example, GM belongs to the auto category and would be affected by developments affecting all auto stocks, but not railroad issues. Stocks usually belong to

---

[1] For a detailed discussion of the theory underlying this concept, see Robert L. Hagin's *Modern Portfolio Theory* (Homewood, Ill.: Dow Jones-Irwin, 1979).

more than one group because industry classification is only one form of grouping. Autos are also durable goods stocks and are interest-sensitive stocks, too. All three of those categories may present some risk or reward potential at different times. However, this form of risk can be controlled in the same way as specific risk—by diversification, cash balancing or intermarket transfer. Thus, only the systematic form of risk is not diversifiable and all three risks can be handled by cash and intermarket adjustments.

Other forms of risk are commonly cited in discussions of the topic: inflation risk, banking system risk, etc. These are all risks which are *external* to the markets. Therefore, these are managed by proper control of market risk within the portfolio. Forecasting higher inflation? Increase your risk exposure to inflation beneficiary investments.

In addressing what to *do* with this risk knowledge, we must bring volatility back into our discussion, since it is the actual measurement of risk in investments. Volatility is predjudiced. It is the measure of just one form of risk acting on a particular issue at a given time: systematic risk. As noted earlier, when risk is specified numerically in stocks, it is termed beta.

The beta of a stock is a decimal relationship of that stock's historic volatility compared with that of the overall market as measured by the S&P 500. Market volatility is assigned a value of 1.0, and stocks with less volatility are ranked lower, from 0.99 down. Those with greater volatility are above 1.0. To utilize a stock's beta, simply multiply the beta in question by the anticipated risk (or gain estimate) for the market as a whole.

Thus a stock with a beta of 1.8 would be expected to move with 1.8 times as much volatility as the overall market, assuming no other company news developments or group action affected that stock's movement. If the market declined or was expected to fall 10 percent, this stock could be expected to drop about 18 percent.

This measurement allows a ready method for calculating the risk in the common stock segment of any portfolio—multiplying the average beta of that segment by the estimate for the overall market's vulnerability. To the answer may then be added any expected risk from an individual stock or stock group. The result is a volatility (risk) estimate for the portfolio stock segment. If the market declines (or rises) x percent, the stock segment will be expected to change by a decimal multiple of that amount, depending on the beta of its components. This gives us a first practical method of risk assessment and estimating.

Controlling Risk with Cash

Now let's deal with one risk control method in some detail. Utilizing cash equivalents, such as T-bills, money market funds, and commercial paper to cushion the impact of adverse market moves can be neatly quantified.

Suppose an investor had committed all his/her funds to buying an equivalent of the S&P 500 at the 118 level where that index sold in October 1981, about the time the MCI crossed below its 11-month MA. The buy signal was a proper one in theory, as the table at the end of Chapter 6 showed. Unfortunately, the stock market didn't see it that way and kept right on falling until the following August, when the S&P 500 bottomed at about 104. Thus the decline in more than 11 months was an annoying 12.5 percent coupled with a long wait.

Had the investor divided the funds half and half between cash in the mattress and the S&P 500, the loss would have only been half, or 6.25 percent, to the total "portfolio." More sensibly, had that cash portion been invested in one-year T bills, which at that time were yielding about 15 percent, the *total portfolio* return would have been *plus* .25 percent in that 11 months. A market-risk loss could have been turned into a "portfolio" gain through the simple expedient of balancing market risk with a cash-equivalent earnings certainty.

In fact, growth-market risk can always be controlled through the use of cash equivalents. The question is only how much of each to hold and at what return?

In a two-part portfolio, cash equivalents and growth, an easy formula can be used to determine the balance. For a $1,000 portfolio:

$$C(1 + i) + G(1 - r) = 1,000$$

where

C = Cash-equivalent amount.
G = Growth amount.
i = Interest rate on cash equivalents.
r = Estimated downside risk on growth amount.

As an example, let's assume an investor who can obtain a highly secure return of 12 percent on his/her cash equivalents for a year has his/her portfolio balanced 60–40 percent in favor of the cash equivalents

over the growth segment. As a result, he/she can absorb a loss of 18 percent of the growth segment in that year *without overall portfolio loss.*
    Proof:

$$1.12 \times 600 + (1 - 0.18) \times 400 = 1,000$$
$$672 + 328 = 1,000$$

To determine the amount of downside protection the same cash
equivalent-to-growth balance will achieve with a 10 percent annual cash
return in just *six months,* solve the equation for r using half the annual
cash yield:

$$1.05 \times 600 + (1 - r) \times 400 = 1,000$$
$$400(1 - r) = 370$$
$$r = 0.075$$

The portfolio balanced this way in a 10 percent-yield world can absorb a
7.5 percent loss in its growth assets over six months and still break
even.
    To determine the correct *portfolio mix* when the estimated growth
risk is 20 percent and the cash yield is 10 percent (over a period of one
year) requires two variables and use of simultaneous equations, where C
+ G = 1,000. Solving for C:

$$1.1C + 0.8(1,000 - C) = 1,000$$
$$0.3C = 200$$
$$C = 666.7$$

Thus a portfolio having two thirds in cash equivalents at 10 percent
and one third in growth investments that lose 20 percent in a year would
break even.
    It is obvious that the goal of investing is not just to break even. No one
would attempt to structure a portfolio in this way only. However, the
protection-first concept does require looking carefully at the *downside*
risk in growth investments and not becoming so heavily committed in
one investment that the portfolio would show a substantial loss if the
identified risk were realized. The value of balancing is in ensuring that
an investment position doesn't get carried away.
    Two questions immediately flow from this: How does one know that
the upside potential is sufficient to make the investment? How does one
estimate downside risk? The answers are found more in the realm of art
than science, to be sure, but rules of thumb are available. So is the intriguing world of serious technical analysis.

Upside and Downside Potentials

There are two brief rules that I've found most useful in deciding whether to look seriously at a given investment.

First, study that issue's systematic and specific risk levels to determine whether or not it has the right mental comfort characteristics for you. If it doesn't, there's no point in digging further. Cross it off promptly. If stock XYZ has 60 percent greater volatility than the market and you can't sleep with anything greater than 25 percent *less* volatility, forget it. There'll be a right one along soon.

A second rule addresses the matter of comparative growth potential. It says that over a reasonable time period of 6 to 12 months the upside estimate for gain should be at least double that of the downside risk. I'd even prefer 3–1 when I can get it. This condition is useful because it forces the investor to make numerical estimates of both upside and downside potentials before investing. And that means focusing on just how far this growth item might fall if things don't go quite according to Hoyle. There's nothing like a dose of contrary opinion to alert the caution senses.

The techniques for determining *upside* potential in any given growth investments are discussed in the respective chapters on those vehicles. Usually the vendor or analyst recommending or bringing the issue to your attention will devote considerable effort to convincing you about it, as well.

Making a *downside* risk estimate must rely largely on the world of technical analysis since few brokers care to make loss estimates when recommending a buy. However, in falling markets, some "support" estimates are given by technical analysts. They are looking for a chart pattern that offers a sound basis for believing that good buying support will come into the issue or market at a specific level or trading area.

Support Levels

The Dow Jones Industrial Average (DJIA) from 1977 to 1980 (Figure 7–1) shows the most prominent type of probable market support—a chart area that moves horrizontally within a relatively narrow range. It is usually preceded by a general market decline to that area from higher levels. From mid-1978 to late 1979, the 780–825 range was one that pro-

FIGURE 7-1
DOW JONES INDUSTRIAL AVERAGE, 1977–1980

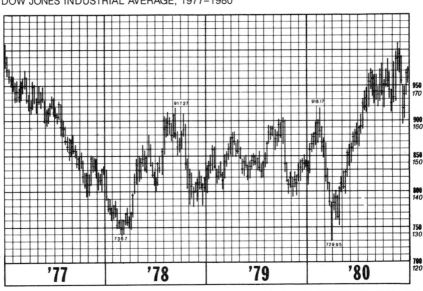

vided great support. It contained (stopped) five declines in those two years. It was ultimately pierced in 1980, but by only 5 percent.

Once the market has treaded along a generally narrow path for a period and then launches an upward move from it, chartists consider that it has built a base from which new gains can be made. In fundamental terms, the market has been simply marking time prior to developing a new advance. Since it is from this apparent base that the new rise ascends, in charting theory it is also at this base that a future falling market has support: Investors were willing to buy there to stop the prior declines, and so, supposedly, they will be willing to do so again.

For the purpose of this discussion, support areas are those against which to measure potential declines. The longer the period of time during which these supports were formed, the better they provide worthwhile points at which a decline from a current level might be expected to stop. For example, if the market in terms of the above DJIA is at 1000 and an important base extends between 850 and 900, an estimate of a potential decline would be 100 or 150 points, or about 10–15 percent.

This is the range that can be used in the previous formula for estimating downside risk. It's rough, but we're not looking for precision here.

Bases are not the only forms of chart support. A second one is the multiple-bottom formation, evident in the pattern of Global Marine stock (Figure 7–2). Note the August and September 1982 downthrusts to 7¼ and 7½ and the third spike to 7⅜ in March 1983 (a triple bottom). These are important signs of a bottom in a stock on the theory that investors have been willing on three occasions over several months to buy the stock sufficiently heavily between certain prices (7¼ and 7½) to turn it up from there. Those are good indications of support and are therefore points at which future declines may be expected to stop, or at least pause.

On the same chart is yet a third form of support. It takes the shape of overhead resistance that is later pierced and becomes a new support level. In this case it is the 10–11 range into which the stock penetrated in July–August, October–November 1982, and May and July 1983. Once decisively broken on the upside, that 10–11 area will become a support level, just as the 7¼–7½ did earlier.

In fact, there's a fourth support, one that is less impressive but there nevertheless. That's the 8–9 range, to which the stock declined from the 10–11 highs paused in the October–April 1982 period. However, since the stock broke that level in March to make its final bottom, it is not a strong support level.

Summing up the Global Marine picture, there has been strong support at 7¼–7½, minor support at 8–9 and, once through to a new high, good probable support at 10–11. This sort of support series is typical in chart patterns, and whether it is seen in a single stock, a stock market average, or in a precious metals or bond futures contract, it delineates probable price ranges that should arrest any declines.

In estimating pullbacks for portfolio-balancing purposes, it is usually with the first support, and occasionally the second, that one will deal.[2]

Support Calculations

Now imagine you've identified a support range of 10–15 percent below the current level for the stock market as a whole, and an average beta for the portfolio stock segment of 1.2. The stock *segment* in a market

---

[2]Many advisory services also identify important areas of market support on a continuing basis and should be used for this purpose. For other chart patterns identifying areas of market support, see Robert D. Edwards and John Magee, *Technical Analysis of Stock Trends* (Springfield, Mass.: John Magee, 1957).

FIGURE 7-2
GLOBAL MARINE, 1982–1983

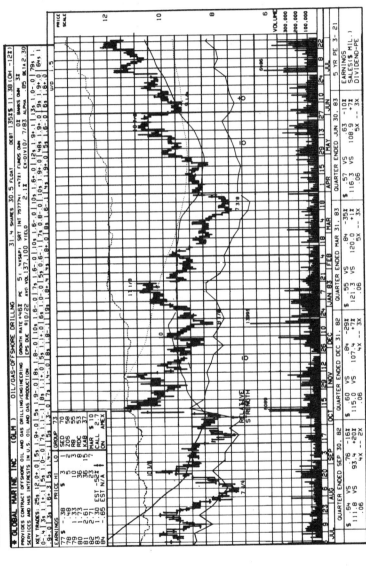

Source: Daily Graphs, P.O. Box 24933, Los Angeles, CA 90024.

correction could see 1.2 × 0.15 = an 18 percent decline, or a 1.2 × 0.10 = a 12 percent drop to lower market support. It would be stated as a downside risk of 12–18 percent.

These numbers could then be fed into the balancing formula to determine what portfolio balance of stocks and cash equivalents for any given interest rate and time period would create zero portfolio loss with this risk. To offset an average 15 percent risk over one year with a 10 percent interest rate, the portfolio balance would be at 60 percent of portfolio in cash equivalents and the 40 percent remainder in stocks.

To protect against this sort of market decline potential under the conditions above, you would balance the portfolio with those percentages. This type of reasoning is useful for determining how well protected your portfolio is from unexpected losses.

A portfolio constantly kept in such balance would of course be unusual. These are necessarily rough estimates of market declines, and there is truly little point in focusing only on the downside when gains are the desired results. Nevertheless, it is wise to consider these factors when establishing a portfolio structure and at times during which the market(s) appear vulnerable to declines.

Comparative Results

To estimate what would be achieved with a given portfolio balance if the growth segment were to show either a gain or loss of a certain amount, let's take a 2–1 cash-equivalent-to-growth balance in a 10 percent interest rate environment with a 20 percent gain in comparison to the 20 percent loss noted a few pages back. Here the arithmetic is simpler than in the formula. A $1,000 portfolio to start and a 2–1 balance would call for $667 in cash equivalents and $333 in growth. Adding 10 percent interest to the cash segment and a 20 percent gain to the growth would make the total portfolio worth $1,133.30 at the end of a year. The gain would thus be 13.3 percent. Comparing this with the prior loss protection shows the trade-off. We've traded a downside protection of zero overall portfolio loss against a potential gain of 13.3 percent under conditions of a 20 percent growth segment loss or gain, respectively. Not a bad trade-off.

These examples have shown that:

- Upside gain potential is not the only sensible side of the market to weigh.

- In high-interest rate times, the returns on cash are a valuable portfolio-management ingredient.
- A given market risk that cannot be diversified away or eliminated by making investments in other markets, can be controlled by portfolio balance.
- The trade-off for reduction of market risk is reduced upside gains, but only if rebalancing action is not taken before gains occur.

Practical Rules

Let's set this knowledge into the context of practical portfolio management by specifying a few action steps.

1. Compile a list of all your liquid financial assets, excluding all items that do not have ready markets—such as real property, insurance and annuities, or such collectibles as art or Chinese ceramics. This is your present investment portfolio.

2. Organize this list into the two broad categories of cash equivalents and growth per the above discussion. Some items won't quite fit—for example, investments made primarily for income, such as bonds or utility stocks. A good rule here is that any investment that has a widely fluctuating market or a maturity date longer than about three to four years cannot properly be purchased for income alone. Even low levels of inflation will eat away at the market value, and high rates will destroy it. Accordingly, cash equivalents should contain two sections: (1) daily availability assets, such as money market funds, plus that paper with maturities up to one year, and (2) those assets with one- to four-year maturities. All other income items belong in the growth category along with true growth stocks and metals bought for price appreciation.

3. Once your portfolio is organized as above, figure what percentage of the total is in each and what the average rate of cash return is on the cash and growth segments. The growth segment cash return includes only dividends and interest.

4. With these figures in hand, estimate the risk that your portfolio is now taking. The following example should help.

Suppose your portfolio shows 33 percent in cash equivalents (both sections combined) and 67 percent in growth of all types. Assume cash returns are 11 percent on cash equivalents and 8 percent on growth. For a $1,000 portfolio, at the end of a year the cash items will be worth 11 percent more, or $366.30 in total, and the growth items 8 percent more (assuming no market change), or $723.60. The new portfolio total is

$1,090.20. In other words, the portfolio will have a positive return of just over 9 percent in the year ahead if the market in the growth items doesn't change. It will also withstand about a 9 percent decline in the combined markets over the year without net loss per calculations explained earlier.

5. You are now in a position to determine whether this portfolio structure and its planned returns are adequate compared with your market forecast. Do you expect an 8 percent inflation rate? There's almost no room in this portfolio for a market decline on top of that inflation cut in real return. Do you anticipate that several months from now the growth markets' downside risk will be 12 percent from current levels? The portfolio will be in a losing position if that occurs. In both cases, increased cash equivalents might be called for unless the markets' upside potentials appear more significant. Estimate those for comparison.

In sum, you should now be in a position to manage your portfolio instead of having it manage you. Before long, especially in using some of the portfolio-management techniques discussed below, you'll be surprised how your feeling of control over your financial destiny increases. Using such techniques will also produce measurable results in ease of decision making and performance.

Cash Management

The objective of managing cash is of course to obtain the highest return on it while keeping sufficient liquidity for other portfolio needs, such as growth buying opportunities. Cash should also be available for personal emergencies or, in the case of institutions, for general business or retirement contingencies.

As simple as that sounds, cash management is a whole investment discipline that is attracting some of the best investment industry talent and computer backup available. The money market itself is sufficiently complex and important not only to have spawned a new industry around it in the past decade with assets in the hundreds of $ billions (the money market mutual funds and money market deposit accounts combined), but also to become the centerpiece of major brokerage firms' cash-management "sweep" accounts.[3] It is also the subject of numerous major books of worldwide interest.[4]

[3]"A Buyers Guide to the Financial Supermarkets," Forbes, August 1, 1983.
[4]The most comprehensive is Marcia Stigum's The Money Market, rev. ed. (Homewood, Ill.: Dow Jones-Irwin, 1983).

There is one important cash management technique that can be refined and expanded as your portfolio grows. It approaches "interest rate nirvana," or more simply put, not caring about interest rate trends as they might affect your cash equivalents.

If you have the knowledge and ability to trade the money and note markets to obtain a maturity schedule that keeps you on top of interest rate movements, this hedging procedure is child's play. You're already doing something more than is involved in this procedure. However, if that expertise or time to pursue it is not available, this method is an easy way to obtain a moving average of short-term rates, no matter how they move. What's more, it doesn't matter if you begin it during a high- or low-rate period.

The plan is to obtain both a fixed-rate commitment and a daily rate change on different parts of your cash equivalents. To accomplish this, I prefer to use the two- to three-year Treasury note market for one portion of the funds and an all-Treasuries money market fund for the other part. Working this requires a minimum of $20,000 cash equivalents, so that the fee to buy the note doesn't destroy the yield.

Simply placing half the cash equivalents in each vehicle hedges against both upward and downward movements in interest rates. Assume you have $10,000 in a two-year Treasury note yielding 11 percent (11 percent coupon at par) and a money market fund currently yielding 10 percent. Table 7–1 shows the effect of a 500 basis point (5 percentage points) increase and decrease in market interest rates after 18 months.

In a rising-rate environment the average yield on your cost also rises, albeit to a level a bit below the current market of 15 percent. The trade-off for that rise is a decline in the price of the note (see table footnote).

TABLE 7–1
A CASH EQUIVALENT HEDGE

| | Start | | 18 Months Later | | | |
| | | | + 500 Basis Points | | − 500 Basis Points | |
Vehicle	**Price**	**Yield (percent)**	**Price***	**Yield** (percent)**	**Price***	**Yield** (percent)**
T-note	100	11 %	68.75	11 %	183.33	11 %
MMF	1	10	1	15	1	5
Average		10.5%		13.0%		8.0%

100 basis points = 1 percent.
*Prices shown would not actually be achieved in the time frame indicated because of the pressure of the note's *yield to maturity*. Investors would bid up the price in rising-rate periods and sell it lower in declines, but the direction of movement is correct.
**Yield is current return on cost—not current yield or yield to maturity.

However, since it matures in a relatively short time (six months later in our example), the price drop is of no real import for holders to maturity.

On the other hand, in the falling-rate period, your cash return remains above the new market level of 5 percent, and your note appreciates in price. You then have the delightful choice of deciding whether or not to sell the note at a profit. If you strongly believed that rates were about to rise again, the sale would make sense, even though it would reduce (temporarily, you hope) your cash return, since the proceeds would be re-invested at only 5 percent.

The keys to success in this strategy are its simplicity, the use of a Treasury note that matures in a couple of years, and the modest discipline it requires in rolling it over at maturity. Taking a long maturity would reduce the value of the automatic bail-out in rising-rate periods and make the choice of whether or not to take the note profit in declining-rate periods more difficult.

Since this strategy is so simple it becomes obvious that varying two elements will make the hedge a more active one: Select an earlier maturity for the note when rising rates are forecast, and vice versa, or increase the amount committed to the note when declining rates are forecast, and vice versa. Using the Money Cycle Index to aid in rate projections should be of help. Also, multiple-note maturities may be used if sufficient cash is available, committing to one-, two- and three-year maturities, for example. Still holding an amount in the money market fund that's roughly equal to the note total will achieve a similar balance. Splitting the total amount invested into equal thirds is the procedure that became known as the "Kinsman Spread" on my CBS talk program in 1984.

There's nothing magical about the foregoing cash-management procedure, but its simplicity is a major plus in this otherwise complicated financial world.

Summary

This and the preceding three chapters have taken the money-management problem from the recognition stage through a discussion of the tools needed to establish a management strategy. They discussed a strategic framework in terms of investment emphasis during the stages of wealth accumulation, the concept of achievable return, and the formulas that make it work. They've shown that cyclical phenomena are both widely used and often flawed in the investment world but that recognizing the limitations of some cycles can make them extremely useful, especially the direction-pointing nature of the political cycle, and the moving-force aspects of the money cycle. The portfolio has been presented as a means of organizing and managing investments toward your goals, and more important, as an excellent means for controlling risk. Central to this is the way in which the portfolio is balanced both by estimating risk and then by controlling the prevailing market and nonmarket risk. Cash management is an important part of that process. We now have a sound basis and the tools for an overall low risk investment strategy.

Next, we put these elements together in the key investment markets, based on the first of our three portfolio segments, protection.

PART THREE

Fitting
the
Pieces

Protection First: Insurance

8

*Insurance agents tirelessly argue
that whole life policies are great
for people who lack the discipline to save.
That's a little like saying
the Sahara is a good place for people
too dumb to get out of the rain.*

Money magazine

Protecting investment assets before attempting to profit on them is one of the first principles of low-risk investing in high-risk times. Thus far, the principle has been discussed mainly in terms of portfolio management and risk control in securities. Going a step further, a moment's reflection will raise the point that risk control is principally a matter of risk transfer in some form.

Diversification transfers the specific risk in one stock to several. Cash balancing partially transfers it to the certainty of cash returns. Buying into a second or third market transfers some risks to those markets. Each method changes the risk-reward relationship of the portfolio in which it is utilized.

There is very little that is different in these principles where insurance is concerned. Life insurance transfers a particular kind of risk—interruption of an income stream—in a different way from the methods used in a portfolio, but the concept remains the same.

Risk Transfer through Life Insurance

There are many forms of insurance, of course. Although casualty insurance on your home or car has little to do with investments, that type of insurance illustrates risk transfer best.

To avoid the risk of paying the potential replacement cost of a car or home or the cost of personal liability, the insurance buyer transfers most of the risk to an insurance company in return for an annual fee, the policy premium. The insurance company spreads the risk from one client's home or car among thousands of other owners and their premiums by calculating what its likely payoff risk is for each and then charging appropriate fees. Simple enough.

With life insurance, the risk-transfer principle still applies, but the nature of the risk to be transferred changes. Life insurance takes a novel approach to the risk-transfer process because it can't protect against the risk to the insured person's life by paying that person when loss occurs. It pays someone else for the loss. (Endowment or annuity-type policies alter this and pay whether or not the insured has died by the end of the policy period.) Of course, casualty insurance can be written in the same way, naming a third party as the loss payee, but with life insurance there typically is no other choice.

Since life insurance protection is not for the insured but for someone else, what is being protected is not a life, but rather the earning power of that life: *personal earning power.*

Going further, it is obvious that the risk to life is not the risk that is being transferred, since death is a certainty. The critical matter is timing of it. Timing is the aspect of the earning-power risk that is transferred to the insurance company. This fact has important implications as to the type of insurance purchased and its cost.

For example, compare a young person who has family dependents with a middle-age, post-family-dependent person. Since the younger person has less risk of dying in that age bracket, insurance rates will be cheaper. Yet, (s)he probably has a greater family-protection need. The two interact to suggest more inexpensive insurance is needed for the younger person than an older one.

In contrast with other types of insurance, life insurance further adds the novel element of return on the money that has been paid to the insurance company. That return, earned over the life of the policy itself, is the savings feature of the policy. It becomes an investment matter.

Estimating Life Insurance Needs

Earning power to be protected, timing, and the savings feature must be considered when choosing a policy. These key questions will help determine how much and what type of life insurance is appropriate for most people. Life insurance buyers should consider these matters.

1. Who is it you wish to protect against earning power loss?
2. What specific goals should this accomplish?
3. For how long should this protection last?
4. To be effective, what dollar value should this protection have? Will the necessary dollar value change with time?
5. How much of the total amount of protection needed is covered by your current assets?
6. Will other assets, such as a pension or profit sharing plan or Social Security bear on the future value of this protection, and how much?
7. Does this total protection value require a savings feature in the insurance?
8. What type of insurance can best meet these protection and value goals?
9. What is the lowest-cost method of buying this insurance?

From these questions, you can clearly see that the savings aspect of life insurance should not usually be the primary reason for buying it. Savings should be considered only in the valuation or investment part of the determination, since it has no bearing on protection. To those who argue that the enforced payment attribute of life insurance is important, I reemphasize the quote from *Money* at the beginning of this chapter. There may be exceptions, and a certain type of policy might be able to provide all life insurance features at a combined lowest cost. However, to purchase the policy primarily for its savings feature misses the most important reasons for it. (The tax advantage of one category of life policies make it an exception. See below.)

In answering the questions above, for number 1 suppose you are a successful midlife person with two grown children and no spouse. Who should you protect with insurance on your life? Maybe no one, assuming that the grown children don't require some special funds. If you own a business upon which many others depend for their livelihood, "key man" insurance might be appropriate. If not, you may not need life insurance at all, especially if burial costs are provided for in a joint savings-type account with a close friend or relative. However, the addition of a spouse or younger children radically changes these answers and shifts the focus to the questions on amounts.

In question 2, goals to be accomplished and time frame raise some important points. They should be answered as specifically as possible. If you die while your children are still school-age, should their schooling be funded by insurance, at least in part? How much would your spouse need to live on in today's dollars? Should your spouse have the same protection throughout life, or more or less, and for how many years?

Questions 3 through 6 deal with the basic idea of how much insurance is appropriate. Herein lies the greatest disagreement among insurance specialists. The fundamental points of view largely revolve around two different methods of calculation: life value and programmed needs.

The life value approach, which generally results in a higher insured amount than does the programmed needs method, depends primarily on how great a rate of discount on expected future income is chosen, and is less widely used than programmed needs. In brief, life value requires estimating aftertax, after-living-expense, average annual income for the remainder of your productive life and then selecting an appropriate discount rate for the value of those earnings. Then an annuity table (with a future value of 1), gives an estimate of the future value of those earnings. Presumably, life insurance should make up the difference between your discounted worth to your family now and the family's current investable net assets.

This insurance estimate method suffers from a need to update data frequently because of changes in real earnings and because it's based on multiplying earnings by the number of productive years remaining in life, which obviously declines annually. Contrast this with the need to purchase life insurance on a long-term contract basis (even if it's decreasing term insurance), and you can see why this approach is not favored by many experts.

The programmed needs approach is more accurate but can be carried to such an extreme in detail as to glaze the eyes of most insurance buyers. Fortunately, insurance company computers will provide all the details ever wished for if you'll just provide the inputs. It's the providing of facts and discussing them with an agent that are the drawbacks here.

The needs method attempts to categorize and then estimate the family's specific needs at various future times in the event of the death of the covered wage earner. It takes into account such diverse needs as (1) dependency income to support the family until the children grow up; (2) a life income for the spouse after this dependency period; (3) a readjustment income to ease the potential burden of a change in living standards upon death of the principal earner; (4) children's education, mortgage payoff, and an emergency fund; and (5) lump-sum expenses, such as illness and burial costs and probate expenses, if any.

Once these items are estimated separately, a time graph is plotted versus these income or capital needs. It includes factors for future payments for pension/profit sharing, IRAs, Social Security, and the like. The result is then funded on paper by each available asset, including a selection of types of life insurance.

Since insurance agents provide this information without cost (except for your time), it makes sense to let them do so. In fact, once the basic information is gathered, it makes sense to have at least three specialists provide their estimates and insurance product recommendations. At minimum, two of these estimates should be obtained from certified financial planners. They are better equipped to view your full insurance needs within the context of other investments than are most insurance agents. Unless your situation is complicated neither by income taxes nor a multiplicity of investments, make a note now to obtain this insurance review, or roughly estimate it yourself from Table 8–1.

The remaining questions in the list, 7–9, deal with types of life insurance.

Types of Life Insurance

Term Insurance

Term insurance is the basic form of pure protection. It represents a direct transfer of the insurance risk to the underwriter of the policy, and it requires the insured to pay only for that protection for a specified time. There are no savings features unless the policy is a modified form of term insurance. The beneficiary receives the face value payment only upon death of the insured. When the term is complete, the protection ceases, and the policy is void.

Term life may be in the form of *level* term, which means that the face amount of the policy is unchanged for the specified term, or it may be *decreasing* term, wherein the benefit declines in value over the term of the policy. The latter form is most useful for young, growing families whose need for protection will logically drop as the children become independent. It might also be useful in a variety of special cases of temporary

TABLE 8–1
A SIMPLE "NEEDS" METHOD FOR ESTIMATING INSURANCE REQUIREMENTS

Lump Sums

Final settlement expenses.*	$_____
Three-month emergency fund for spouse.†	_____
Special fund for education, etc.‡	_____
Total 1–3.	_____

Annual Living Expenses

a. Spouse's gross expenses estimate.	_____
b. Less: Spouse's aftertax income.	(_____)
c. Less: Social Security benefits.§	(_____)
d. Net expenses.	_____

Investment Returns

Years until spouse reaches 90 = _____. If this number is 40 or more, write ½ of it here:	_____
If not, and it is 20–39, write in 70 percent of it:	_____
Multiply this number by net expenses in d above. This is the *total* living expenses factor.	_____
Add total lump sum 1–3 above.	+ _____
Subtotal	_____
From this, subtract total net investment assets you now hold.	(_____)
Total life insurance required	$_____

*This amount should include funeral expenses, estate taxes, and any nonmortgage debt. For estates under $250,000, it should be a *minimum* of $7,500, and for those over, at least $12,500.
†This sum should be three times current monthly take-home pay.
‡This should include any special family financing requirements, such as children's education (estimate $10,000/year per child), grandparents care, etc. If you wish your present home mortgage to be paid off by insurance, include that total amount here or include its annual payments under living expenses (a).
§A rough estimate of Social Security payments will be $4,000 to $5,000 per year. Refine as necessary.
Source: *The Wall Street Journal* and Kinsman Associates, Inc.

needs. However, it does deal at the insured's expense with a basic problem: rising premiums as mortality risk increases with age.

Term insurance is still the cheapest form of insurance that can be bought because of its lack of savings or other special features, but it varies widely in cost based on different actuarial tables used by various companies. When buying term life, you may find some policy premiums are 50 to 70 percent lower than others. In fact, some companies now promote whole life policies with premiums below other firms' term rates.

Whole Life Insurance

Whole life insurance provides protection along with a savings feature for the insured's entire life, even though policy premiums may be paid either for the insured's lifetime or for a specified period of years. Newer forms have annuity provisions built in, along with lump-sum premiums and tax-deferred market rates of return. These offer highly advantageous policies for persons within 5 to 10 years of retirement who are in high tax brackets.

The savings aspect of whole life is controversial these days, primarily because the policy underwriting company is able to pay *unidentified* rates of return on the portion of the premium in excess of the pure actuarial protection amount. These yields are known to be nowhere near current market rates in these high-interest rate times. The result is that the savings element is generally an unsatisfactory use of capital.

The whole life policy basically sets a level premium for an expected future period that is higher than actuarially required in the early years and lower than needed in the later years. However, the interest-compounding aspect of yields on the paid premium more than compensates the company for the later part. This permits the underwriter to offer an attractive cash value to the policy (the savings feature) even in its early years. But the insured person could carry out this savings function with a better return than the insurance company pays if (s)he wished to and had the discipline to do so. The discipline factor is often raised by insurance agents, as noted earlier. If you want the enforced savings feature, just realize you are paying a significant price for it. Sound common advice is "Buy term and invest the difference."

Another disadvantage of whole life is that sales commissions are usually very high—typically 70 percent of the first-year premium and 7½ percent annually thereafter.

Endowment

An even worse form of letting the insurance company do your savings for you is the third type of basic life policy, the endowment. This is a savings program with term insurance protection added on. It works by modifying the third-party-payment concept of life insurance by allowing the insured to be the beneficiary for the risk taken and by establishing a period of time for an insurance contract and accepting specified premium amounts for that time. If the insured lives past the contract end date, the face amount is paid either in a lump sum or in installments over another period of years.

The problem with this form of insurance is that, as with whole life, the premiums are set at levels well in excess of the actuarial protection required. This means the savings account portion of the premium is high. But, the undisclosed compounded return on it is in fact extremely low. If whole life has its justification problems, endowment is a quagmire of them.

Variations

The inflation era has combined with consumer education to spawn literally scores of new insurance policies. Yet almost all of these are some variation on the three basic types just surveyed. The most widely used types of these new policies are called modified life, variable life, adjustable life, and the ultimate (in name at least), universal life.

Modified life is nothing more than a whole life policy with the premiums reduced in early years of the contract and raised later to aid the younger, lower-income earner in affording the policy. Since it generally doesn't improve the savings yield, modified life still suffers from the fault of other whole life policies.

Variable life is a bolder attempt to boost the return on the savings portion of the insurance by permitting policy cash values to be invested in common stocks or other high-potential-return investments. In trade for this attribute, however, most variable life issuers require that the cash value itself or the death benefit rise and fall to some degree with the success of the chosen investment vehicle. This requirement has caused the plan to be sometimes thought of as too much of a good thing. What if the policyholder died or needed to borrow during a bear market?

Adjustable life is sort of a "change when you want" answer to the arguments against other forms of life insurance. It generally permits the policyholder to switch back and forth from term to whole life, or to change the amount of premiums paid with a consequent change in the death benefit, under certain conditions. Often the conditions are the trouble spots, and the first-year sales load is usually deducted from the initial premium, leaving a small initial pay-in.

Universal life is the newest and—since its tax questions were resolved by the 1982 federal tax law—the most popular form of life insurance. Yet, it has its problems, and the variations on it are great.

In simplest terms, universal life provides in one policy two separate accounts: a term insurance program plus a market-rate tax-deferred return on a savings fund for a stated period. The better of these plans allow withdrawal of funds from the savings or adding greater amounts to it, a variable premium in case the budget is tight one year or even a payment of the premium from the savings, and increased insurance protection as desired (usually if medically approved). It's sort of an "all things for all people" policy concept. The plan definitely addresses the important objections to other forms of life insurance.

One point to watch in comparing various universal life policies is the size of the first-year commission to the agent, which is often tacked onto the first-year premium. It can vary by 200 percent even among the better-known companies. Another is how much of the first-year guaranteed return on the savings account applies to all of the account. Typically, there's a lower rate paid on a certain portion. A similar condition may occur in later years. Another point to think about is the annual fee taken by the company from the premium. A recent study found the range to be from 3 percent to 10 percent.[1]

Other points should also be considered with universal life: (1) the surrender charges for taking money out and (2) the aftertax and total cash values at key dates (say, at years 5, 10, and the end of the plan). Look for lowest charges and highest cash values.

When all is considered in the enormously detailed life insurance field, universal life may be the most useful form for the most people because there are more younger persons than older ones around. That doesn't mean that there aren't significant advantages in other life insurance forms, especially term, for the rest of the population. To meet individual or family needs, shop the market, and study the alternatives.

Table 8–2 is a useful comparison of three different insurance plans and their terms.

Single-Premium Variations

The clear pattern of life insurance product development over the past decade has been toward a savings (investment) orientation. As a result, life insurance at its best has ceased to be purely a vehicle for earning power-risk transfer and is becoming more of a financial/retirement planning tool. Nowhere is this clearer than in the newest products, even though they're just new wrinkles in old cloth: the single-premium annuity and single-premium life.

These products were developed to meet two important goals in financial management: tax deferral and market-rate returns. Both are true

---

[1] A highly useful independent review of universal life and other policies is "How To Save Money on Life Insurance" (National Insurance Consumer Organization, 344 Commerce Street, Alexandria, VA 22314).

TABLE 8–2
COMPARISON OF THREE TOP INSURANCE PLANS ($100,000 face value)*;
20-year results

	Cash-Withdrawal Features	Aftertax† Cash Value	Total Cash Value	Aftertax† Death Benefit
Universal Life (USAA CO.)	No penalty for withdrawal; not taxable unless exceeds premiums paid.	$38,555	$55,310	$155,310
Term Plus Annuity (Metropolitan Life)	No cash value on term, penalty for withdrawal from annuity for 10 years and taxable unless exceeds interest earned.	38,203	60,798	138,203
Whole Life (Northwestern Mutual)	Must cancel or borrow against cash value at 8 percent; to withdraw; reduce death benefits even if repaid.	36,027	50,655	133,046

*Assumptions: Premiums set at $1,070 annually, the amount required by the whole life policy based on a 35-year-old nonsmoking male paying for 20 years. Dividends paid by mutual company based on 11 percent investment portfolio annual return and reinvested in additional whole life. Annuity and universal life returns based on investing the difference between term and whole life premium in 11 percent annual yield accounts.
†Assume 50 percent top federal tax bracket.
Source: Edward E. Scharff, "How Sweet Is Universal Life?" *Money*, May 1983.

objectives of investment management, since taxes directly cut available net income/capital, and market-rate returns aid in management of inflation risk. The big disadvantage of these products from a risk standpoint is their pronounced lack of liquidity.

Single-Premium Annuity

The single-premium annuity underwent a significant transformation in the early 1980s. Initially, it was sold as a method of accumulating market-rate, tax-deferred income on the premium up to fulfillment of the annuity contract. There was also an important feature that permitted any funds withdrawn, up to the amount of the original premium, to be considered a repayment of capital and thereby nontaxable.

True, these annuities generally had certain withdrawal penalties, but they were modest and usually extended only the first five years or so. Most important, the penalties were levied by the insurance company, not the IRS. This meant that, until the law was changed in 1982, these annuities often functioned as tax-deferred checking accounts and as such were obviously very popular—except with the tax collectors.

The 1982 federal law changed two facets of annuity operations and resulted in the new generation of them. It specified that initial amounts withdrawn were to be considered interest, not capital, and would therefore be taxable. It also levied a separate 5 percent tax penalty on all money withdrawn before the annuity term expired. The insurance company withdrawal penalties, or lack of them in some cases, became irrelevant. It was the tax that was the problem.

This spawned what the industry has called the post-TEFRA annuity, in reference to the title of the 1982 Tax Equity and Fiscal Responsibility Act. Subsequently, there were both fixed-rate and adjustable-rate annuity contracts, both with limitations on withdrawals. These modifications generally permit investors to switch out of a fixed-rate form into other contracts with the same or even a different insurance company and with no taxable event. If the fixed rate originally specified falls below market rates, the investor can opt for either a new, higher fixed rate or an adjustable one tied to some market measure, such as Treasury bills. Another variation automatically raises the initial fixed rate by a fraction of a percent each year for the annuity term. In almost all cases, variable or fixed, the beginning rate is usually above current money market rates.

Post-TEFRA annuities can be sensibly used in long-range retirement planning as vehicles for obtaining tax deferral on high income from accumulated capital, where that income is not currently required by the owner and is not expected to be required for the term of the contract, usually 10 years. Funds can be withdrawn in an emergency, subject to the company's and tax collector's penalties. This is not a wholly attractive situation, but a positive one.

Single-Premium Life Policy

The single-premium life policy is even better. By adding a death benefit for a beneficiary, dropping the annuity title and attendant stretched payout, and allowing liberal borrowing, this new product has obviated the 5 percent tax penalty for fund withdrawal.[2]

What single-premium life has thus accomplished is (1) insurance protection at very low cost (only that equal to what the insurance company can earn on the premium above the market rate specified in the policy); (2) a choice of market-related or fixed return; (3) tax deferral on that re-

---

[2]In matters on the cutting edge of tax policy (where these products rest because of the recentness of TEFRA), change may be in the wind. However, in 1984 the borrowing of cash value up to the full amount of the paid-in premium was not considered taxable.

turn as earned; (4) very low borrowing costs on both capital and income; and (5) relatively low withdrawal penalties, commonly up to 5 percent for the first five years held. Also, the front-end fee is a moderate 3 to 4 percent of the premium.

For persons with the capital to commit, and especially those in higher tax brackets who don't require current income, single-premium life policies are now a preferred form of retirement-planning vehicle, and a low risk one at that.

A final risk to consider in life insurance that is often overlooked by purchasers is the insurance company. Historically, life companies have enjoyed great profitability due to their product-pricing structure and a favorable tax load. Because of extensive state regulation and reserve requirements levied on them, the question of insurance company safety has rarely been validly raised.

In 1983 a holding company named Baldwin-United changed that. State insurance regulators seized six of the Baldwin companies following disclosure of serious financial problems with the parent and put some 160,000 annuity policyholders on ice while they determined the extent of the damage and what rehabilitation work would have to be done. Baldwin itself later filed for bankruptcy protection under Chapter 11 of the federal bankruptcy laws. Those Baldwin policies had been sold extensively by the largest stock brokerage firms in the country until the Baldwin troubles surfaced publicly in 1982, and neither those firms nor the various state insurance regulators involved questioned the insurance companies' viability until then. In fact, the firm that rates insurance company finances, A. M. Best Co., rated some Baldwin companies in 1982 with its A level, the second highest available.

If the organizations with the closest look and best means to analyze insurance company strengths and weaknesses misrated Baldwin, the average investor has almost no chance in digging through financial records for safety clues. In most cases, the information available is invariably too old to provide any early warning, and it's designed for obfuscation, not simplicity.

Methods of self-protection fall back on commonsense ideas:

1. Deal with products from known insurance companies. If you've never heard of the firm, ask for assurances about its age and financial stability from your financial planner or insurance agent. Require that the company have an A + rating by A.M. Best Co.
2. Invest in smaller policies and use more than one company rather

than one larger policy with one firm. This is a common risk-diversification strategy.
3. Check your state insurance department to determine whether it has a policyholder's "rescue" fund that's been created by insurers to pay off policyholders of failed insurance companies. If not, you may want to purchase an insurance product through a state that does and permits nonresident policyholder protection.

Reinvesting Cash Value

Many older persons own whole life because it was the most popular and heavily promoted form of insurance prior to the 1960s. Most of these have relatively substantial amounts of cash built up in them. Since that's their money and it's earning so little where it is, it makes sense to get it out and reinvest it elsewhere. However, since that withdrawn money will usually be deducted from the policy's death benefit, it's important that it be invested with utmost safety.

One alternative is buying Treasury notes having maturities ranging between two and four years. To proceed, first check the interest rate the insurance company will charge to withdraw the present cash value of the policy. In recent years the rate has varied from 5 to 8 percent. Next, check the *yield to maturity* for the appropriate Treasury note in your newspaper. (The yield shown is almost always the yield to maturity for government notes.) The difference between the borrowing rate and the T note yield is the rate to be gained by borrowing the policy cash value and investing in the note, assuming that the T note yield is higher. You won't borrow if it isn't.

Let's assume that the net in favor of borrowing is 5 percent, made up of a 6 percent borrowing cost and an 11 percent note yield. With this net interest spread, by buying notes you'll gain $50 per year for each $1,000 lying idle in a policy account, less taxes on that amount. The total may not be a great deal, but you're throwing it out with the trash if you don't act.

If the insurance policy is *owned* by someone other than yourself, make sure that person puts the new T note investment in his/her name to ensure that it's in the right hands in the event of your demise. If the policy is owned by you, check with your estate planner as to whether the policy or this borrowed sum should continue to be in your name.

Summary

Insurance plays a vital role in protecting assets by transferring risk. Choosing a life insurance policy and coverage should begin with estimating earning power to be protected, and for whom, considering the goals and timing factors, and looking critically at policy savings features. The latter can often be achieved better by nonpolicy investments.

The basic types of life insurance are still term, whole life, and endowment, but there are many newer variations of these basic forms. The best of these is probably universal life, due to its flexibility. The newest products, single-premium annuity and single-premium life, are intended to combine tax deferral with market-rate returns, the latter most successfully.

A second type of asset protection is available in the markets rather than in contract form. Gold and other precious metals have significant market risks as a result, but remain the purest form of inflation hedge.

Protection Second: Gold

9

*My advice is to put 10 to 15 percent of your assets
into gold and hope that its price goes down.
The world of $100 gold is marked by
happy and trusting people living in peace and plenty.
The world of $1,000 gold is marked by
war, famine, and human misery.*

Nicholas Deak

Gold is virtually indestructible. Gold coins 200 years old found on the ocean floor are as bright as the day they were minted. It is estimated that nearly 90 percent of the gold unearthed in the past 6,000 years is still in existence today—nearly 3 billion ounces, or almost 94,000 tons. All of that mined in the past five centuries, about 60,000 tons, would fill a room less than 55 feet on a side, or about equal in volume to twice the airspace in an average home.

Gold is also one of the most workable of metals. It can be wrought into an almost endless variety of shapes, from sharply angular to gracefully curving sculpture, from absorbing the tiniest details of artistry to filling every crevice and cranny in a tooth cavity. This workability arises out of gold's impressive malleability and ductility. One ounce has been beaten into a sheet covering more than 100 square feet and to a thinness 1,000 times less than that of ordinary paper. Another ounce of it can be drawn into a thread 50 miles long. Gold's electromagnetic reflective qualities have spawned paints now used for shielding electronic circuitry from random interference. At the same time, its electrical conductivity has made it commonplace in high-reliability electronic circuitry.

The key point to note about the five-millennium history of gold is that the world's belief in it for its so-called store of value developed both slowly and voluntarily. When Menes, the first-dynasty Egyptian Pharoh, produced gold for his own use and adornment in the 32d century B.C., it was undoubtedly not an item of public interest. As successive royalty and governments gave it importance and then based their money systems on it, gold grew in public esteem. In fact, public confidence grew to such an extent that when governments eventually reduced their monetary reliance on the metal, as in the case of third-century A.D. Rome, people lost their faith in the government instead of in gold.

The history of gold is replete with examples of debased currencies that coincided with eras of revolution, war, and more decline; and periods of peace and prosperity have tended to occur when money was based on some gold backing.

It would seem that this "barbarous relic," as it was termed by Keynes, has been more desired as a stabilizing force in people's lives than have their governments, which is strong evidence of the voluntary nature of public faith in gold.

These factors of historical permanence, reliability, workability, and beauty have given gold properties unique in comparison with any metal. They are sufficient alone to prompt a demand for the metal. Gold is also scarce and difficult to obtain. Gold has been discovered in quantity on all the five major continents of the world, but demand for it over broad periods has usually exceeded supply, with only temporary exceptions.

Whatever is happening to the world and the price of gold when you read this, one thing is certain: If gold is important in the markets and is rising sharply in value, economic times will be looking worse. Perhaps much worse. If few people care about gold, and its price is stable or declining, economic times will be steady or improving. That's the nature of gold, and it has been so for nearly 5,000 years.

Implications

Some of the important implications of gold's use do not fit the standard views of gold. The first noted below is common and correct. The second is not widely held, but is also correct.

Inflation Related

First, when gold price forecasts economic bad times, that forecast is apt to be inflation related. Gold is an inflation bug. It has risen substantially in price as inflation prospects worsened throughout recorded history, and it will do so again. Figure 9–1 shows this for the 1970s inflation.

FIGURE 9–1
GOLD PRICES VERSUS U.S. CONSUMER PRICES, 1969–83

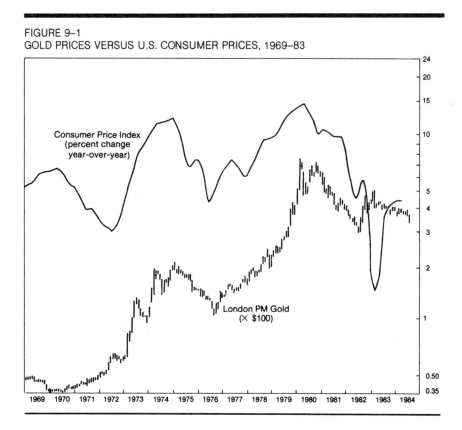

Falls in Price during Deflation

Second, it is very doubtful that gold has any positive protective value in a serious economic depression. It's always possible that some governmental authority will use gold to political ends, as Franklin Roosevelt did in 1933, and thus cause the price to soar. However, deflation per se is not halted by a change in the gold price. A sound theory of economic cause and effect backs this up. That which reacts positively to one set of economic circumstances will not also react positively to the opposite conditions. Accelerating rates of inflation mean a *loss* in the buying power of money. To this, gold reacts positively. The opposite situation, a deflation, is an *increase* in money's buying power. How can one expect gold to react positively to that, too? In fact, it does not. During the disinflationary or deflationary periods since the Great Depression, gold has fallen in price. Each recession beginning with that of 1946 has clearly shown this tendency in a free gold price, as the slump brings about the reversal of the prior inflation.

Figure 9–2 shows the performance of U.S. gold-mining stocks during the 1930s depression. It appears that they performed exactly opposite to what I'm saying (some after 1930 and others after 1932), but this action was caused by other factors. From 1930–32 mining costs were falling while the price of gold was fixed. Mine profits thus rose, and so did their stocks. The gold price was then forced higher by President Roosevelt starting in 1933, when he began setting the gold price over breakfast each morning in an attempt to bolster sagging commodity prices. The process was accelerated by the gold embargo in March 1933 and completed with the new 70 percent higher official gold price of January 1934. Small wonder gold-mining stocks rose in this environment.

Many people believe that gold prices must rise in as serious an economic contraction as the 1930s depression because people will turn to gold as a store of value when other values are collapsing. This may occur if the Federal Reserve Board or some future president takes action similar to Roosevelt's, but it will not be a normal free market reaction to the circumstances. Economic forces will not bring about a gold rise in a depression, but political forces could.

Sensitive to Bad News

This is the third point that develops from the nature of gold. It is highly sensitive to all sorts of political as well as economic bad news. Roosevelt proved that politics can't be separated at will from economics because they are closely intertwined. So, the gold price is apt to fluctuate sharply on news or worries over war or famine or totalitarian political drives. This susceptibility means that the economic forces behind gold price movements are occasionally obscured and even reversed by political actions or forces.

Here the doom-and-gloom folks have a point. A complete economic collapse is an event that every politician, economist, and bureaucrat will attempt to prevent, but since people are fallible, a collapse could arise

FIGURE 9–2
GOLD STOCKS IN THE DEPRESSION

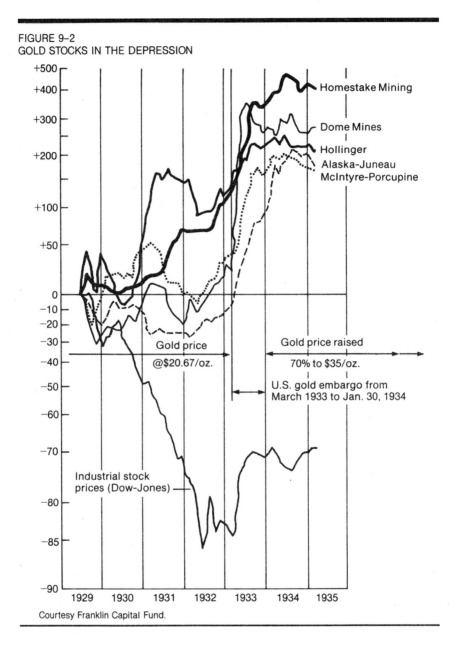

Courtesy Franklin Capital Fund.

out of uncontrollable events. In such an extreme, normal money might have no value, and people might turn to gold or silver to live on. The fact that such a collapse hasn't happened in the United States is no assurance it won't, however low the probability. For this small chance, as is done in other countries, the holding of some gold for protection purposes, without regard to price action, is just prudent. The above political caveat remains.

Protection Potential

The truly significant point that separates gold from any other commodity is that, given its reaction to extremes, its ultimate protection potential is not unlike that of a specialized insurance. Whereas life insurance offers protection to a beneficiary against loss of *personal* earning power, gold offers a similar protection against a loss of *money's* earning power. As insurance in its newest forms also adds investment potential to the protection, so does gold. In fact, a close look at the parallels between gold and life insurance in terms of protection against premature loss of earning power reveals important similarities.

The historically demonstrated ability of gold to rise in price when inflation cuts the buying power of money means that the long-term holder of gold has a real degree of protection against this financial disaster. Gold performs this function by the mechanism of price change. Life insurance does the same thing for a family's financial assets in the event of loss of the principal support to those assets, the insured's income stream. It does this by providing a previously agreed upon amount of capital. Thus, the principal protection differences between gold and life insurance are (1) the nature of the earning power protected, personal earnings or money's earnings and (2) by what means the protection payoff occurs, in gold, whose price may have changed, or cash from insurance where the number of dollars is set, but where the buying power may have changed. Yet, the ultimate protective function is quite similar for both.

Investment Potential

As to the investment characteristics of the two, gold is the purer form because its investment performance is entirely in terms of its own price, whereas insurance-investment values are measured in various ways, including price and yield on accumulated capital. The similarity is that both gold and insurance can be purchased for protection *and* investment values if one wishes.

To see this investment aspect of gold above its protection quality, refer again to the gold/CPI chart in Figure 9–1. It is plotted on a semilog scale, which means that any given vertical distance on the chart represents the same percentage movement as any other equal vertical distance. Note that the CPI rate quadrupled between its 1972 low and its 1974 high. However, measuring the vertical distance move of gold shows it to be *greater* than fourfold from the 1972 low. This excess gain of gold over inflation is a measure of gold's excess investment value over its protection quality.

This quality was shown even more dramatically in 1976–80. From the 1976 low, gold soared nearly eightfold by the 1980 peak. The CPI rate jumped to only three times its 1976 low over the same period.

To be sure, these excess rises of gold over inflation were blamed on numerous fundamental reasons, including the Iranian hostage affair in the later period. Yet, the fact is that historically there are always explanations as to why gold overruns inflation. Whether it is called overexuberance, overreaction, or whatever, the phenomenon occurs.

One useful result of this knowledge is the certainty that during significant gold upmoves, an investment premium is being built into the gold price over its protection value, rather like the premium on whole life insurance where some part of it represents savings rather than protection. So, with gold there is the opportunity to identify times during which it is a much better protection purchase than at others. Such times occur when gold's investment value is minimal; that is, it is out of favor, world inflation prospects are improving, and the gold price is down.

Gold's purchase price under these conditions can even be thought of similarly to an insurance premium expense, and its after-purchase price action can be largely ignored. In terms of pure protection, the buyer wants to know that the inflation insurance is there, and only secondarily what it's worth. Protection purchases of gold should be thought of in the same way. Then, purchases of gold or another precious metal such as silver for *investment* purposes can be made in the same way as any other growth asset purchase, keeping in mind sound timing techniques and a specific selling-price objective.

Gold can also act as a protection for life insurance protection. The insurance benefit is usually paid in a lump-sum, fixed amount, (plus any investment value increase, as with universal life). Since this sum loses earning power over the term of the life contract in inflationary times, it can be protected from inflation like any other asset. Gold can fulfill that function. Of course, since total return is sought as inflation protection, gold is not the only way to achieve that protection. If your insurance benefit is already being protected by tax-deferred market rates of return, it will probably be adequately preserved without gold. If not, using gold's protective qualities would make great sense.

To do this, you must make some assumptions: (1) the number of years until the insurance face value is paid to your beneficiary, (2) the average rate of inflation over that period, (3) that gold will appreciate at about that same rate. Then calculate what the reduced buying power of that insurance will be at the inflation rate assumption over the term of years. Subtract that from the original face value of the insurance to obtain its *loss* in buying power. From an annuity table select the amount of gold to buy now that will appreciate to equal that buying power loss at a discount rate equal to the inflation rate.

These are not all standard views of gold. The common viewpoint is that well-timed purchases of gold represent an excellent inflation hedge because gold is a store of value that has been trusted over the centuries. As far as that goes, it is true, but gold can be a good deal more than that if thought of in the proper way.

Buying Gold—What Form?

As befitting a commodity that has such a wide international acceptance, the variety of forms in which gold can be purchased is great. The forms range from physical types, such as coins and bullion, to the paper forms, such as mining stocks, options, and futures contracts. Table 9–1 shows the principal forms grouped by investment objective with comments on each type. The groups follow my rules of thumb for such purchases: When buying for gold's protection (insurance), buy it in physical form and keep it as close to you as possible. When buying for speculation, use the paper form for ease of transactions.

When buying for protection purposes, it's wise to hold physical gold because one important purpose of such a purchase is that economic events *could* lead to a hyperinflation or an economic collapse that would make the actual use of the gold as money necessary. Unlikely scenarios, yes. Impossible, no. You don't buy life insurance because you expect to drop dead soon, either.

On the other hand, when purchasing for investment gains or outright speculation, it makes little sense to bother with the physical metal. Ease of transaction is the objective, and paper entries on broker's statements are the easiest.

TABLE 9–1
GOLD PURCHASE CATEGORIES

Protection

Gold bullion	This is the most widely accepted form in which to hold gold. In this refined form, the metal is shaped into bars or wafers of varying size. Each is graded in gold parts per 1,000—995 being the minimum acceptable level. The refiner's hallmark and the weight and fineness are stamped on the bars. Disadvantages are bulk, weight, and possible need for assay upon sale if held in personal possession. This form requires secure storage.
Gold bullion coins	These coins are minted by national governments in fractions or full one-ounce weights and have become the most popular and practical form of gold holding by the public. Most sell for a small premium above their gold content, typically 3–5 percent, and are readily traded through coin dealers. The most popular are the South African Krugerrand, Canadian Maple Leaf and Mexican 50 Peso denominations. Hungarian and Austrian one-ounce coins sell at a small discount to their bullion value. This form also requires secure storage.

Investment

Gold certificates	Certificates are issued by coin dealers, banks, and brokers. Available for bullion or bullion coins, they evidence ownership of the metal stored in the certificate-issuer's vault or bank vault. They require storage and insurance fees in addition to the per-ounce price.
Gold-mining stocks	Mining stocks may be purchased through banks or brokers by individual company through exchanges in the United States, Canada, Australia, South Africa, and London. They are also available through mutual funds. Although more volatile, prices tend to parallel the bullion price and also relate to such other factors as grade and life of ore mined, management, and dividends. Individual stocks can be highly speculative.
Gold collector's coins	Collector's coins, also termed *gold numismatic coins,* are priced on the basis of their age, rarity, and condition—rather than the bullion price. This is a highly specialized investment.

Speculation

Gold futures or forward contracts	Futures, or forward contracts, are the most speculative means of participating in the gold market because of very high leverage and trading rules that usually require adding more cash to the original purchase if price drops 10–20 percent, even if the contract cannot be liquidated.
Gold options	The option is the most recently developed form for market participation. Options are available from individual companies, such as refiner-dealer Mocatta, or on exchanges, including the Comex in New York, plus those in Vancouver, Montreal, and Amsterdam. The advantage of options over futures contracts is that the amount invested in the option is the total that can be lost on adverse price moves. (For greater detail, see Chapter 13.)

The groupings reveal where these various forms fit into low-risk investing considerations. Protection is the first relevant form and bullion-type coins should be purchased for this purpose and held by the owner, either at home or in a nearby bank vault. Recalling the March 1933 bank holiday when many bank vaults became inaccessible (in a minority of locales, their contents did remain accessible), storing of coins in a secure place at home is preferable. The emphasis must be on *secure*.

As to amount, a rather arbitrary portion of 3–5 percent of investment portfolio seems sensible as a rock-bottom minimum holding for protection purposes. Higher levels will be appropriate only if inflation again threatens to approach 1978–80 levels.

A second purchase in the form of either gold certificates or gold-mining stocks will be appropriate during gold bull markets, especially in their latter stages (1974 and 1979, for example). During these times the most money is to be made from gold, and the risk is actually lowest then due to public fervor over the accompanying inflation problems. However, since no bells ring and no alarms sound at the beginning or end of gold bull markets, timing investments in both bullion certificates and mining stocks make sense. (The no-load mutual funds that specialize in mining shares are particularly useful for diversification.) Rarely should total asset exposure to certificates and mining stocks exceed 15–20 percent of portfolio.

The gold-mining stocks significantly outperform bullion in gold bull markets because they are highly leveraged plays on the gold price. All mines have a gold price breakeven point above which company profits soar and below which they disappear for each additional ounce sold. When it appears the gold price is not only headed higher, but will remain there for some extended period, the mines' profit expectations explode higher—and so do their stocks.

A good example of this occurred after the 1982 gold price bottoming and during the subsequent trading rally into 1983. The bullion price increased on the order of 70 percent from June 1982 to February 1983, but the split-adjusted stock of Homestake Mining, the largest domestic U.S. producer, zoomed from 8 to 37, a 362 percent increase.

Of course, this leverage works just as dramatically in reverse, as leverage always does. In the 1980–82 gold bullion price plunge of 65 percent, Homestake stock sank 81 percent.

The caution is there in the figures. The mining shares, whether U.S. or foreign, are not for the fainthearted, but they can greatly springboard profits during the long-wave bull markets.

Knowing what form of gold to purchase under which conditions is one thing. Knowing how to do so with safety is quite another, as the year 1983 attested. Although 1983 was probably the worst year for gold since the free market for it developed in the late 1960s, it wasn't the year of the largest decline in the bullion price. That honor goes to 1981 when the calendar-year dive was $189.50 per ounce and 32 percent. However, it was 1983 that saw the demise of two of the largest U.S. gold dealers, both under odd circumstances, including the suicide of the chairman of one, at a cost to the investing public of something approaching $100 million. Those figures undoubtedly set the record for personal pain in the gold market. It's one thing to lose 32 percent of an investment on paper, but quite another to have that investment disappear altogether.

The collapse of International Gold Bullion Exchange and Bullion Reserve of North America deeply underscored the importance of buying gold and silver carefully. Both firms were well known nationally. Both promised gold buyers prompt delivery or adequate safety of storage. The month that the Bullion Reserve company chairman committed suicide, two well-known investment advisors recommended doing business with the firm. That was undoubtedly a better comment on the coverup capability of the gold company than on the inadequacy of the advisor's search. The critical message for investors is "buyer beware." Follow sensible bullion and coin-buying procedures.

Cash-and-Carry

The oldest shopping method known, *cash and carry*, should be used if at all possible when purchasing metals. Find a reputable local dealer, go there and pay cash for the items, and leave with them. For added counterfeit protection, obtain a return guarantee from the dealer, and take the metals to another local dealer for a bid to buy them. That dealer will inspect your items in offering the bid, and you'll know then with good probability whether you've gotten honest goods.

This method has its drawbacks, of course:

1. It is time-consuming.
2. It subjects you and your purchase to some risk as you cart the metals around.
3. In many states it might require payment of sales tax on the purchase.
4. Not all dealers will permit a return policy.
5. You'll still have to store these items later.

Any or all of these factors have led many buyers to prefer dealing either by mail or over the phone.

The Sight Draft

The best way to deal with any unknown vendor for shipment of goods is another old method, the *sight draft*. It guarantees buyer protection in the critical problem area of remote purchases—by calling for physical delivery and inspection at the time of payment. This method inserts a respectable third party into the process and thereby offers the protection.

Before ordering the goods, arrangements are made with a third-party bank to have good funds from the purchaser on hand at the time of receipt of the metals purchase and to be prepared to pay for the goods. These goods should be insured by the dealer and sent to arrive at the bank for sight-draft payment. The bank will notify the purchaser when the gold arrives for inspection and, upon purchaser approval, will forward its draft payable to the dealer for the amount involved.

Later, the carrying and storage matters must be arranged, but this is far preferable to the risk of the dealer delaying payment while purchaser's money goes to other uses (the IGBE problem) or of the metal involved not being segregated at the storage facility as the buyer had directed, which was the Bullion Reserve difficulty. Of course, there is still the counterfeit matter to face.

Storage by the Dealer

For those purchasing gold coins or bullion who don't wish to bother with the physical metal (such as with purchases made for capital growth), or those wanting to avoid the counterfeit or storage problems, there are many large and long-established dealers, banks, and brokers from which purchases can be made. Major banks on both coasts and in the Midwest and South, several nationally known and long-established stock brokerage firms and international foreign exchange dealers offer metals certificate programs and/or physical metals purchase/storage programs. However, even with them it is wise to ask for independent all-risk insurance on the purchase and to deal with only the best-known and largest firms.

Still, risks of unforseen developments exist. Anytime someone else buys and stores the metal for you, the acquisition and holding risk level must be higher than for either of the first two buying methods above. Those two are therefore preferable to the third in virtually all instances.

When to Buy: The Big Question

Professional advisors, average investors, and gold bugs alike have long sought a technique that can forecast the trend in gold prices with adequate early warning. The series of indicators shown in this chapter should accomplish that task. It provides forecasting signals for inflation, the force that most consistently moves the gold price. These signals or "gates" function just as a computer does, flashing plus or minus signs depending on indicator trends. When a sufficient number of signal gates point in the same direction, a favorable or unfavorable mode is created for gold investments.

Several key problems are inherent in developing a forecasting series for inflation that is adequately linked to gold prices. The principal problems are (1) verifying the theoretical and practical evidence that gold always reacts to inflation, (2) choosing which inflation measure or measures to use, and (3) knowing how to forecast future gold price moves based on only the relatively short period of experience with inflation and a free gold market price since the late 1960s. Let's explore these problems to determine the adequacy of the basis for my series.

Evidence of an Inflation-to-Price Link

There is substantial historical evidence to support a theory of why gold reacts to a falling value of money. As we've seen, the public came to trust gold more than it trusted rulers or government officials who debased the currency at will (and coincidently, the public was usually right to do so). The idea of debasement, barbarous as it may be, has stuck through the ages.

More important, the price mechanism, as always, functions through supply and demand. When a currency depreciates through price inflation, investors (later, the general public) sell their financial assets and their currency and buy tangible assets for protection, which drives up the price of the tangibles and tends to further depreciate the currency. Since gold is the premier tangible asset, it rises in price as the movement becomes increasingly self-fulfilling.

The theory to this point is sound. Regrettably, statistical evidence is lacking because the gold price has been an administered or dictated number for most of the past 150 years from which good data exist, other than Canadian gold mining stocks, as shown in Figure 9–3. This leaves only a very brief period since the late 1960s upon which to base an ob-

FIGURE 9–3
TORONTO GOLD MINES INDEX (1934 TO 1984) LOG SCALES

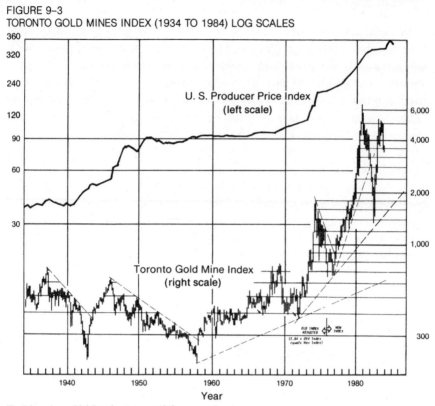

(Each bar shows high/low for *two months*)
Source: Ian McAvity's *Deliberations*[1] and Kinsman Associates, Inc.

served relationship between the *free gold price* and any inflation index.
Nevertheless, the evidence available from this time span is strong. Gold
has clearly followed the smoothed U.S. CPI during the years since 1969.
(See Figure 9–1.)

A second factor that might come into play here is whether or not interest rates as the rental price of money do in fact reveal the value of
money and thereby predict the gold price. Any correlation that might
have existed has been clearly flawed at the recent high-interest rate levels, as discussed in Chapter 6.

U.S. wholesale prices and international gold-mining stock prices
have the advantage of being trackable back to the 1930s, with the Toronto
Gold Mines Index in Figure 9–3.

[1]This excellent charting-based advisory letter is available from P.O. Box 182, Adelaide
St. Station, Toronto, Canada, M5C 2J1.

The greatest problems with this chart seem to be (1) the sharply rising U.S. price index 1940–50 accompanied by the seesawing Mines Index, and (2) the relatively level nature of the wholesale price index from the early 1950s to the mid-1960s compared with the notable drop in the mines price index. Surely the difference wasn't caused by delays in transmittal of the U.S. prices to Canadian mining stocks. More likely, we see in the stocks first a wartime profits squeeze, and then a steady decline in inflationary expectations as prompted by a lack of significant price increases in the world's premier (U.S.) economy from about 1948 to 1959.

A more complete study of this chart brings us several relevant conclusions:

1. Probably due in part to the enforcement of an official world gold price at $35 per ounce from early 1934 to 1968, movements in U.S. wholesale prices did not correlate with rising and falling expectations in international mining stocks until after 1968.
2. Significant percentage movements in the mining stock index can occur without a change in the long-term trend—for example, the rise from 1943 to 1946 within the long decline from 1937 to 1958 or the 1969–71, 1974–76, and 1980–82 declines in the enormous rise from 1958 to 1984.
3. Beginning in 1958, a cycle of roughly five to six years is evident in the stocks' price movement.
4. War periods of 1940–45, 1950–54, and 1964–72 show no single pattern in mining stock price movements.
5. Recessionary periods—1937–40, 1946–50, 1957–58, 1960, 1969–70, 1974–75, and 1980–82—have had a pronounced negative effect only at certain times on U.S. producer prices, e.g. in the 1930s and 1940s. The Mines Index reacted negatively on each occasion.

In sum, only in the post-1968 era, where U.S. inflation rose steadily, was there a long-term correlation with Canadian mining stocks. This suggests that we're on some thin ice in drawing long-term parallels between the two.

Data Shortcomings

One shortcoming of the above data is that they offer no measure or estimate of absolute value. That is, rising inflation rates correlate with rising mining stock prices after 1968, but that fact does not suggest at what point the stock prices are anticipating too much or underestimating too far the actual inflation. Moreover, they relate U.S. prices to Canadian stocks which, as noted earlier, is not a direct link. In short, is some international standard of value also a useful gauge of where the gold price might be headed?

This idea is espoused by several experts, significant among whom are analysts Christopher J. D. Murphy, a former partner of James Capel & Company, London, who is now a senior metals analyst with the firm, and Joseph C. Wyman of Shearson American Express.[2]

Since the money to purchase gold comes from the total pool of capital available in all Western industrial nations, Murphy and Wyman believe that some measure of the pool compared with the amount of gold reserves those nations hold to back the pool should be used to give a benchmark value for gold. In other words, if one ounce of gold backs $200 in the capital-reserve pool on day 1, that ounce is "worth" $200. If on day 2 gold is not increased in amount, but capital reserves are doubled, each ounce of gold is worth $400. That's fine in theory, but in practice it's a bit tough to calculate.

Murphy terms his version of this relationship the *Eurocurrency-gold parity*—which is the ratio of (1) the outstanding Eurocurrency totals (a figure provided quarterly by the Bank for International Settlements in Basel and refined by Morgan Guaranty bank) to (2) total gold reserves held by Western commercial and central banks and the International Monetary Fund. Murphy believes this ratio provides an excellent proxy for the parity value of gold at any time. "When gold is below this value," says Murphy, "it is undervalued in the market; and when above it, it's overpriced."

Wyman reaches a similar figure by beginning with the total *monetary* reserves of IMF countries as expressed in special drawing rights (SDRs).[3] He then subtracts from this total the actual *gold* reserves of IMF nations in SDR value, leaving a net amount that must be covered by those same gold reserves.

From these methods Wyman and Murphy conclude that the gold price should have been as follows. From Wyman: December 31, 1970— $60.20 per ounce; December 31, 1980—$435.72; November 1, 1982— $373.20. Murphy's calculations yielded $45 for year-end 1971 and $485

---

[2]See J. C. Wyman, "Gold, The Investment Case" (New York: Shearson American Express, April 1983).

[3]SDRs are central bankers bookkeeping money, originally based on gold but now calculated on a "basket value" of five leading industrial currencies.

for year-end 1980. A glance at the actual prices in Figure 9–1 shows that the market did not quite agree with these figures, but that only in 1980 was it significantly off, and to the high side.

However, these calculations suffer from two significant practical problems: They are only available on a quarterly basis, and they project benchmark values, not market forecasts. Thus, although interesting, these analytical tools for relating monetary levels to the gold price may not be available quickly enough nor be sufficiently predictive to be of great use for day-to-day investment decisions. Still, when one buys an asset, it should be bought with some regard for real value.

These figures have another value in that one can extrapolate these benchmark estimates into the future, as analysts are wont to do. It's a speculative idea, but let's see where it gets us.

Taking the mid-1983 net world monetary reserves at Wyman's figure of approximately $367 billion, with a backing of approximately 1 billion ounces in official gold reserves, gives a gold price of about $370 per ounce. The figure is remarkably close to the level reached during the fall of 1983.

Moreover, Wyman says one may assume that nearly all nations' financial deficits end up being monetized (turned into printed money, not borrowed). That's what, he says, occurred during the 1970s. If they are monetized, and if U.S. deficits represent the great bulk of these sums— projecting $200 billion-per-year U.S. deficits in both fiscal 1984 and 1985 could translate into a gold price in excess of $750 per ounce by October 1985. Of course, this conclusion also assumes that there will be no net deflation in reserves—as might be caused by a default on sovereign debt—and it does take liberties with both the size of U.S. deficits and the amount monetized.

Given the antimoney-creation stance of both the Reagan administration and Fed Chairman Volcker, a more conservative approach might well be closer to the mark. The broad U.S. money supply (M2) increased about 8 percent from mid-1983 to mid-1984. If that equalled the net addition to world monetary reserves and the gold supply did not rise measurably, the June 1984 gold value was $396 per ounce. On June 29, 1984, London PM gold was $374 (albeit before a sharp break to $338 the following week). That's a statistically close approximation.

In our investigation of the support to my gold price series, so far we've seen: (1) that U.S. inflation-rate changes correlate directly with gold-mining stock prices internationally (and by inference, with the gold bullion price) only since 1968, and (2) that the ratio of world monetary reserves to gold reserves provides some measure of the level at which the gold price adequately supports these reserves. The key question remaining is how to use this knowledge to derive a gold-forecasting method that functions well in the real investment world.

Tracing gold prices from the most recent free gold bullion price in 1968, only three price cycles have been completed, plus the beginning of a fourth. No statistician worth his/her salt would base future predictions on the behavior of three cycles alone.

A Solution

The proper way around these difficulties is to take advantage of them to the greatest degree possible. To do so we should utilize indicators with longer accurate predictive records for inflation, then add to them carefully constructed measures of inflation itself, and then require as a cross-check that these indicators move in tandem before a trend is considered valid. By then factoring in the U.S. producer price figures since 1968 and the world monetary resource value, we could use the three recent cycles as tests, rather than drawing complete proofs from them. Exactly which indicators should be selected? Table 9–2 and Figure 9–5 show four indices have met these tests well.

It has long been claimed by Dr. Milton Friedman and others of the monetarist economic school that the broadly defined U.S. money supply, M1, is a good forecaster of the inflation trend in the domestic economy. It is unnecessary to argue the merits of this thesis, nor the precision with which the M1 changes reflect later inflation, in order to see from Figure 9–4 that a lead factor has existed between the dotted M1 plot and the solid CPI line. However, to verify this potential predictive ability, a second inflation precursor must be located, one that functions independently of the money supply. Fortunately, Dr. Geoffrey Moore of the Columbia University Graduate School of Business has recently developed the Leading Index of Inflation. Its reconstructed long-term record is also shown in Figure 9–4 by the dash-dot line near the bottom of the chart. It also leads the CPI by a comfortable margin.

By combining the above inflation forecasters with the CPI and the PPI, which have already been shown to parallel the gold price in recent years, we can create an integrated *experimentum crucis*. When these indicators are smoothed to remove excessive fluctuations and when a methodology is developed to ensure that real trends are underway before signals are given, we should have a series of inflation indicators that

FIGURE 9–4
THE GOLDEN GATES (1967–1983)

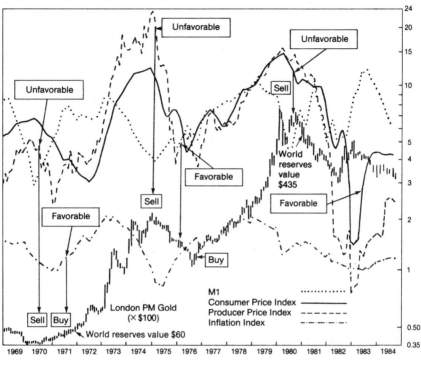

relate well to the gold price. A signal process that requires a majority of the indicators to point sequentially in the same direction before triggering action will complete the program.

However, even this is not quite enough. No law *requires* that the gold price move *precisely* with inflation. It can and does lag by many months, as the charts show. What's more, nothing says a given inflation trend cannot be *reversed* before the long-term factors involved play themselves out. True, inflation has tended to move in a steadily accelerating or decelerating trend for medium-length terms of at least two to three years. However, that is more by dint of Federal Reserve Board policy than by some sort of economic law.

For these reasons and because the gold price has exhibited some reluctance to react to early inflation trends during the past seven years,

one more test is added to the above four indicators. The test is a requirement that standard technical analysis of the gold price chart must also
confirm the trend called for by the other indicators. The gold chart pattern must be trending the same way as the gates. This becomes the final
gate . . . and the final test. (Use the same technical analysis techniques
referred to in Chapter 7.)[4]

Before turning to the record, one last question should be raised: "Why
not just use the chart pattern and skip the other bother?" Short-term
traders with good chart-reading experience or assistance can do that
with all the risks of frequent in and out trading. In fact, although tracking of past moves in the gold market has been done successfully with
mainly technical analysis by a few experts, the medium- to long-term
buyer needs something more to go on and a stronger basis for commitment. (S)he needs a *lower-risk approach*. This new series should finally
provide that basis because it demands that both the *fundamental* pressure of inflation and a *technical* position that confirms it be present.
That's the soundest analytical combination possible in any market. It
doesn't make the series infallible, but it does give it true strength.

The Record

The rules for using the Golden Gate series are straightforward. When
three of the four indicators are positive (rising), inflation is accelerating
sufficiently to create a favorable period for gold prices. When this is discovered by the market and confirmed by a positive gold price chart pattern, a gold *buy* signal is triggered. A negative indicator series and a declining gold price chart trigger a gold *sell*.

With these forecasting rules in mind, look at Table 9–2 and the Golden
Gates chart in Figure 9–4 for the period 1967–1984. In the table, note
that the sequence of gates is numbered/lettered so that 1–2–3 leads to *favorable periods for gold prices*, and A–B–C leads to *unfavorable periods*.
Each triggered gate in the chronology table corresponds directly to the
chart designations so you can check them yourself. Where favorable and
unfavorable points differ from buys and sells, it is due to the gold price
chart delaying action.

---

[4]See also *The Futures Guide To Technical Analysis*, (New York: Merrill Lynch Futures,
1982).

TABLE 9-2
GOLDEN GATES CHRONOLOGY

Gate Openings	Gold Price/Action
1967	
1. M1, June 1967	
2. CPI MA, September 1967	
3. Inflation Index, October 1967 (favorable)	Buy $35
PPI, December 1967	
1969–1970	
A. M1, June 1969	
B. CPI MA, May 1970	
C. PPI, June 1970 (unfavorable)	Sell $35–$36
Inflation Index, June 1970	
1970–1972	
1. M1, July 1970	
2. PPI, May 1971	
3. Inflation Index, June 1971 (favorable)	
World reserves value	
12/71 = $45. Buy confirmed.	Buy $40–$41
CPI MA, October 1972	
1973–1975	
A. M1, April 1973	
B. Inflation Index, November 1973	
C. PPI, December 1974 (unfavorable)	Sell $176–$200
CPI MA, March 1975	
1975–1977	
1. M1, May 1975	
2. Inflation Index, November 1975	
3. PPI, March 1970 (favorable)	
CPI MA, October 1976	
Chart uptrend October 1976	Buy $110–$122
1979–1980	
A. M1, June 1979	
B. Inflation Index, November 1979	
C. CPI MA, August 1980 (unfavorable)	
PPI, September 1980	
Chart downtrend November 1980	
World reserves value	
12/80 = $435. Sell confirmed.	Sell $600–$645
1982–1983	
1. M1, September 1982	
2. Inflation Index, March 1983	
3. CPI MA, July 1983 (favorable)	
PPI, August 1983	
No chart uptrend by June 1984.	
World reserves value 7/84 = $396.	

Recent History

Looking at what happened to the Golden Gates chart in 1983, it's obvious that the one entity that didn't get the word about the inflation buildup of the indicators is the gold market. All the indicators fell into line as they had over the previous 16 years on rising inflation pressures, but the gold market ignored them. That isn't unusual. Look back to either the table or the chart during the last inflation buildup in 1976. The rising inflation pattern was signaled in March, but the chart didn't confirm a gold price bottom until October, seven months later. Still, had one bought gold in March 1976, the price would have been in the range of $129–$137 per ounce, only moderately above the October range of $110–$122 and 18–25 percent above the low of $104 in August.

Could there have been a similar situation in 1983–84? The rising inflation pattern in 1983 was signaled as of July, with a London PM gold price range that month of $410.75–$430.50 per ounce. So, it was not until the end of February 1984 that the market had ignored the inflation pressures as long as it had in 1976. Of course, nothing requires the market to respond within any specified time frame. Six months is as good as 3 months or 12 or more months as far as the market's inattention is concerned. What's more, the price drop from the inflation signal in July 1983 wouldn't match the 1976 postsignal *percentage* decline until it reached $305–$310 per ounce. As of July 1984, with a $338 London PM low, it was coming close. Interestingly, it was also well below the extrapolated world reserves value at around $396.

This time delay factor does confirm the need for a final chart pattern confirmation. One can shout until blue in the face about the budding inflation pressures, but if the market wishes to ignore them for good (or bad) reasons, the shouting doesn't matter. The market must ultimately become convinced itself.

The indicator series appears to have met the tests required. It is sound in theory and has independent variables that cross-check one another. It has operated profitably throughout the test period in both accurate purchases for profit and avoidance of losing times. No claim can be made for its infallibility, but it can obviously be most useful.

Summary

The Golden Gates series has provided a discipline to use when acquiring gold for either growth or protection purposes, since it signals favorable periods for gold price movements and announces action triggers. As with all such disciplines, it must be remembered that in this case the gold price itself is also a discounting vehicle. That is, the price forecasts what it believes will happen to inflation. The series attempts to forecast what the gold price itself will forecast. This means that a given gold price may already be accurately predicting all of the inflation increases or decreases that the gates are foreseeing. It doesn't mean that a *further* price acceleration must occur just because an acceleration in inflation has been correctly forecast by the gates.

The above is a reminder that it would not be unusual to see a decline in the gold price at the same time an increasing inflation pressure is predicted. All that is required for this to happen is for the gold price to have incorrectly predicted a higher level of inflation sooner than was the case. This is precisely what occurred in 1976 and 1983 as rising inflation rates were correctly forseen by the Golden Gates series—but gold had already expected more of it, and sooner. Gold then corrected its wrong assumption.

With this caveat in mind, one can give gold its place in the portfolio-balancing process. It may be used as a protection or growth vehicle after its price is unduly depressed, as in 1982. It may be used as a growth investment when the markets temporarily believe it is some sort of universal salvation—especially when inflation is accelerating dramatically and other growth markets are having problems such as in 1978–79.

Gold is therefore a multifaceted extra arrow to have in the investment quiver. It clearly marches to a different drummer than do stocks, bonds, or the money market, and that drummer is the value of money, not just its rental rate.

This chapter and the preceding one have explored the protection segment of a low risk portfolio. Let's now address the cash equivalent portion in some detail.

Winners and Losers: Notes versus Bonds

Do you know that the large brokerage firms—
the big wire houses—
have whole departments around
just to take bond losses at yearend?

Venita Van Caspel

How good are long-term bonds for your financial health? Except for short periods, they are not good at all in an inflation-expectation era. The past 25 years' trend of top-quality Treasury, corporate, and municipal bond prices has been down. Not since the late 1950s has there been more than one consecutive three-year period where those bond prices rose.

Recently, the contrast between the rises and falls has been particularly great. The worst declines were in the 1980–81 period. But then, according to Lipper Analytical Services, the well-regarded tracker of mutual fund performance, the 1982 average total return (price plus interest) of funds invested in long-term Treasuries was + 23.9 percent. From May 1983 to June 1984 the average total return from the funds investing in AA corporate bonds *fell* 1.05 percent. The long bond market continues to be a good place for the fainthearted to avoid. What's the alternative for investors who need a safe income stream?

Chapter 7 stressed the value of Treasury notes and showed how they can be used in a very simple strategy to hedge interest rates. This use represents a key part of a sound long-term portfolio strategy, because it allows the portfolio constantly to achieve high relative return on the cash portion of its assets as those same items balance market risks in growth vehicles. Notes deserve fuller discussion because they can accomplish even more. They also allow improvement in capital safety and may even gain tax advantages in portfolio management.

By definition, notes mature 1–9 years from original offering, the shorter end of which is not a long period compared with the 20- to 30-year maturities of long-term bonds. Since my strategy calls for investing most heavily in the two- to four-year Treasury note maturity range, I am stressing a virtually risk-free return with a highly acceptable money-back time horizon. In other words, buying a T-note with a two-year maturity makes the wait to maturity very pleasant when rates are declining (the note price rises), and it's not an uncomfortably long wait if rates rise against you. In the latter case, all that's happening is that the capital isn't earning as much income as it could, but there's really no risk to the capital itself, even though the note price declines: The capital will be repaid at par in two years. What's more, keeping a significant portion of other capital available in a money market fund or bank money market deposit account, earns the rising rates while waiting. Thus, the short T note maturity provides a near-perfect balance with your money fund.

The Trouble with Bonds

Compare this maturity advantage to a long-term bond—even a government bond. If rates rise after purchase, the investor is stuck. The maturity is too far away to wait for, and there is no certainty that the rising rates won't go to a new plateau, leaving the bond at a permanent loss and the income well below available rates. Of course, one can always leave the bond at a loss in an estate, which is just the same as having thrown some of the money away: That's probably not calamitous, but it's hardly wise either.

Because of this long-term lock-in problem, which occurs partly because the capital in bonds constantly loses buying power at the rate of inflation, long bonds carry the constant problem of when to sell. That turns out to be much more of a problem than it might at first seem (unless inflation turns into long-term deflation, as in the 1930s).

A little background illuminates this point. Since purchasing a note or bond is nothing more than lending capital to the issuer (or previous owner if bought in the open market), to be smart you must be assured that the capital will be returned in full at maturity and that it obtains a fair return until then. With inflation this won't hapen unless the interest rate paid is above the inflation rate for the *full period*. Naturally, the longer the period before maturity, the more difficult it is to determine what will be an adequate inflation-beating rate. So, over the years of the inflation era, lenders of money have come to demand more of a rental price for their cash and a shorter time until it's repaid. They have stopped believing the government's promises that inflation will be permanently reduced and that any paper promises to pay cash in the future will be worthwhile. In short, investors have become smarter.

Bond Timing Problems

Long bonds are almost always bought by investors in periods of falling interest rates, when the short-term rate levels are depressed and longer rates become most attractive. The natural inclination of the investor is to reach for the higher rates. When this is done reasonably early in the rate downtrend, usually very nice things happen for awhile: The bond price moves up smartly as yields drop further, and the bond buyer has the best of both worlds. About that time a dilemma creeps in, almost unnoticed and certainly unheralded. Interest rates bottom out and begin a long, slow (at first) ascent. This bottoming process is historically a multimonth affair, and with long bond rates it often stretches out for a year. Thus the best time to sell bonds, before the next rising interest rate cycle harms the bond profit, usually passes by unnoticed. Thus, the investor becomes "locked in," not wanting to take either a reduced profit or a loss. Besides, the bond income still looks pretty good.

Reinvestment

Then comes the major problem of reinvestment of the proceeds from selling at or near bond market price highs (low yields). The return received on the bond before sale is inevitably going to be more than on the short-term instruments that should be bought with the bond proceeds in order to take advantage of the rate rise ahead. Typically, at real bond market price highs, the spread is three to four percentage points between long government bonds and 90-day T bills. Making the switch involves a *certain* loss of income in the belief that rates will rise to replace it. That makes the decision to sell much tougher.

One way to deal with this problem, overlooked by most investors, is to consider what would be the *total value* of income from the bond compared with the total income when capital is reinvested in the lower short-term rates. If the bond has *appreciated in price before sale*, the *total income* gap between bonds and bills probably won't be too great; for example, 100 bonds, bought at par, produces a cash return of $10,000 annually. They are now selling for $1,200 each. A short-term bill or note yields 7 percent, and $120,000 invested at 7 percent equals $8,400. That switch represents a cut in real income but perhaps an acceptable one.

In any case, picking the best time to sell bonds, even knowing they must be sold before another rate rise, is a tricky task. It's tough even for pros—witness the huge bond portfolios held by most institutions during the soaring rates of 1978–81, and the $60 million bond loss taken by the city of San Jose, California, in 1984. The timing is almost always missed by amateur investors.

Accordingly, a low-risk investing rule is *not* to buy long-term bonds as a *cash-equivalent* item but rather to hold in that segment only those securities that are immediately exchangeable for cash at full value or that can be so exchanged within one to three years. *Long bonds should be purchased for growth of capital, just like stocks, at or near the bottom of the interest rate (money) cycle and earmarked for sale at the opposite end of the cycle.* The Money Cycle Index is again most valuable in determining such purchase and sale points.

The advantage of looking at bonds in such a way is that their income yield will not be the principal reason for purchase and should accordingly not be a main deterrent to their sale. Considering long-term bonds from this standpoint will be a big step toward avoiding the problem of being stuck with those bonds at depressed prices.

Figure 10–1 shows bond yields for the three principal bond categories from 1969 to 1984 along with my MCI signals for falling *short-term* interest rates (buys) and rising short-term rates (sells). Note that since yields are plotted, price gains would be made in buying at high yields and selling lower.

Since short- and long-term rates don't move precisely together, making long-term calls based on short rates isn't exact. Still, the signals would have created profits in all buy-sell pairs except 1980. More important, it would have kept investors out of the long bond market when it counted most: from late 1972 to late 1974, and from mid-1977 to late 1981 (except briefly in 1980).

FIGURE 10–1
LONG-TERM INTEREST RATES

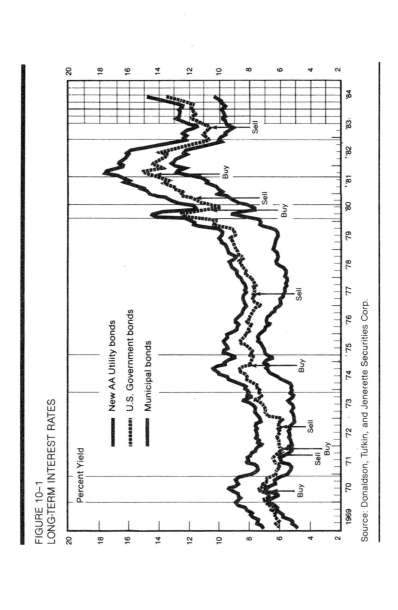

Source: Donaldson, Tufkin, and Jenerette Securities Corp.

One possible exception to the above discussion occurs with zero coupon bond packages offered by the major brokerage firms since 1981. (See pp. 24–25 for description.)

While "zeros" are extremely volatile—more so than coupon issues of the same maturity—and therefore share the negative qualities of other bonds on the long end, they have one comparative advantage. The price at which they trade at a given moment assumes a constant compounded reinvestment rate equal to the yield to maturity at that time. If the yield to maturity is 12 percent for a zero one day, that is the compounding rate until maturity. Because of this fact, an investor is better off with that zero than any coupon issue of the same maturity *if* the *average* yield on issues of that maturity falls below the purchase price yield to maturity anytime prior to maturity. That's compounding for you.

The effect of this is to make zeros that have been bought and held just a few years highly resistant to price declines below cost, even if interest rates rise moderately above the zero's original yield to maturity. However, during the first two to three years after purchase (depending on maturity), they are very price vulnerable.

Treasury zeros deserve serious thought for inclusion in retirement plans where the tax treatment of imputing interest to them will be nulified. Under my portfolio methodology they are still growth vehicles not cash equivalents when so bought.

Buying Treasury Notes

Treasury notes with maturities in the two- to four-year range have an important feature which comes from the way in which prices move compared with their maturity price of 100. Table 10–1 from *Barron's* shows note prices and yields to maturity as of July 1, 1983. Selecting the two- to three-year maturity range, we have maturities in the period of summer 1985 to summer 1986 for this list. In that period, the coupons ranged from a low of 7 ⅛ percent in May 1986 to a high of 15 ⅜ percent in September 1985. Since the market was pricing all the period's notes in a yield-to-maturity range of 10.1 percent to 10.53 percent, the prices varied widely, given that great range of coupons. These price variations can be taken advantage of.

Investors wishing the highest possible yields would prefer either the 15 ⅜ note of September 1985 or the 14 ⅜ note of June 1986, the latter offering about a quarter point better yield to maturity and the former a bet-

TABLE 10–1
NOTE PRICES AND YIELDS TO MATURITY

GOVERNMENT BONDS

U.S. TREASURY BONDS AND NOTES

Over the Counter U.S. Government Treasury bonds, weekly high, low and closing asked prices, the net change from the previous week's closing asked price and yield.

Rate	Maturity		High	Low	Last	Chg	Yield
15⅞s	Jul	1983 n	100.20	100.18	100.18	− .2	7.19
9¼s	Aug	1983 n	100.3	100.2	100.3	+ .1	8.10
11⅞s	Aug	1983 n	100.14	100.13	100.14	....	7.53
16¼s	Aug	1983 n	101.6	101.4	101.4	− .4	8.29
9¾s	Sep	1983 n	100.6	100.5	100.6	....	8.71
16s	Sep	1983 n	101.21	101.20	101.20	− .4	8.57
15½s	Oct	1983 n	102	101.31	102	− .3	8.79
7s	Nov	1983 n	99.10	99.8	99.10	+ .2	8.89
9⅞s	Nov	1983 n	100.8	100.5	100.8	+ .2	9.03
12⅛s	Nov	1983 n	101.4	101.3	101.4	....	9.11
10½s	Dec	1983 n	100.19	100.16	100.19	+ .1	9.20
13s	Dec	1983 n	101.23	101.20	101.23	+ .1	9.27
15s	Jan	1984 n	103.2	103	103.2	− .2	9.36
7¼s	Feb	1984 n	98.24	98.20	98.24	+ .3	9.40
15⅛s	Feb	1984 n	103.16	103.15	103.16	− .1	9.48
14⅛s	Mar	1984 n	103.7	103.5	103.7	....	9.51
14¼s	Mar	1984 n	103.9	103.7	103.8	....	9.58
13⅞s	Apr	1984 n	103.13	103.10	103.13	+ .1	9.46
9¼s	May	1984 n	99.31	99.26	99.31	+ .3	9.29
13¼s	May	1984 n	103	102.29	103	....	9.54
13¾s	May	1984 n	103.16	103.12	103.15	+ .2	9.65
15¾s	May	1984 n	104.31	104.26	104.31	+ .3	9.60
8⅞s	Jun	1984 n	99.17	99.11	99.17	+ .4	9.38
14⅜s	Jun	1984 n	104.12	104.6	104.12	+ .4	9.62
13⅛s	Jul	1984 n	103.11	103.6	103.11	+ .2	9.76
6⅜s	Aug	1984	97.12	97.5	97.10	+ .6	8.97
7¼s	Aug	1984 n	97.23	97.16	97.23	+ .4	9.46
11⅝s	Aug	1984 n	101.28	101.22	101.28	+ .3	9.87
13¼s	Aug	1984 n	103.20	103.14	103.20	+ .2	9.73
12⅛s	Sep	1984 n	102.16	102.8	102.16	+ .1	9.93
9¾s	Oct	1984 n	99.25	99.18	99.25	+ .6	9.93
9⅞s	Nov	1984 n	99.29	99.20	99.29	+ .7	9.94
14⅜s	Nov	1984 n	105.14	105.8	105.14	+ .5	10.00
16s	Nov	1984 n	107.13	107.6	107.13	+ .2	10.05
9¾s	Dec	1984 n	99.7	98.31	99.7	+ .5	9.96
14s	Dec	1984 n	105.19	105.12	105.19	+ .5	9.85
9¼s	Jan	1985 n	99.2	98.24	99.2	+ .8	9.91
8s	Feb	1985 n	97.12	97.3	97.12	+ .8	9.80
9⅝s	Feb	1985 n	99.10	99.1	99.10	+ .8	10.09
14⅝s	Feb	1985 n	106.20	106.14	106.20	+ .6	10.07
9⅝s	Mar	1985 n	99.8	99	99.8	+ .6	10.11
13⅜s	Mar	1985 n	105.1	104.28	105.1	+ .3	10.14
9½s	Apr	1985 n	99.4	98.26	99.4	+ .8	10.04
3¼s	May	1985	95.4	94.12	95.4	+1.9	6.06
4¼s	May	1975–85	95.15	95.2	95.15	+ .27	6.89
9⅞s	May	1985 n	99.15	99.7	99.15	+ .5	10.19
10⅜s	May	1985 n	100.18	100.8	100.18	+ .8	10.04
14⅛s	May	1985 n	106.15	106.7	106.15	+ .7	10.22
14⅜s	May	1985 n	106.30	106.24	106.30	+ .5	10.19
14s	Jun	1985 n	106.19	106.10	106.19	+ .5	10.24
10s	Jun	1985 n	99.23	99.8	99.23	+ .14	10.16
8¼s	Aug	1985 n	96.18	96.12	96.18	+ .4	10.10
9⅝s	Aug	1985 n	99.1	98.26	99.1	+ .5	10.15
13⅛s	Aug	1985 n	105.13	105.4	105.13	+ .7	10.22
15⅞s	Sep	1985 n	110.31	110.24	110.31	+ .5	10.27
9¾s	Nov	1985 n	98.30	98.20	98.30	+ .8	10.27
11¾s	Nov	1985 n	102.29	102.21	102.29	+ .6	10.33
14⅛s	Dec	1985 n	108.6	107.30	108.6	+ .10	10.31
13½s	Feb	1986 n	106.29	106.23	106.29	+ .5	10.41
9⅞s	Feb	1986 n	99	98.20	99	+ .7	10.32
14s	Mar	1986 n	108.11	108.2	108.11	− .1	10.42
7⅞s	May	1986 n	94.4	93.24	94.4	+ .8	10.30
9⅜s	May	1986 n	97.22	97.8	97.22	+ .14	10.33
13¾s	May	1986 n	107.29	107.22	107.28	+ .3	10.49
14⅞s	Jun	1986 n	110.28	110.21	110.28	+ .5	10.53
8s	Aug	1986 n	93.28	93.16	93.28	+ .10	10.35
12¼s	Sep	1986 n	104.17	104.9	104.17	+ .5	10.56
6⅛s	Nov	1986	92.14	90.11	91.26	+1.22	9.00
13⅞s	Nov	1986 n	109.2	108.26	109.2	....	10.60
16⅛s	Nov	1986 n	115.10	115.2	115.10	+ .2	10.59
10s	Dec	1986 n	98.21	98.8	98.21	+ .7	10.47
9s	Feb	1987 n	95.23	95.11	95.23	+ .7	10.45
12¾s	Feb	1987 n	106	105.13	106	+ .8	10.70
10¼s	Mar	1987 n	99.1	98.13	99.1	+ .7	10.57
12s	May	1987 n	104.5	103.24	104.5	+ .5	10.66
14s	May	1987 n	110.1	109.20	110.1	+ .9	10.76
10½s	Jun	1987 n	99.22	99.1	99.22	+ .15	10.60
13¾s	Aug	1987 n	109.23	109.7	109.23	+ .4	10.76
7⅝s	Nov	1987 n	90.19	90.4	90.19	+ .7	10.36
12⅝s	Nov	1987 n	106.6	105.24	106.6	+ .4	10.81
12⅜s	Jan	1988 n	105.18	105.2	105.18	+ .4	10.79
10⅛s	Feb	1988 n	98.3	97.14	98.3	+ .5	10.66
13¼s	Apr	1988 n	108.24	108.10	108.24	+ .10	10.86
8¼s	May	1988 n	91.12	90.26	91.12	+ .6	10.56
9⅞s	May	1988 n	97.2	96.18	97.2	+ .8	10.66
14s	Jul	1988 n	111.30	111.8	111.30	+ .10	10.86
10½s	Aug	1988 n	99.4	98.12	99.4	+ .14	10.73
15⅜s	Oct	1988 n	117.14	116.30	117.14	+ .8	10.94
8¾s	Nov	1988 n	92.16	91.30	92.16	+ .3	10.62
14⅝s	Jan	1989 n	114.24	114.8	114.24	− .1	10.99
14⅜s	Apr	1989 n	113.30	113.10	113.30	− .6	11.05
9¼s	May	1989 n	94	93.24	93.30	− .2	10.66
14½s	Jul	1989 n	114.30	114.22	114.30	+ .4	11.04
11⅞s	Oct	1989 n	104	103.9	104	+ .4	10.97
10¾s	Nov	1989 n	99.14	98.29	99.14	− .2	10.87
10½s	Jan	1990 n	98.8	97.15	98.8	− .1	10.88
3½s	Feb	1990	92.16	91.22	92.12	+ .29	4.86
10½s	Apr	1990 n	98.8	97.20	98.8	....	10.87
8¼s	May	1990	89.3	88.4	89.2	+ .14	10.52
10¾s	Jul	1990 n	99.10	98.15	99.10	+ .16	10.89
10¾s	Aug	1990 n	99.11	98.22	99.11	− .1	10.88
13s	Nov	1990 n	109.17	108.28	109.17	+ .10	11.07
14½s	May	1991 n	117.2	116.11	116.22	+ .2	11.25
14⅞s	Aug	1991 n	119	118.6	119	+ .8	11.24
14¼s	Nov	1991 n	115.31	115.4	115.30	+ .4	11.26
14⅝s	Feb	1992 n	118.12	117.20	118.12	+ .10	11.24
13¾s	May	1992 n	113.28	113.2	113.28	+ .12	11.24
4¼s	Aug	1987–92	92.7	91.26	92.7	+ .19	5.33
7¼s	Aug	1992	80.27	80.16	80.16	− .17	10.65
10½s	Nov	1992 n	97.12	96.24	97.12	− .5	10.95
4s	Feb	1988–93	92.7	91.1	92.6	+ .29	5.04
6¾s	Feb	1993	77	76.12	77	+ .16	10.62
7⅞s	Feb	1993	82.25	81.30	82.25	− .6	10.79
10⅞s	Feb	1993 n	99.18	98.20	99.18	+ .19	10.95
10⅛s	May	1993 n	95.10	94.12	95.10	− .9	10.91
7½s	Aug	1988–93	80	79.16	79.30	− .1	10.81
8⅝s	Aug	1993	86.10	85.22	86.10	+ .7	10.89
8⅝s	Nov	1993	86.4	85.18	86.2	+ .2	10.91
9s	Feb	1994	88.4	87.11	88.4	+ .4	10.91
4⅛s	May	1989–94	91.30	90.30	91.11	+ .15	5.18
8¾s	Aug	1994	86.7	85.16	86.7	+ .8	10.92
10⅛s	Nov	1994	94.31	94.6	94.31	+ .6	10.90
3s	Feb	1995	91.28	91.2	91.14	+ .12	3.92
10½s	Feb	1995	96.28	96.2	96.27	+ .3	10.98
10⅜s	May	1995	95.28	95.2	95.27	+ .2	11.01
12⅝s	May	1995	109.10	108.16	109.7	+ .5	11.20
11½s	Nov	1995	102.18	101.25	102.16	+ .6	11.12
7s	May	1993–98	72.14	72	72.13	− .12	10.77
3½s	Nov	1998	91.31	90.23	91.7	+ .1	4.29
8½s	May	1994–99	82.16	82.7	82.15	+ .1	10.84
7⅞s	Feb	1995–00	76.14	75.8	76.14	+ .9	10.99
8⅜s	Aug	1995–00	79.23	78.18	79.22	+ .10	11.04
11¾s	Feb	2001	103.22	103	103.22	+ .8	11.26
13⅛s	May	2001	114.7	113.10	114.7	+ .17	11.26
8s	Aug	1996–01	76.17	75.20	76.17	+ .9	11.02
13⅜s	Aug	2001	116.1	114.27	116.1	+ .14	11.29
15¾s	Nov	2001	134.22	133.15	134.22	+ .12	11.25
14¼s	Feb	2002	123.10	121.27	123.8	+ .24	11.25
11⅝s	Nov	2002	102.28	101.19	102.28	+ .9	11.25
10¾s	Feb	2003	96.20	95.14	96.20	+ .10	11.18
10¾s	May	2003	96.27	95.16	96.27	+ .13	11.14
11⅛s	Aug	2003	99.16	98.1	99.16	....	11.19
8¼s	May	2000–05	78.18	77.19	78.16	− .2	10.84
7⅝s	Feb	2002–07	73.1	71.31	72.31	− .3	10.80
7⅞s	Nov	2002–07	75.8	74.5	75.5	+ .7	10.78
8⅜s	Aug	2003–08	78.20	77.16	78.20	+ .13	10.87
8¾s	Nov	2003–08	81.12	80.9	81.11	+ .11	10.93
9⅛s	May	2004–09	84.10	83.7	84.10	+ .19	10.96
10⅜s	Nov	2004–09	94.16	93.13	94.16	+ .18	11.01
11¾s	Feb	2005–10	104.14	103.6	104.14	+ .14	11.20
10s	May	2005–10	91.15	90.13	91.14	+ .14	10.99
12¾s	Nov	2005–10	112.6	110.25	112.6	+ .15	10.25
13⅞s	May	2006–11	121.11	119.26	121.11	+ .15	11.26
14s	Nov	2006–11	122.22	121.3	122.22	+ .20	11.24
10⅜s	Nov	2007–12	94.22	93.11	94.22	+ .16	10.98

Prices quoted in dollars and thirty seconds. Subject to Federal taxes but not to State income taxes.

n— Treasury Notes.

Source: *Barron's*, July 1, 1983.

ter current yield.[1] However, both these notes were selling above 110, which means that by maturity their prices must drop, since they are paid off at 100. Such a price decline is figured into the yield to maturity, whereas the current yield ignores that fact. The decline will produce a capital loss for tax purposes, but that's usually an undesirable condition since only a maximum of half of it is recouped by tax deduction.

Conversely, those notes selling below 100 must increase to that level by maturity. This means that such notes have a built-in capital gain going for them, and if the maturity is more than six months away, it will be a long-term capital gain for tax purposes.[2] This means that buyers of all the notes selling below 100 are *guaranteed a profit* as part of the stated yield to maturity.

Other Advantages

The above fact permits an unusual statement to be made: Any note bought at or below par (100) that declines in price prior to maturity will offer a greater guaranteed gain at that point than when originally purchased. There aren't any other securities that *guarantee* a greater gain after a *decline* in price except notes and bonds. Some may offer a *possible* gain, but not a guarantee. In this case it's a U.S. government pledge besides.

If that note's original maturity is within two to three years, it is then possible to purchase such discount notes and view any subsequent price declines caused by rising interest rates as just more attractive buying opportunities. The worry about price declines is eliminated and turned into a potential advantage. Of course, if interest rates rise shortly after purchase and continue higher until maturity, buyers have an extended period of lower-than-market returns on capital. However, by judiciously selecting a new buying point to add to the position, you can achieve a greater gain than that on the initial purchase. (Try doing that with long-term bonds.)

Another advantage stems from these same considerations. Investors in high tax brackets will find that the aftertax yield to maturity on dis-

---

[1]Yields to maturity are those quoted in the list and are determined by calculator or bond-yield table. Current yield is figured by dividing the coupon by the offered price.

[2]The 1984 Tax Reform Act changed this for notes issued after the effective date in the act in July 1984. The gain for those issues will be taxed as ordinary income. Therefore, there will be two classes of notes traded for a time—one with and one without the long-term capital gain feature.

count notes issued prior to July 1984 is often very favorable because of the lower tax rate on the capital gain portion of the yield. (Treasury note interest is taxable neither at the state nor local level.) For example, the 8 percent note due August 1986 was offering investors in a 44 percent top federal bracket a 6.37 percent yield to maturity aftertax on the list date. That was nicely more than the current seven-day yield on tax-exempt money market funds, and it made the consideration of such a note worthwhile.

The list of advantages of regularly buying T notes of two- to three-year maturities is quite formidable:

Capital safety.

Livable maturities.

Further gain advantages after price declines.

Profits on interest-rate declines.

Possible tax advantages.

To these we can add the fact that T notes are readily marketable at daily-quoted prices, they can be bought for relatively low commissions of $40 to $50 per lot or a low fraction of a percent (depending on the broker), and they can be purchased in bearer form.

Disadvantages

There are some disadvantages, but they pale in comparison with the pluses. Probably the biggest disadvantage is that full-service brokers don't like to deal in T notes because they tie up capital for an extended period for a very low commission fee. The solution is to use a discount broker.

Second, even though the commission is relatively small, it does cut into yield. A $50 fee on a $10,000 purchase means a 1/2 percent cut in yield. Therefore, T notes are not very suitable for the smallest investors. But, for those who can purchase $10,000 lots, or preferably in $15,000 to $20,000 face value size, the fee should be acceptable in light of the other pluses.

Finally, T notes bought through a broker and delivered to the purchaser are in bearer form. This form makes transport easy but has the disadvantage of making other brokers wary of accepting the notes for later resale. There has existed a thriving business in stolen securities. The best procedure is to have the purchasing broker hold them in safekeeping under the firm's securities insurance policy. This is especially important if the notes might be sold prior to maturity, and it offers the convenience of broker collection of the semiannual interest payments.

Since Treasury notes are useful in a long-range portfolio strategy because of their hedge nature, they can be used in all four stages of wealth accumulation, as discussed in Chapter 4. However, they will be most important in the latter two stages as current income increases in importance. Discount T notes have been most useful to investors in the prime wealth-accumulation stages because of their usually strong need to reduce tax impact. In those stages a hedge combination of a tax-exempt money market fund and discount notes has served the function properly.

Notes of other issuers can also fill the T note role. Such tax-exempt entities as cities, counties, school districts, and states issue notes regularly, and often in the form of tax- or revenue-anticipation notes. Corporations issue them from time to time, although the maturity range of their notes lately has been five to seven years. Further, previously issued bonds that currently fall into the useful maturity range of two to four years can be used in the same way as notes.

However, in all the alternate instances, the quality of the issuer is of critical importance. You must not be worried about the safety of your capital when using notes to hedge cash equivalents against interest rate swings. Risk of default must not be an operative concern. Accordingly, only prime quality-rated notes/bonds should ever be considered as a viable alternative to Treasury notes.

An important cash management technique for T notes and money-market funds was discussed in Chapter 7, pp. 94–96. Review of it may be useful here.

Summary

The principal problems with long-term bonds as investments are three-pronged. Their high volatility and long-term declining price trends imply they should be traded, not bought and held. Figuring the proper time to sell is tough for the pros, let alone the average investor, partly because of the very slow turns the bond market makes. And even if a "good" time to sell is selected, the action is difficult to take because it almost invariably means an important cut in current income.

On the other hand, short maturity Treasury notes of two to four years' maturity have significant advantages over longer bonds, including maturities you can live with, added gain opportunities after price declines and a fine hedging capacity when used with money funds. The latter ranges from simple 50-50 splits of capital to three- and four-way balances depending on one's outlook for interest rate trends. If the investor can make the required maturity rollovers in such hedges, there is no risk to capital no matter which way interest rates move. At worst some income may be forgone. Withal, Treasury and other prime grade issuer notes deserve to be utilized in cash equivalent management by all investors of even moderate means.

With our discussion of the portfolio segments of protection and cash equivalents now completed, we can move on to the most widely studied area of growth investments—stocks. Here our Money Cycle Index gives us an important advantage.

Equities: The Market and Money Cycles

11

*The one thing we learn from history
is that we do not learn from history.*

Milton Friedman

At the beginning of what has become a much longer career in finance than I originally expected, I received a world-class course in stock market extremes. In 1961 while I was learning the ropes as a stock broker, the stock market exploded and took everything in sight with it. For the year, the S&P 500 rose more than 25 percent, but that was small potatoes compared with the real action, which was in IPOs (initial public offerings, better known as new issues.)

Almost anything that had *data* or *tronics* attached to its name was brought public by ever-more ambitious underwriters, and the public wildly bid up the issue prices. A company named Dynatronics was sold originally at 7 and rose immediately to 25. Risitron Laboratories spurted from an offering price of 1 to a 4 bid the same day. That's four times your money in hours! Even some stocks that had been first issued a few years before 1961 hit outrageous highs that year. Control Data, a 1958 IPO, reached a price 120 times its initial offering price during 1961.

151

Exemplary of the times was Foamettes, another company that went public in those days. It manufactured a foaming tooth cleaner and breath freshener for the canine set, a product that prompted stock traders to nickname it "mad dog." On the initial offering, there wasn't enough stock to meet demand. Soon after, there wasn't enough demand for the company's product. One wonders whether there ever really was. The fact that the company could go public at all was a measure of the new-issue mania.

Late in 1961 the bloom began to fade. Yet, hope remained fervent into early 1962, long enough for a major printer of new-issue prospectuses to run off a circular for a firm named Reuseable Pie Crust Company of America. It fully conformed to standard prospectus requirements by highlighting the nature of the company's business, its pro forma earnings, the officers' backgrounds, and the like. But the data, as you might guess, was wholly fictional. For a smile, I sent copies of the circular to a half dozen of my clients with the comment that it looked "interesting." Four called back wanting to buy stock. Most investors still believed that a 50 percent annual gain was the norm for any stock, no matter what its business.

Naturally, the bubble then burst. During my first six months as a broker in 1962, the Dow Industrials plunged more than 200 points. By May it was difficult to find a buyer for anything in the stock market. The investment mood was as black then as the 1961 mood had been rosy.

Underscoring the collapse, and especially the demise of that outrageous new-issue market, was an SEC study published a year or two later on some 500 new stock offerings that came to market in the late 1950s and early 1960s. The study found that 43 percent had gone bankrupt, 25 percent were operating at a loss, and 12 percent had simply disappeared. Only one in five was showing a profit. Tough odds. The reality of market returns over time had entered the marketplace.

Of course, this boom-and-bust scenario has been played out with almost clocklike regularity over the next two decades. The S&P 500 Composite more than *doubled* in value from the 1962 lows to 1968 highs, only to lose nearly 40 percent of it by the 1970 low 18 months later. The 1973 peak was 10 percent above the 1968 high, but the 1974 low was barely half that level.

The 1974–77 recovery added 74 percent to the index, and the next three years were spent in a trading range of just 22 percent, from 90 to 110 on the S&P 500. The rush to the 1983 peak added nearly 70 percent to the index from its 1982 lows.

The clear pattern of the overall market remains one of euphoria and despair with only the time frame varying from cycle to cycle. As the French proverb says, "The more things change, the more they remain the same." Knowing that fact is indeed helpful in dealing with the stock market because it keeps the ardor and apathy in perspective.

In this important and rather lengthy chapter, we'll cover (1) The long term expected returns on stocks, (2) a reprise of our MCI, now with a stock-market average included to show how the market itself aids in MCI use—and the exceptions, (3) a detailed market buy-sell method using stages of risk, and (4) how to select the right stock-market vehicles—mutual funds and individual stocks—to match our risk-stage method.

Anticipating Returns

Since making money is the game in the stock market and low-risk investors have no reason to accept less than fully adequate returns for the risk they're taking—it's worth considering what realistic return can be expected from stocks.

Despite some claims of high performance in the 50 percent per year range over the short term of a few years, history says that our expectations should be far more modest. Those big results most always reflect principally the boost from a single bull market, not performance through good and bad periods.

The definitive study of investment returns in U.S. securities was completed in 1978 and covered the years from 1926. It was updated recently through 1982, some 57 years in total.[1] It calculated the total return on the S&P Composite Index (composed of the 90 largest companies prior to March 1957 and the 500 thereafter) and compared those results to a constant 20-year maturity U.S. government bond, three-month Treasury bills, and the rate of inflation. The results are shown in Table 11–1.

Authors of the study found that the total return on common stocks, including dividends, was an annually compounded 9.3 percent. (That's the equivalent of an 11.6 percent arithmetic return per annum.[2]

---

[1]Roger G. Ibbotson and Rex A. Sinquefield, *Stocks, Bonds, Bills and Inflation: The Past and the Future,* (Charlottesville, Va.: Financial Analysts Research Foundation, 1982).

[2]The compounded annual return differs from the average or arithmetic return as in the example provided by the authors: "Suppose $1 were invested in a common stock portfolio that experiences successive annual returns of + 50 percent and − 50 percent. At the end of the first year, the portfolio is worth $1.50. At the end of the second year, $.75. The annual arithmetic mean is 0 percent gain, whereas the geometric (compounded return) is − 13.4 percent. Naturally, it is the geometric mean that more directly shows the change in wealth over more than one period . . . ."

TABLE 11–1
TOTAL ANNUAL RETURNS, 1926–82

Series	Geometric Mean	Arithmetic Mean	Standard Deviation
Common stocks	9.3%	11.6%	21.5%
Long-term corporate bonds	4.2	4.4	7.6
Long-term government bonds	3.5	3.8	7.4
U.S. Treasury bills	3.1	3.2	3.2
Inflation	3.0	3.1	5.0

When figures for the bull market of 1983 are added in, the *compounded* return will likely rise to above 10 percent per year. Interestingly, that is still well below the annual return the team projected in a related study of future-return probabilities through to year 2000, 12.5 percent per annum.

In comparison, T bonds and T bills were definite losers, rising only 3.5 percent and 3.1 percent per year, respectively, compounded through 1982.

The stock market figures were borne out by a recent study by Frank Russell Company, a pension fund consulting firm. They revealed that over the 10 years through 1983, independent investment advisors earned an *average* annual return of 12.6 percent and banks earned 8.3 percent on funds under management in stocks.[3]

Those numbers are hardly great shakes. Although they seem too small to accept for a future goal, they represent a half-century record through thick and thin and a practical confirmation of the stock market returns over a fair recent period. For a long haul, these time-tested, definite returns, must be accepted.

However, these averages don't tell what to expect in *any given year.* Shortsighted as it may seem, performance needs to be measured in less than decade spans. The trick is in finding the fair periods, a point already addressed in Chapter 6.

Appropos of fair periods, Ibbotson and Sinquefield found that the data they studied exhibited a convenient characteristic: The actual results clustered nicely in a bell curve around the average performance. This "normal" distribution permitted calculation of a statistical quantity known as standard deviation (the measure of variability around the mean). From these calculations arises a handy rule of thumb for expecta-

[3]"The Billion-Dollar Boys." *Time,* January 9, 1984, p. 46.

tions about stock market returns: The chances will be two out of three that any market total return will fall within one standard deviation of its historic mean, and more than 95 percent of the returns will be within two standard deviations of the mean.

The common stock *arithmetic* mean return was calculated at 11.6 percent per annum in the study, and the team found the standard deviation to be 21.5 percent. This means that two out of three annual mean returns should be expected to fall between the extremes of one deviation on each side of + 11.6 percent—that is, between + 33.1 and − 9.9 percent.

What this boils down to is that the average (and long-lived) investor during the 56 years shown could have expected the odds to be about two out of three that his/her stock market return (including dividends) in any one year would have varied between just over + 34 percent and just under − 10 percent and would have had an arithmetic average around + 11.6 percent. If the Ibbotson-Sinquefield study projections for the future work out, the average annual arithmetic return should come in around + 15 to 16 percent.

Obviously, with the standard deviation for stocks as large as it is (it's only 3.2 percent for T bills), investors cannot expect a narrow range of stock market results in any year. (The smaller the standard deviation, the greater the probability of achieving the expected or average result, and vice versa). Still, we now have a set of probabilities and a related range of returns to look for.

The appropriate query is: How does one achieve solid consistent returns toward the upper end of that range?

Cycles Revisited

Those who wish to invest in the stock market should recall the discussion of the political and money cycles in Chapters 5 and 6. Three important conclusions were drawn. First, the four-year political cycle has taken on greater importance in recent years as a weather vane to watch for expected market trends. Second, short-term interest rates have a strong bearing on the direction of stock prices in general. Third, the measure of those rates, the Money Cycle Index, has been a most useful monitor in this regard when combined with such statistical smoothing techniques as moving averages and momentum. It's now time to refine that Money Cycle Index usage to create concrete, useful signals for the stock market.

Figure 11–1 shows the months in which MCI moved through its 11-month moving average to the accompaniment of its 3-month momentum moving in the same direction. These are plotted versus the S&P 500 Index from 1955 to 1984.

The theory backing use of the 11-month and 3-month data is this: The Federal Reserve Board attempts to make major policy changes in the interest rate market that are relatively infrequent in order to avoid serious market upsets and to allow its policies time to work. Therefore, the major changes in interest rate trends that are shown by a long-term (11-month) moving average and a short-term (3-month) momentum gauge in a viable index of short-term interest rates will be relatively infrequent and will reflect those major policy changes. When the stock market fully perceives these changes, it should respond negatively to a rising cost of money and positively to a falling cost.

It is important to allow for the delay in the market's recognition of the major rate-trend changes and to allow for the fact that periods immediately following those changes are usually characterized by disbelief on the part of market participants. Therefore, the signal points on the chart for those cyclical-rate changes have been labeled in terms of risk. *High* risk for upturns in rates and *low* risk for downturns. Those terms indicate that the climate for stock market participation is *moving in the direction* of a high- or low-risk mode.

For example, all of the periods that begin with declining interest rate signals are designated low risk, but six of the periods were characterized by further stock market declines of from 1 to 11 months. Also, most rising-rate signals were followed by a rising stock market for a few weeks or more.

In short, the changing force of interest rates on the stock market will make itself felt relatively sooner than later, but the *initial* market reaction is usually the opposite to its longer-term reaction. This may be a function of the Fed's ability to disguise its policy changes to avoid great market disruption, or it may be a matter of stubbornness or mind set on the part of stock market investors. Whatever the cause, the result is like a ship steaming south: Inertia keeps it moving in a straight line for a time even after the wheel has been turned for a new course to the north.

Notice on the chart that this inertia phenomenon was applicable to only a small degree in 1980, the most rapid turnaround year in Fed policy shown. The rising market of 1979 (an inflation market fed by oil price rises) did not exceed its June 1977 high-risk signal level by more than 10 percent until October 1979 and again in January and February of 1980. The severe credit controls imposed in March 1980 then caused a

FIGURE 11–1
THE MONEY CYCLE INDEX VERSUS THE S&P 500 INDEX

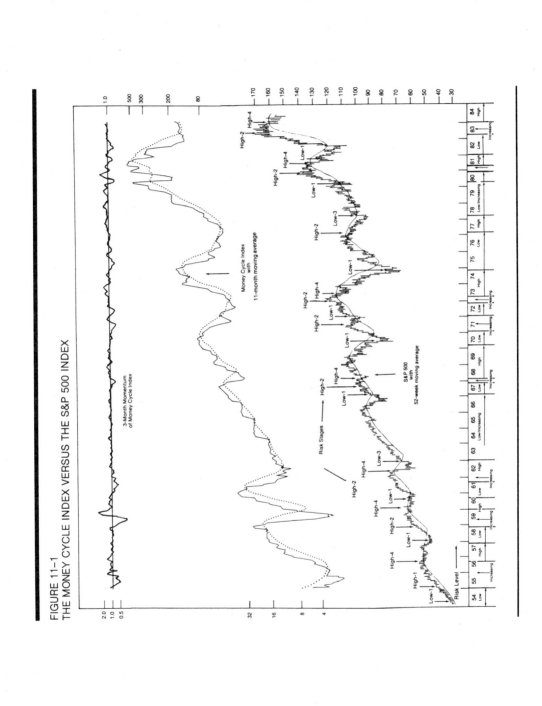

sharp market plunge that lasted through April. It was reversed by a declining interest rate signal in May. Lower rates quickly propelled the stock market sharply higher to the November high at another high-risk signal. Such turn-on-a-dime days are rare in the risk-signal history.

A study of the chart should make the lessons of this 30-year period clear as far as a low-risk approach to the stock market is concerned.

1. The Money Cycle Index definitely identifies periods in which interest rate changes will significantly impact overall stock prices.

2. Momentum or disbelief most often carries the market in its *existing direction* for anywhere from a few weeks to several months following the rate turn.

3. This slow-motion reaction belies the conventional wisdom that one must act quickly in the stock market in order to capture sizable profits. In truth, investors can usually act rather methodically when they are forewarned of important new interest rate pressures developing on the market.

4. Investors can increase cash-equivalent reserves in high-risk periods and decrease them during low-risk times without making fast all-or-nothing stock market commitments for fear of missing a turn. This permits easy adjustment of cash-equivalent and growth positions in portfolios.

It follows that if changes in cash-equivalent positions are made methodically after high- and low-risk signals, they can cushion market moves that continue after the signals: The cash position should still be high when approaching market bottoms; and stock holdings should still be extensive, if decreasing, as market tops approach. Thus the MCI signals provide a method that works as a dampening force to prevent unexpected events or predictive errors from doing major damage to a portfolio.

It may also be understood from this market approach that one can utilize any number of more precise market-timing indicators to refine tops and bottoms once the broad interest rate picture is clear. Those indicators provided by the most successful market-timing services can be helpful indeed.

Adding the Market's Opinion

One way to apply the information shown in Figure 11–1 is to let the market itself tell more about what is occurring. Note that the long-term S&P Index's moving average shows when that broad index has moved above or below its long-range trend—in this case its 52-week-average level. Using the S&P MA in conjunction with the Money Cycle Index is a way to temper the overrun characteristic of the stock market at MCI signals, both as to time and magnitude, without missing major market-trend changes. In short, the S&P Index's long-term trend can be used to indicate when the overall market has recognized the significance of the interest rate change shown by MCI.

Now let's look at Table 11–3 (pp. 166–67), which summarizes the signal pairs from Figure 11–1.

The Selling Side

The average gain per period invested in the "whole market"—just over 29 percent in each of nine consecutive winning periods—suggests that paying attention to these signals is a worthwhile exercise. The average gain per month of 1.36 percent (not including dividends) is moderately above the average monthly total return from stocks observed by Ibbotson and Sinquefield.

Looking behind these numbers, better returns could have been achieved than those above by an investor who sold the market at the first high-risk signal, after having bought at the first low-risk signal. The gain would have been 231.3 percent in 122 months, for a sparkling 1.9 percent gain per month, excluding dividends.

The results imply that MCI's ability to identify true low- and high-risk periods is better than the secondary top signaled by the S&P 500 MA. Tending to confirm this is the fact that six of the nine market tops called by MCI occurred *between* the MCI high-risk signal and the S&P 500 MA penetration ("bracket tops"), but none occurred within six months *after* the S&P MA breakthrough. What's more, of the three remaining peaks, two were before simultaneous MCI and S&P MA signals (1971 and 1977). Only the sequence of 1967–68 was an oddball, and it was followed by the only significant market turnaround to new highs within 12 months time.

This interesting perspective suggests that the initial MCI high-risk signal functions best as a serious warning indicator, and the second signal, given by the market itself, acts best as a final confirmation that a major top has occurred. Since there were clear timing differences between the signals and the tops, both signals appear to be needed to ensure a reasonable probability of success in determining major peaks. To wit, investors would have left a great deal of market growth on the table if they had sold at the first signals in 1955 and 1958.

160

TABLE 11–2

Market Peak	High-Risk Signal	Final-Risk Signal
September 1967	December 1, 1967	January 31, 1968
April 1971	August 10, 1971	Simultaneous
December 1976	June 3, 1977	Simultaneous

Table 11–2 shows the three periods during which the market topped *prior* to the two signals.

The striking point about all three exceptions to the bracket-top formation is that interest rates were rising notably before the high-risk signal. There is a satisfactory explanation of this condition that also fits with the bracket concept. A moving long-term average or momentum measure of an index has limitations. One of those is that the events that cause the index to move in the direction of its MA (e.g., here rising interest rates) may be perceived by a market before a long-term MA is broken. In short, quick reversals in a long-term trend may cause the MA penetration to occur late. The best example of this happened in 1971, when MCI itself and its momentum clearly began rising in late spring but didn't break the 11-month MA until the end of July.

There are, of course, fundamental factors at work. In 1971 it was rising interest rates and rising inflation that caused President Nixon to impose wage/price controls in August, just after MCI's long MA was broken. His action reversed the trend and later caused the low-risk signal of December 1971.

The rising interest rates of late 1967–68 were, on the other hand, simply not a worry to the stock market for long. The great bull market from 1962 died very hard, a fact that anyone who experienced that market will recall. More to the point, 1968 was a presidential election year during which it was widely believed that nothing critical would be done to disturb the economy until after the election—and nothing *was* done.

Summing up on the high-risk side of the stock market, the Money Cycle Index trend provides the first clues to market danger, and its long-term MA and momentum measures signal important practical high-risk periods ahead. The S&P 500 Index long-term MA then acts as a confirmation of the topping process.

Finally, the pattern of the top formation in relation to the signals, (bracketing or near-simultaneous configurations,) can be useful in telling how serious the final downturn might be. To see this latter point clearly, notice in Figure 11–1 that the five bracket tops of 1955–56, 1958–60, 1961–62, 1972–73, and 1980–81 saw greater market declines following them (an average of 20.6 percent) than did the three late-signal periods in 1967, 1971, and 1977, which averaged 6.7 percent. Of course, part of the reason for this is that a portion of the market decline had already occurred by the date of the simultaneous high-risk/final-risk signals. Nevertheless, that knowledge is still valuable: If you have reason to believe that a market has a greater downside potential following one type of signal compared with another you can certainly act accordingly.

The Buying Side

The low-risk signal aspect of this discussion and its relationship to stock market lows is also revealing. Excluding the market low-risk posture in February 1954, and the special case of mid-1971, MCI low-risk signals found the stock market at a bottom in the same month on three occasions. It was late in its call four times and early in another three. But only the early calls tended to miss by more than 1 or 2 months. (The late 1962 signal was 7 months off.) The 1960 signal was 5 months and 2 points early. The 1967 signal was 9 months and 14 S&P points early. But the worst was 1981.

After the October and November rally of 1981, which followed the low-risk signal of September, the market subsequently fell to its lows at the beginning of the recent bull market in August 1982. The decline from the first signal to the actual S&P 500 low was 12.8 percent, not a great amount, but nevertheless a bothersome one.

The reason for it was very simple: The market didn't believe that rates were falling. It was gripped by the forecasts of a handful of economic gurus that rates would ultimately rise. For its own purposes, the Fed chose not to dispel that thinking. These conditions then set up the buying panic of August 1982, when the gurus changed their tune. These circumstances provide another reminder that no matter how well the MCI works in both theory and practice over time, sometimes the stock market will ignore its signals. Therefore, despite the inefficiency of the added S&P Index signal, it must be an indispensable part of any true measurement of stock market risk. Note that it confirmed the interest rate low-risk signal only two weeks and 15 points after the panic buying in mid-August 1982. That allowed a 51 S&P point profit by the time of the subsequent high-risk signal of June 1983.

Two rather glaring gaps in the 30-year market record need discussion before turning to practical steps for utilizing market-risk signals. These are the bull markets of 1962–66 and 1978–80, during which the Money

Cycle Index gave only later stage low-risk signals. One might argue that these were not low-risk periods despite the rising stock prices. That argument can be made with merit about the latter era. Both inflation and interest rates were soaring during 1978–80, and it was increasingly perceived that both were out of control, at least until 1980. This situation provided very definite alternative investment markets to stocks—namely precious metals, property, commodities in general, in fact all forms of tangible assets. Under the low-risk scheme of things, it was those markets that were the lowest risk places to be. The forces driving them were much stronger and more positive for their price appreciation than were the forces shoving stocks higher. Inflation *must* lift the prices of tangible assets higher; that is the definition of price inflation. However, it will do so to stocks only as long as it feeds corporate earnings in aggregate and then only if the market is at historically modest price-earnings multiples and low in relation to stock book values.

A sound basis for this point of view is found in comparing the effect of inflation on the stock markets of 1969–70 and 1973–75 with those of 1978–80 in terms of book value multiples. See Figure 11–2. Stock prices had been pushed to more than 220 percent of book value before inflation soared in 1968 and 1973. From 1978–80 stocks ranged between 110 percent and 140 percent of book, a low valuation for an inflationary economy.

The other gap in the low-risk signal record 1963–66, also has a simple explanation: Interest rates were rising sufficiently to obviate any chance for a low-risk signal, but the rise was very slow. In fact, during the four years from January 1963 to January 1967, the three-month Treasury bill-rate rose only 170 basis points (1.7 percentage points), for an average rise of under .5 percent per *year*. It was pretty hard for the stock market to get bothered about interest rates under those conditions, especially when its main fuel, corporate profits, were rising dramatically due to increased Viet Nam and Great Society expenditures.

So, although the stock market chooses to ignore rising interest rates in some low-risk periods, it does so for special reasons. Naturally, the investor must be alert to conditions that might cause future exceptions, especially those that make alternative investments viable, such as were precious metals in the 1977–79 era. (The Golden Gates Series should be useful in this regard, per Chapter 9.)

It is also worth remembering that, at worst, the lack of a low-risk signal might keep investors out of stocks during a market rise. It would not

FIGURE 11–2
S&P 400 INDUSTRIALS—PRICE VERSUS BOOK VALUE

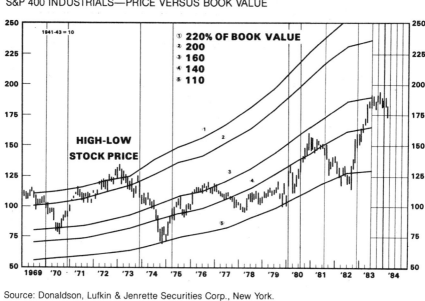

Source: Donaldson, Lufkin & Jenrette Securities Corp., New York.

have gotten them into the market during a period of collapse, and the high-risk signals would have told investors when to avoid the collapses for the past 30 years. It is difficult to expect more from broad market indicators. Refinements other than those we'll address shortly are of such a technical nature as to be beyond the objectives of this book.

This exercise with interest rate and market-trend signals provides a most valuable insight into the interest rate pressure as it drives the stock market. It achieves something for the investor that is critical in winning with the low-risk concept—namely, an ability to know when the market is most vulnerable to negative developments and, conversely, when it is most inclined to accept favorable news and conditions. This increases the investor's odds of missing major market collapses and of participating in great bull runs.

A practical method for optimizing performance based on ability to identify high- and low-risk market eras is developed by adjusting the size of growth portfolio positions as the following signals are received. We'll add other methods for increasing results shortly.

MCI Signal Useage

As has been seen, the value of the MCI and S&P 500 Indexes and their related smoothing and movement measures are greatest in identifying broad market movements, not in pinpointing exact buy and sell points. There is a need for more accurate tuning of the transactions. I've developed a more comprehensive set of MCI use rules based on the evidence just discussed. Table 11–3 shows how you would have fared taking these actions.

Low-Risk Signals

Each series of actions is divided into stages based on the market's history following the key past signals.

Stage One. When the MCI moves *downward* through its long-term MA, accompanied by falling short-term momentum, a first low-risk signal is given.

Action. Buy initial (or add to existing) selected conservative and defensive stock positions by reducing cash reserves one quarter to one third.

Stage Two. Following the MCI low-risk signal, when the S&P Index rises above its most recent chart down *trendline* (not its long-term MA), and an important *alert* signal is given.

Action. Buy additional positions in broad based, no-load mutual funds and interest-sensitive stocks with an additional one quarter of reserves.

Stage Three. When the S&P Index rises above its 52-week MA after the MCI low-risk signal and trend-change alert, the second low-risk signal is flashed.

Action. Take maximum bull market positions, including aggressive growth funds/individual stocks, bringing total to the range of 60–80 percent of portfolio, depending on your personal comfort level. This is the potentially most profitable period in stocks, and these positions should be maintained until the high-risk sequence develops.

High-Risk Signals

Stage One. When the MCI moves upward through its medium-term (6-month) MA, a rising-risk *alert* is given.

Action. Investors should then sell into periods of market strength all aggressive growth funds/stocks, raising cash reserves with the proceeds. It is these aggressive issues that are most vulnerable to any market downturn.

Stage Two. As the MCI moves upward through its long-term MA with rising short-term momentum, the first full high-risk signal is generated.

Action. This depends on the prior action of the S&P 500 in relation to its 52-week MA. (*a*) If the S&P index is *above* this MA at the time of the MCI signal, *and* has not been declining for a month or more—as on all occasions shown in the figure except 1971 and 1977—a bracket-type top is forming. Investors should sell stocks to increase cash reserves moderately (20–30 percent) and prepare for a complete sell. (*b*) If the S&P Index is already *below* its 52-week MA at the MCI high-risk signal or if it has been declining for two or more months, low-risk investors should liquidate only their weakest stocks and those in which any further losses will become problems (i.e., those approaching long-term holdings for tax purposes). Hold the balance.

Stage Three. Following the preceeding alert and high-risk signals, if a bracket top is forming, added sales of positions should be made any week the S&P 500 closes *above* the level at which the stage two high-risk signal occurred.

Stage Four. This also applies *only to bracket tops.* It is the final high-risk stage and coincides with the signal numbered 4 in the Table 11–3 summary of signals. It occurs when the S&P 500 breaks below its own 52-week MA. It is the mark of completion of the major top. What lies ahead is a period of trouble, be it short and sweet or long and nasty. Which of these it will be is unknown at this point, but it will be a difficult time: Historic losses ranged from just 8.6 percent to more than 42 percent below this signal level.

TABLE 11-3
STOCK MARKET MCI SIGNALS, 1954–1984

Market Risk/Stage	Date	S&P 500 on Date	Subsequent S&P High/Low NA	Average Percent Gain*	Months Total	S&P 500 Three Months Later (percent change from final high signal)	S&P 500 Six Months Later (percent change from final high signal)
Low 1	2-8-54†	26.23					
High 1	1-3-55	36.75					
High 4	9-20-56	46.25	49.7 (7-56)	+76.2%	31	46.07 (−.4%)	44.10 (−4.6%)
Low 1	12-2-57	41.36					
Low 3	5-2-58	43.69	39 (10-57)				
High 2	11-3-58	51.56					
High 4	1-20-60	57.07	60.5 (7-59)	+37.9	25	55.44 (−2.8)	55.61 (−2.8)
Low 1	5-2-60	54.13	52 (10-60)				
Low 3	8-12-60	56.66					
High 2	9-1-61	68.19	72 (12-61)				
High 4	4-25-62	67.71		+25.1	24	56.46 (−16.6)	54.69 (−19.2)
Low 3	12-62	Special conditions: See text.					
Low 1	2-1-67	86.43	72 (11-67)				
High 2	12-1-67	94.50					
High 4	1-31-68	92.24	102.3 (8-68)	+6.7	12	93.47 (+1.3)	100.91 (+9.4)
Low 1	5-1-70	81.44	69 (5-70)				
Low 2	10-9-70	87.08					
High 2 (b)	8-10-71	93.54	104.8 (4-71)	+14.8	15	93.41 (−.14)	105.59 (+12.9 see next signal.)

Low	1	12-1-71	95.54	94 (12-71)				
Low	3	12-17-71	100.26					
High	2	9-1-72	111.51					
High	4	3-23-73	108.88	120 (1-73)	+13.9	16	103.70 (−4.8)	107.36 (−1.4)
Low	1	11-1-74	73.88	62.5 (10-74)				
Low	3	2-14-75	81.50					
High	2	6-3-77	97.69	107.4 (12-76)	+32.2	31	97.45 (−.25)	94.67 (−3.1)
Low	3	4-78	Special conditions: See text.	98.2 (3-80)				
Low	1	5-12-80	104.78					
Low	3	5-16-80	107.35					
High	2	11-3-80	129.04					
High	4	7-2-81	128.64	140.5 (11-80)	+22.7	14	119.36 (−7.2)	122.69 (−4.6)
Low	1	9-21-81	117.24	102.3 (8-82)				
Low	3	8-27-82	117.11					
High	2	6-20-83	168.74					
High	4	2-3-84	160.91	172.65 (10-83)	+37.2	28	161.13 (+.01)	157.99 (−1.8)
Totals					266.7%	195		
Ave. per period		29.6%						
Monthly Ave.		1.36%						

*S&P 500 from Low (1) to final high signals.

†The first signal would have occurred before all of the present components of the Money Cycle Index existed, as the federal funds rate was not quoted until August 1954. Therefore, this date is the first market trading day after a downward reversal in the Federal Reserve discount rate following a rising pattern. Discount rate changes under such circumstances are valid indications of Federal Reserve Board intent, as discussed in Chapter 6.

Action. If this signal *occurs simultaneously* with the stage-two signal, (MCI crossing above its 11-month MA), as it did in 1971 and 1977, sell positions per stage two, action *b*. Otherwise sell all but minimum stock positions (10–20 percent of portfolio) and switch remaining holdings into defensive issues. If, following a further market decline, a secondary rally off an interim S&P low fails to carry to new highs, it is usually wise to then move completely out of stocks. This decision should be based on a full range of additional technical indicators.

Added Timing Details

Discussion about breakthroughs and MA penetrations above has touched on the most difficult part of this stage-investing process: The exact buying point. It's difficult because at important market turning points there are enormous and conflicting pressures, and there usually will have been several prior occasions when a bear market rally has tempted investors greatly, only to later disappoint. Here, sticking to the technical discipline will pay off. For stage two low-risk signals, insist on a week's breakout above the S&P Index's recent multimonth down trendline to give you a strong probability (in conjunction with the already defined interest rate downturn) that a real market uptrend is in place. For stage three low-risk signals, require a week's breakout above the long-term S&P MA. If all these indicators are not in place, jumping the gun is speculating: A false start can be very costly.

On the other hand, if the bull market is truly underway, this caution will give away some upside profits. Low-risk investors let them go. It is almost a rule of thumb that the amount missed before technical confirmation of an up move is a modest part of the whole bull market. The reward for waiting is usually great, and the risk of losing important profits is small. Even in the great bull move that began explosively in August 1982, the gain before stage three confirmation was about 14 percent. But the follow-on gain to the October 1983 highs was an additional 41 percent.

Occasionally, other market or economic indicators will also prove useful in verifying the signals given by the interest rate and chart tools. For example, both the smoothed track of M1 money supply and the recently developed *Business Week* (magazine) Leading Index of the economy should be pointing higher at the time of the low-risk interest rate downturn *and* the technical confirmation. Also valuable will be one of several measures of market downside exhaustion, such as Prolonged Liquidation.[4]

The next stock market stage to look for is the "midcourse correction" that so often occurs in major bull markets. The trick in identifying this stage is differentiating it from the beginning of a new bear market because both may be heralded by a high-risk interest rate signal. This occurred at the end of July 1971. That was followed immediately with a nonconfirming decline in momentum and in the rates themselves, even though the long-term interest rate MA wasn't rebroken on the downside until that autumn. Throughout the period the MCI long-term MA continued to fall. Meanwhile, stocks slipped about 10 percent from peak to trough after the high-risk signal. This qualified as a bull market decline, not as new bear market. However, at the time of the first high-risk signal, that matter was in question.

What tells the difference? Although there can be no certain set of rules that will apply in all circumstances, that year there were several clues.

First, interest rates began their rise from an MCI low in March, even though the MA breakout didn't occur until July. That sharp, long rise raised the potential problem that the stock market could be discounting the rate dangers and that the MA crossover was simply late. The fact that the S&P Index was already down about 10 percent from April to July supports this contention.

More important, a closer look at the behavior of MCI's long MA and its momentum trends shows that they were moving in the *opposite direction* to the breakout by August. That's not enough to obviate the breakout signal, but it is a very strong caution sign whenever it occurs. By this juncture an investor would have thus had two strong warnings that the MCI sell signal should be viewed with skepticism.

Third, the market had been declining for two months by July 1, a condition of high-risk stage two (b), which calls for only modest stock sales.

Then came the fundamental surprise: President Nixon announced the wage-price freeze and the closing of the gold window to foreign governments. This was sufficient to turn the stock market around until early October when a new set of worries over the economy sent the list plunging to its November lows. By that latter point, most market technicians and traders had had it with the whipsaw of decline, rally, decline. Naturally, that was the bottom.

---

[4]See "Prolonged Liquidation, A Market Timer's New Buy Signal," *Barron's*, March 19, 1984.

An investor adhering strictly to the high-risk, sell signal at July month-end would have had no choice but to sell some stocks prior to the Nixon announcement. The differences between this and other high-risk signals, especially the bracket-top variety, should have been sufficiently clear to make that selling selective and to alert the investor to a possible early turnaround. From mid-August to mid-October, that selling would have appeared wrong. By late October vindication came through.

Look again at the MCI chart in Figure 11–1. October saw a falling MCI along with a still-falling momentum and a declining 11-month MA. By the end of November, there was an MCI break below that MA, and the bull market of 1972 was set up.

What are the lessons of this hindsight?

1. Beware of steeply rising interest rates even if they don't cross the long-term MCI-MA. A sharply rising trend and a break above a 6-month MA are good first warnings that all may not be normal. Especially if confirmed by a falling stock market.
2. Beware of simultaneous MCI and S&P MA crossovers or an MCI breakout with two or more prior months of declining stock prices. As in 1977 the battle may be largely over when the signal is flashed in these cases (but not in the case of bracket tops).
3. When the trend of the long MCI—MA and momentum—is opposite to the direction of an MA breakout, consider it a notably weakened signal.
4. When a reverse MCI signal is given after the above cautions, (as in November 1971) respond to it immediately and strongly. It is correcting the garbled information given earlier and is to be respected.

In short, no bells will ring or sirens wail when bull market corrections in stocks occur in lieu of new bear markets starting. The MCI-S&P signals should be followed as received. Just be alert to any cautions and weakened signals as revealed above and temper your actions accordingly.

The foregoing refinement of the Money Cycle signals has been applied to create a functional stock market strategy. It now permits the following: (1) Dealing with all three major forms of risk—systematic, extra-market, and specific—by increasing cash reserves toward 100 percent in stages after a high-risk signal and thereby reducing the need for stock diversification, and (2) reducing cash reserves toward zero by stages after a low-risk signal but allowing some reserves to remain and using diversification to manage risk while also increasing stock and industry selectivity to enhance performance in the favorable markets that accompany lower interest rates.

Vehicles versus Risks

Having found a reasonable method for identifying favorable and unfavorable periods for the overall stock market, the next step is to determine how to choose the appropriate vehicles within the market.

A first consideration in that regard is determining what the risks in stock investments actually are and how to reduce them on the downside and take advantage of them on the upside. As we've seen, volatility is the most reliable statistical measure of stock market and portfolio risk. Since it has a down component and an upward one, volatility is both foe and friend. Therefore, knowing what forces cause this stock price volatility will be helpful in selecting volatility reduction and enhancement actions.

Long-term studies of the stock market have confirmed that there is a notable tendency for stocks to move with the market as a whole and a lesser tendency for factors related to the individual company to affect a stock's price.[5] These tendencies have been estimated for the average stock price change over time at 31 percent market-related and 20 percent company-related, respectively. Industry, industry subgroup, and other common factors account for the largest price component, some 49 percent of an average price change and significantly even more in some industries.

Considering the importance of these estimates in connection with earlier discussions on risk types and how to balance them leads to the conclusion that the 31 percent market-following (systematic risk) component of price action may be offset to any degree desired by increasing cash equivalents up to 100 percent. That is, when increasing market risk is perceived, we increase cash equivalent positions in proportion to the risk.

The large price risk components of industry group and subgroup may also be offset by the same cash-equivalent balancing. Thus an average 31 percent plus 49 percent, or an 80 percent component of the downside price risk may be tamed by cash equivalent adjustments. This leaves the 20 percent price risk that's related to individual company factors, which of course can be managed through stock diversification by owning many stocks in a portfolio or by owning mutual funds.

Therefore, by adjusting cash equivalents with market timing, individual stock selection becomes the least important factor in market perfor-

---

[5]Robert Hagin, *Modern Portfolio Theory* (Homewood, Ill.: Richard D. Irwin, 1980), pp. 38–39.

mance in *terms of downside risk*. Utilizing this fact is important to a low-risk portfolio approach. It is exactly what we've done with the MCI stage actions.

On the appreciation side of the equation, the broad market component of price action can be *enhanced* with the most market-sensitive stocks or with an indexed stock fund (one that matches the composition of a market index, such as the S&P 500), or with broadly based and aggressive growth stock funds. Utilizing specialized stock funds that concentrate on individual industries (i.e., energy, utilities, or technology) should enhance the large, industry price movement component (with proper timing, of course). At appropriate times in bull markets, individual stock selection can also enhance upside potential by recalling our discussion on beta and selecting, for example, high beta stocks in low-risk stage three.

To address these elements, there's an extension of our beta-volatility idea that is most useful, even if it comes with the ponderous-sounding name, standard deviation. It allows risk measurement to be applied to any market, not just stocks, and to advisory portfolios that invest in multiple markets. It is an extension of the standard deviation discussion in this chapter.

The standard deviation of any portfolio is a numerical measure of how much that portfolio varies in value from its own mean return. That sounds complicated, but it is not.

For example, if an investment portfolio showed a mean return of 4.33 percent per month or 15 percent for all of 1983, and mathematically varied around that monthly mean by 10 percent, its standard deviation is the latter number, or 10 percent. Combining the two numbers, we then obtain a return/risk ratio: a 1.5 percent return for each percent risk taken by that portfolio. That is a number that can be very helpful, especially if we relate that return per risk to a benchmark index such as the S&P 500.

The 1983 standard deviation of the S&P 500 was 9.64 percent around its monthly mean, with a total return of 22.5 percent. That equaled a 2.33 percent return for each percent risk taken. Now we've got a basis for comparison among all mutual funds, the overall market, individual stocks and advisory portfolios for which the data are published. We do this by risk adjusting each.

Making Risk Adjustments

There are two published sources of useful risk data available to all investors. *The Individual Investors Guide to No-Load Mutual Funds* is published each August (the first was in 1982), by the American Association of Individual Investors and includes both beta rankings of mutual funds. The monthly *Hulbert Financial Digest* has, since February 1984, included risk-ratings for some 90 advisory letter portfolios. Each rating is the respective portfolio's standard deviation. (He calculates them on a monthly basis, so each must be multiplied by 3.46 to obtain the annual rate.)

Use of the pertinent data is simplicity itself but the results will tell you a potentially very profitable story. The following table is taken from the two publications above, plus *Barron's* 1983 mutual fund results. I've selected only three funds and three advisors for simplicity of comparisons. Names have been changed to protect both guilty and innocent. The following comments refer extensively to Table 11–4.

The basic questions we want answered are, "Which fund and advisor provided the best return in 1983 *for the risk taken?*" and, "Which ones will be most likely to produce the most satisfactory return for either high or low risk tolerance investors in the next bull market?" Finally, we should know which ones to avoid if we believe the market still has real downside risk in it.

While the data shown don't take into account every factor that goes into answering these questions, they go much further than the average investor does. For example, the return per risk columns show how good the results were in terms of the risk taken by the manager/advisor. Yet, total return is the figure most commonly used by investors to rank funds or advisors. Clearly, the differences between the two measures are sharp. Fund Chi and advisor Delta had the outright best returns, but as the first column shows, investors following them took lots of risk to get those results—the highest in each category. That placed them third and second respectively on a return-for-risk basis. What's more, due to their high volatility numbers, chances are they'd be among the worst performers in the next down markets.

The risk-reward winners were fund Pi and advisor Sigma as they obtained notably greater results for the risk taken than did the best outright performers. Pi's return/risk was more than double Chi's, despite a one-quarter lower total return. As we'll see in a moment, Pi and Sigma are probably the best selections for early in a budding bull market.

But a logical question here is, why invest with an organization that underperforms, even if it does better for the risk taken? For one, the predictability of future results is better with managers/advisors who have lower relative betas and standard deviations. That's the nature of those risk measurements. Related to this is the fact that when those risk fig-

TABLE 11–4
RISK COMPARISONS

Fund	Beta (Risk)	1983 Return	Market Return/Risk	Risk-Adjusted
Kappa	1.0	16.0%	16.0%	– 6.5%
Chi	1.7	24.5	14.4	– 8.1
Pi	.6	18.5	30.1	+ 7.5
S&P 500	1.0	22.5	22.5	0

Advisor	Standard Deviation (Risk)	1983 Return	Return/Risk	Risk-Adjusted
Delta	21.6%	43.5%	2.01%	– .32%
Gamma	16.9	20.2	1.19	– 1.14
Sigma	3.42	9.0	2.63	+ .30
S&P 500	9.64	22.5	2.33	0

Key: The two group's figures are comparable only within their own group and cover 1983. Ideally, longer term results should be used. In the Fund group, Return/Market Risk is the 1983 total return column divided by beta. Risk-adjusted figures subtract the stock market's return/risk of 22.5 percent from the prior column.
  For the advisors, Return/Risk is their total return divided by their respective standard deviation. The risk-adjusted column subtracts the market's return per deviation risk of 2.33 percent from the previous column.

ures are relatively low, the next year's performance is apt to show a smaller swing up or down than will the high beta/deviation organizations. Many investors don't want large portfolio swings as a tradeoff for performance. Protection of capital is at least equal to or of greater importance than future growth of it, albeit with a common caveat that they want some growth.

Third, the period shown might have been a rare slow one for the advisor/manager. Good efficiency shouldn't be penalized on that basis.

Now let's look at the reasoning involved with selections, starting with the "underperformers."

It was a tough year for Sigma. But perhaps not as bad as it appears. After all, he did have the lowest volatility and was the most effective user of risk among the advisors that year. He was also the only advisor to use risk better than the market itself, a fact shared with Pi in the fund group. Pi was also the most effective risk user and had the lowest volatility rating in its group.

The investor with low risk tolerance would have a field day in this universe. The most effective and best risk-adjusted fund and advisor would be the clear selections to follow or invest with early in a bull market where uncertainty is greatest. Not only do the low beta/deviation readings imply some downside protection if the bull should weaken, but those return/risk and risk adjusted numbers are fine for a rising market. Pi would be a better choice than Sigma due to the latter's distant third in 1983 results, but even that may be acceptable in the early, uncertain bull-market days.

On the other hand, when the bull really gets rolling, even a low-risk investor may want to switch to the highest volatility fund and advisor, Chi and Delta. That's the best time to swing for a home run and those two have the best chance of hitting it. But, the low-risk investor would probably also want to use protective stops to control downside surprises with those volatile vehicles.

As to the high-risk investor, he or she would probably want to bet with advisor Delta at the outset due to his combination of near-best return per risk and outright best past return. Delta's risk-adjusted results are a modest problem, though. A murky trading market could give Delta problems. When he's hot, he's very hot. When he's cold, watch out.

A worse difficulty arises with fund Chi as an early bull-market choice even for our plunger. Those risk-adjusted results were notably poor in a bull year 1983, and we're looking for bull performance with a good degree of effectiveness. Fund Pi would again be a sounder first choice, since performance was quite satisfactory and effectiveness was outstanding. Also, a switch to fund Chi is a possibility if the bull market goes rampaging.

We would also note that Kappa and Gamma rather fell through the cracks. Kappa seems to be a nice middle-road fund with nothing to either commend or detract notably from its use. Gamma, however, at least gave us results that nearly matched the market. He just took a lot of risk to get them, and thus suffered.

The clear choice to avoid in down markets is fund Chi with its high volatility beta and its lowest risk-adjusted return. Both Delta and Gamma should be earmarked for careful watching as they could be very inconsistent performers due to their high volatilities.

It should now be clear that the standard criteria that are used to select funds and advisors, such as matching objectives with your own and choosing the amount of current income, can now be expanded to fit closely with your risk tolerance. The same is true about individual stock selection. What's more, the very predictability of future volatility in any stock or multimarket portfolio can be easily meshed with your estimate of market trend to enhance profits or protect assets. The old investment caveat really should read "past performance *is* a reasonable guide to future levels of *risk*." That's about as close as we're going to get to certainty in these high-risk times.

Growth Fund Criteria

One recent study of growth fund performance identified a few related factors in selection of mutual funds.[6] The study was limited to the bull market from April 1978 to April 1983, a period during which the S&P 500 rose nearly 70 percent. As a result, the study ignores the downside performance in this type of fund. Given these funds' volatility, we know their losses would be significant in down markets.

Perritt compared 120 no-load mutual funds of all types over the bull market period noted above and found four characteristics of the funds that performed best.[7] The most interesting finding was that previous performance was *not* among those characteristics. Perritt concluded that ". . . ample scientific evidence exists which illustrates that the use of historical returns alone *is not* a good predictor of future fund performance." Perritt's conclusion is valid per our foregoing discussion, and should be heeded by investors who wish to use growth funds for stage two or three purchases. Expecting a past single-period record to tell what a fund will do in an upcoming period of time asks that the next period be the same as the one just recorded and that the fund managers react in the same way—or that in any different period, the managers will always react in the optimum way. The probabililty of all those circumstances occurring is minuscule. On the other hand, it makes sense not to pick a fund that has a poor record. Accordingly, use a fund's total return as a final veto criteria (as recommended earlier in the discussion of performance), not as the first and strongest selection filter.

What, then, should be used first? Characteristics likely to affect growth in bull markets are these: (1) volatility (for speed and frequency of upside moves), as we've seen; (2) concentration of assets, since heavy asset centering in a few issues affects results; (3) size of the fund itself, since smaller funds can move more quickly; and (4) turnover of the portfolio.

Table 11–5 summarizes three of these four criteria from the *AAII Journal* study. In the table, *systematic risk* refers to degree of asset concentration in few stocks. A high number signifies little concentration and therefore high general market (systematic) risk. Low *systematic risk* means significant asset concentration in a few stocks. *Portfolio turnover* indicates the percentage of assets replaced each year as a measure of management's short-term versus longer-term holding philosophy. *Size*

---

[6]Gerald W. Perritt, "No-Load Mutual Funds: A Little Something for Everyone," *American Association of Individual Investors Journal*, July 1983.
[7]Ibid.

TABLE 11-5
COMMON STOCK RETURN AND PORTFOLIO CHARACTERISTICS

	Number of Funds	Average Annual Return 1978–1983 (percent)
Systematic risk		
High (above 80 percent)	35	20.5%
Low (below 80 percent)	34	23.4
Portfolio turnover		
Low (below 50 percent)	28	20.6
Moderate (50–80 percent)	12	21.7
High (above 80 percent)	28	24.4
Size		
Small (below $100 million)	52	23.4
Large (above $100 million)	18	18.3

Source: Gerald W. Perritt, "No-Load Mutual Funds: A Little Something for Everyone," *American Association of Individual Investors Journal*, July 1983.

refers to size of the fund. *Volatility of the funds* is not included in the table. However, elsewhere in the study the author confirmed the value of volatility as just discussed. However, Perritt stresses that many funds with low volatility (and therefore low systematic risk) can have higher-than-average returns. Naturally, these are the ones to search for. This coincides with our prior criteria of the best return for risk taken.

Thus, the following characteristics are optimum in selecting aggressive growth funds:

- Small fund size.
- Lower portfolio turnover.
- Low systematic risk (high asset concentration).

To these, I would add a verification that the fund(s) total return over three separate periods (one-, three-, and five-year returns) ranked it among the better performers. All five of the above qualities are listed for no-load funds in *The Individual Investor's Guide to No-Load Mutual Funds*.

One variation on these criteria is necessary in order to cover the matter of which fund to select during the so-called second-leg bull markets. I recommend that quality stock growth funds be utilized in this period rather than aggressive growth funds, for this reason: When a low-risk signal follows a high-risk signal by only a short time, there can be no way of knowing whether the low-risk signal represents the beginning of an evolving market top or a sustained bull market. If it develops into a top, the aggressive fund may drop sharply before there's time to get out. The investor is better off with slower-moving, quality funds in those second legs.

Besides, there hasn't been an uninterrupted bull market of more than a couple years' duration since 1963–66. If the odds seem small for a new one, remember in the stock market it is just when the unusual seems impossible that it happens. (Witness the 1982–83 bull market rising from the international debt crisis and the worst recession in 50 years.) So don't rule out a sustained bull. Actually, in the event of such a market with more than one "leg", the quality fund should do quite well because quality stocks often catch up with more aggressive shares in later legs.

A few words must be said about load versus no-load funds.

The author of the fund study notes that no-load funds in general are his recommendations versus load funds for individual investors. The reason given is that the sales commission cost, which usually ranges between 6 and 9 percent of the funds invested on average purchases (up to $25,000), goes to pay for marketing the fund to the buyer, not to pay the investment manager. If anyone deserves rewarding, it should be the successful manager, not your salesman, it would appear. Still, many studies have shown that over long time frames performances of load and no-load funds are not substantially different when they are carefully compared as to objectives and the adjusted for risk. In fact, this study notes that a load fund ranked as number one and slightly outperformed a no-load fund in the 10 years ending March 31, 1983, and that 13 of the top 25 in that period were load funds. That makes it about a draw in that time period.

However, the strategy dealt with here uses shorter time frames, often two to three years between buying and selling, and the sales load looms as a larger factor in total return after such short periods. Therefore I also prefer no-load funds but with a key proviso: If this book's low-risk strategy triggers your purchase, you needn't pay someone else for selling you the fund (assuming you do your own selection homework). When relying on a broker to time fund purchase, don't worry about the load. The broker's time is worth something, and if the timing is right, the load is irrelevant. If that timing is wrong, there are worse problems than just the load. All other things being equal, look for the best no-load fund, and be prepared to use it when broad strategy calls for stock fund purchases.

A good way to handle this timing matter is to make your initial purchase in a mutual fund *family* that includes a money market fund and has telephone switch privileges. Place your initial capital in the money market fund, and plan to telephone your switch to the aggressive growth fund on a stage two or three buy signal. If your selected growth fund isn't part of such a family, open the growth fund account with the minimum amount, and add to it on buy-day.

Specific Index and Growth Funds

The simplest way to participate in a rising market is to own the whole thing, or a proxy for it. Since market averages are used to discuss how the market has done, buying one of those averages or a group of stocks that performs exactly as that average does will give a near-equal market performance. When big things are expected from the overall market—as when all interest rate, economic, and technical indicators are saying go—utilizing such an index is sensible. It may be improved upon, to be sure, but for near-certainty of staying with the market move, you can't beat an index.

Since 1975 there has been a conservative way for the public to utilize a market index, and that is through the Vanguard Index Trust (formerly known as First Index Trust), a mutual fund that keeps its portfolio matched to that of the S&P 500 Index insofar as it is mechanically possible. Dividend and capital gain payments and expenses of operating the fund cause it occasionally to fall a fraction of a percent behind the performance of the index on which it is based. Yet, for all intents and purposes one can own the market by owning this fund. It also gives the advantage of automatic dividend reinvestment, which in rising markets simply provides more shares on which the price gain is based. The fund compounds the rise (and also the loss in down markets) via this reinvestment if the investor wishes.

This kind of index participation is worthwhile in low-risk stage two and sometimes in second-leg up-markets, and it can become the conservative part of a stock portfolio in these stages. There is comfort in knowing that on a day when "the market" is up, your mutual fund must be up, too. The converse is it won't be up as much as the higher risk level funds during the truly major overall market moves. For that, we go back to aggressive growth funds.

There's a box that appears regularly in The Wall Street Journal and Barron's under the heading of "Dual Purpose Funds." This category of fund is known as a closed-end type—meaning it has a set number of shares outstanding. The dual-purpose form of closed-end fund was developed in the 1960s as a means of giving investors a choice between receiving income or receiving leveraged growth on the funds' stock selections. As such, the funds separate the stock growth, if any, to the owners of growth or capital shares and channel the dividends to the second class of shares, the income shares.

The capital shares are useful in the context of our market stages for two reasons. First, they offer leverage on the performance of the stocks owned by the fund due to its income share (dual) structure. Second, they frequently sell at substantial discounts to their net asset values in declining markets, a discount that just as frequently disappears when the market sustains a solid rise. This combination offers buyers who use good timing in the capital shares a leverage of 1.3 to 1.5 times the performance of the fund's underlying stocks, and it makes these funds a most useful addition to an index fund in the portfolio growth segment identified in stage three up-markets. Investors should note that this leverage factor works both ways, however, and that these funds should be the *first sold* during a market-topping process attendant to a high-risk signal.

A good example of this performance is shown by one of these dual funds, Gemini, whose capital shares had a 1982 low of 31 and reached 63 at the time of the October 1983 S&P Index high. That was a 103 percent gain versus 71 percent for the S&P 500 itself, almost 1.5 times the market. However, Gemini capital shares had fallen 39 percent to 20 during the downswing in 1980, while the S&P 500 dropped only about 17 percent, which was worse than double the market loss.

In sum, dual funds' capital shares aren't for the fainthearted, but are excellent vehicles for use well after low-risk signals in this stage approach to stocks. Generally, they also will do best in sustained bull markets, such as the 1963 to 1966 market. Dual-fund shares are usually stock exchange listed.

Industries by Stages

Tracking interest rate signals in Table 11–3 has shown that a stage one bottoming action of a market immediately following the first low-risk signal may be one with further downside to it in terms of both price and time. That point is likely to be inappropriate for buying either interest rate-sensitive stocks or such highly market-sensitive vehicles as growth stock funds or index funds, except when the market move is immediately accompanied by a *major* drop in interest rates (as in May 1980 or August 1982). Instead, investors should be looking for defensive stocks and industries that have histories of bottoming or turning up before the general market. These frequently include foods, finance companies (for personal loans), restaurants, and retail outlets ranging from department stores to drug stores and food chains. These are among the industries (including the funds that invest heavily in them) in which stage one commitments can usually be made safely and with good prospects for ultimate success.

Remember that portfolio cash equivalents will still be high at this time, so any disappointments shouldn't be too harmful to the overall portfolio.

Stage two and stage three investments after the low-risk signal occurs are the exciting ones. At these stages big money begins to be made. They have the most going for them, usually a budding cyclical economic recovery and plunging interest rates, and often good leverage on those prospects. They are also the scariest times. The market has usually been falling for an extended period, and gloom is thick over the economy's prospects (usually a deep recession). This is the wall of fear the market must climb before the economic statistics justify optimism. So make no mistake, it is difficult to commit funds under these circumstances.

However shaky the economy and market appear, stages two and three are the times to buy industries such as autos, homebuilding, savings and loans, REITs and utilities, all highly sensitive to interest rates. Often very attractive as well are auto parts, tires, technology, office equipment, hotels/motels, leisure-time concerns and stock brokerage firms.

Still, there will be investors who wish to remain cautious, wanting further confirmation of a market turnaround. This is especially true at stage two because chart-trend changes are not as explicit as are MCI or S&P-MA signals. For such investors, it is appropriate to wait for stage three or to buy only on market weakness. Cash should still be committed to the best vehicles for this stage, but to those that are on the more conservative end of the above spectrum—that is, utilities and REITs.

When stage three is fully confirmed after a solid breakthrough of the declining chart trendline and the 52-week MA, the market has usually entered the period when the great majority of stocks move in a typical cycle. Investment profits should come the easiest here of any market stage, even though there will be substantial opinion that says this is not a bull market and that offers apparently sound reasons why the dangers are great. Ignore them. No bull market since the early 1930s that was based on an interest rate decline has soon reversed itself after these confirmations.

Individual Stocks

What about the quality versus speculative stocks themselves? Do individual stocks have a place in our broad stock market strategy? As noted earlier, individual stocks play less of a role in this approach than in others because of two factors. First, most of the downside problems in individual stock holdings (such as insufficient diversification or wrong industry selections) have been allowed for by adjusting cash reserves rather than switching stocks or using defensive stock selection. Second, aggressive growth funds give greater gains in strongly rising markets, and thus eliminate the need for "stock picking," with all its attendant research effort and timing problems.

Nevertheless, these aren't totally satisfactory reasons for eliminating individual stock selection. After allowing for and offsetting some of the risks, why not pick individual stocks in this reduced-risk environment? Buying the right individual stocks or the right industries can be most apropos in stage one periods if one chooses to invest early and if the stocks tend to *ignore the market in their movements and march to their own drummers.* A smattering of such stocks is certainly appropriate for low-risk portfolios at proper times. However, selection should be careful, and the size of commitment should not be large. There is no need to achieve great performance heights, and portfolio risk-avoidance is certainly still appropriate.

One important reason that individual stock selection will not be emphasized here (except under very strict criteria) is that stock picking as an art has such an inconsistent and uninspiring record. Two examples suggest the scope of the problem:

- Fifty-two respected surveys have covered well-regarded stock market forecasts for individually selected stocks during 10 different periods from 1929 to 1980. The surveys found that 77 percent of the expert participants *underperformed* the market during the period of their predictions.[8]
- The nation's top securities analysts for 1980, as selected by a major investment magazine for its "All America" research team, were the subject of a study tracking their stock selections for the following year. *Two thirds* of their picks underperformed the next year's *down* market.

---

[8]David Dreman, *The New Contrarian Investment Strategy*, (New York: Random House, 1983).

This is not to say that successful stock selection cannot be done nor that it is all a matter of "random walk" (although it arguably may be) nor that throwing darts at the NYSE stock list is a more productive process. A few mutual funds and money management firms have compiled enviable reasons in stock selection. The fact is that "beating the market" is a problematical criterion for success in any case because it's patently easy to do at certain times, such as with a virtually unmanaged high-cash position in down market years, and it is very difficult to accomplish in others, such as in big reversal years when *everything* must go right for the stock selector. Instead, the record shows that *consistently* selecting the right stocks and doing well with them is not easy for experts, and it will likely be much tougher for the amateur. Those brief numbers are sufficient warning.

Nevertheless, individual stock selections can be a useful addition to the low-risk approach. The single area of stock selection that fits consistently with my broad strategy is the search for *overlooked* stocks. These shares are depressed and essentially neglected by the market for whatever reason, good or bad. My reasons for preferring this type of stock can be boiled down to three: The strategy I employ calls for buying individual stocks primarily in the first stage after a low-risk signal, which often occurs before the overall market wakes up, and it thereby requires stocks that move on their own, irrespective of the market. Overlooked stocks fit this bill well. This early timing also offers the maximum holding period possible in a given market cycle, which many depressed stocks require to realize full recovery potential.

Third, the most interesting fact about overlooked stocks is that a substantial body of data suggests this is the most rewarding of all stock categories in which to work.[9] David Dreman includes a great deal of evidence to support this claim in his excellent book.

A few of Dreman's compilations are worth summarizing here. In several sophisticated studies covering 40 years to 1977, one key measure of an overlooked stock, its low price in relation to its earnings, has been found to be a consistent and prevalent factor in best total return. For example, in a nine-year study from mid-1968 to mid-1977 (a period during which the S&P 500 Index was essentially unchanged), 1,251 stocks representing the largest companies in the nation were ranked into 10 groups of PE ratios from highest to lowest. Total return was then calculated for each group on the basis of holding the stocks for one calendar quarter, six months, one year, three years, and the full nine years.

---

[9]Ibid., pp. 137–50.

The average compounded rate of total return for the whole sample over nine years was 4.75 percent annually. Now note these comparisons. The highest PE group showed *negative annual returns for each period* with the exception of + 0.33 percent return if held the entire nine years. The middle PE-ranked group only exceeded the sample average return in the three-year period. But the lowest PE decile showed a significantly higher *average return in each* of the periods, except the nine-year frame when the return was still a healthy 7.89 percent per annum.

To further deal with market variations over the full period, separate studies were made of the bear and bull market segments in this period, and also the famous "two tier" market of May 1970 to February 1973, the latter because that was when the institutions were buying the "nifty fifty" largest stocks, which sent their prices and PEs soaring. One would have thought that era, if any, would decimate the low-PE idea.

The results in all periods lead to the same conclusion. Low-PE stocks consistently outperformed the high-PE favorites, almost irrespective of the holding period and with generally increasingly favorable results going from highest to lowest PEs.

Considering all the data, further updating to 1980, and his own experience, Dreman concludes, "The evidence strongly supports an investment philosophy of buying solid companies currently out of market favor as measured by their price/earnings ratios."[10]

For all the reasons given above, and many more, such as the inadequacies of both corporate management forecasts and those of Wall Street analysis, this out-of-favor stock strategy fits the stage approach to stocks, and I recommend it as specified below.

How to Find Those Stocks

To find the stocks, first search the NYSE list for PEs *at least one third below* the PE level of the current market. Then look for these additional factors: Dividend yield, track record, and financial ratios, as specified below.

Dividend Yield

Overlooked or underrated stocks tend to have relatively high yields compared with the market if they represent seasoned companies (which

---

[10]Ibid., p. 150.

is the type to consider). The market price for low-PE stocks will have been driven down, perhaps over several years, by any number of factors. Yet, the dividend may have been held or even increased over time, providing the substantial yield sought as a second criteria in overlooked stocks. Dreman's research showed this yield to be one of the key ingredients in the total returns of low PE-stocks, a finding that should be taken advantage of.

Preferably, the dividend for a depressed stock should have been regularly increased in the past, even while the earnings were declining and the stock was otherwise ignored by the market, as shown in Figure 11–3, ARA Services stock. Note the convergence of earnings and dividend lines in 1976–82.

FIGURE 11–3

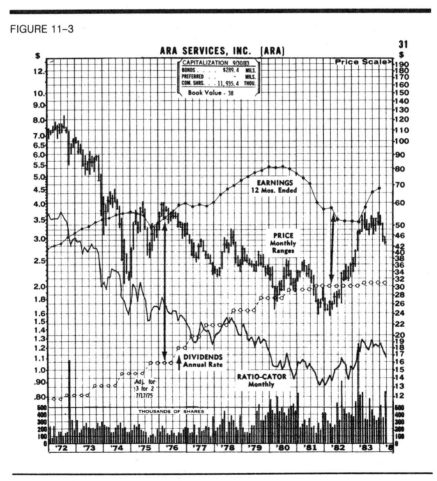

Another criterion is that the dividend should be well covered by current and projected earnings to minimize the surprise potential of a dividend cut. In general, look for yields about one third to one half greater than the current market average when buying, and look for earnings at least 150 percent (preferably 200 percent) of the dividend.

Track Record

An important additional requirement is that the company should be a large, NYSE-listed firm with a public business record going back at least 15 to 20 years. Avoid the smaller, relatively unseasoned companies that bring with them greater risks to achieving successful future operations. This category of junior growth stocks requires much greater specialized knowledge and analysis than we can identify here.

Financial Ratios

The cautious investor will also look into the key financial ratios signifying corporate health when searching for overlooked stocks. The ratios, known as current, quick, acid, debt coverage, etc., will point out sound companies based on standard financial management criteria. These ratios should tip off the inquiring investor as to whether the company is still on an adequate financial footing or whether a slide toward bankruptcy is the reason for the stock being depressed.

With this much fundamental analysis done, you can compile a list of stocks to watch for favorable developments. Then you can add two more filters to find the best opportunities in the list: (1) a sound reason to believe that the operating picture for the company is improving and (2) a favorable price chart breakout to the upside.

The first may come from any number of sources, including new products, new industry operating conditions, sale of unprofitable business segments, product price increases, or even a major competitor's bankruptcy. Securities analysts, or the company itself, should be able to provide this sort of information, as should the larger advisory services. Value Line, for one, regularly searches for low-PE stocks with improving fundamentals.

The price chart breakout is my acid test. One of the definitive characteristics of overlooked stocks is that they are neglected. As long as they remain neglected, they aren't going to rise much in price, if at all, except in very thinly traded issues where even modest buying can drive them higher. Buying too early in overlooked stocks can mean a long, unrewarding wait during a rising market, one of the most frustrating of market postures.

I like to see that somebody else is thinking the same way I am about a given stock and buying it in sufficient quantity to move it above technical resistance levels. Among the most important of these resistance points are the most recent multimonth declining *trendline*, the stock's *200-day moving average*, and the *overhead resistance* formed by previous *tops*, especially double or triple tops. The 200-day MA or the equivalent is available on most chart services. With some experience in charting techniques, you can draw in your own trendlines. The tops are easy to spot, but multiyear charts will identify the most important. As indicated in Chapter 7, a study of charting will be useful.[11]

My rule for identifying clear chart breakouts above these resistance areas for depressed stocks goes like this: "A couple days breakout is no reason to shout, and less than a week is not for the meek. But a full week above is the one to love." That little ditty, like my approach, is on the cautious side. A first test is a minimum of five trading days above major resistance areas and not less than 1½ points when looking for a solid breakout above the level from which the stock previously fell. The more of those three resistance levels that can be crossed, the sounder the purchase and the shorter your wait should be before the stock's recovery proceeds.

There is an important corollary to this breakout rule. When buying a stock under these conditions, place a mental stop signal *just below* recent strong chart support, but in no case should this be more than 15 percent below the buy price. If the stock closes below that mental stop, sell it immediately and accept the modest loss. This should prevent serious losses from developing in your portfolio, which failed breakouts and subsequent support collapses often portend.

A final buying suggestion for overlooked stocks at the beginning of low-risk stock cycles is to locate and purchase several of them, eight to ten being a good number through which to diversify the risk. Neglected stocks tend to be more affected by *specific risk* (related to the company, not the overall market). In addition to holding good cash equivalent reserves at all times, diversification is the direct antidote for this risk, and it's wise to make use of it. Investors without the capital to achieve this sort of diversification should stay with the index and growth mutual funds commented on above for stage two and three purchases.

---

[11]Robert D. Edwards and John Magee, *Technical Analysis of Stock Trends*, 5th ed. (Boston: John Magee, 1957).

One last point about individual stocks is so often lacking in advice given about the stock market: Selling objectives must be developed for your stocks at the time of purchase.

Sell your overlooked stock holdings (1) when the Money Cycle Index has signaled a high-risk period *and* the individual stock has had a substantial (25 percent or more) upmove, or the overall market has technically confirmed a downtrend following stage two high-risk signal or (2) in the absence of the former signals, sell when the stock reaches a dividend yield level that is within 10 percent of the overall current market yield.

As to day-to-day timing, one useful criterion is to remember that historical research has shown that preholiday markets have a pronounced tendency to rise and that the closing hours of the day before a market holiday usually maximize the profits in this regard.[12] In fact, this record has been so good that an investor who had been able to purchase the S&P Composite Index and hold it only during the two preholiday market days for each holiday from 1927 through 1975 would have profited in 45 of the 48 years and made a compounded return of 778 percent, nearly double the 414 percent buy-and-hold return for that index for the whole time. If the foregoing stock market investment suggestions seem to require more effort than you're inclined to expend, there's always that preholiday scenario to try out.

Summary

The astute investor will realize that no mechanical or technical approach to investments—whether it be for stocks, gold, or Chinese ceramics (one of the best performers of the 1970s-early 80s)—can possibly be structured to take into account all conceivable financial conditions that might arise. Therefore, the long-term success of any such method must rest on the probability that the financial circumstances and the reactions of the monetary authorities to them approximate those of the period on which the market investing method is based.

Unless changed drastically, our fractional banking system requires that money creation be controlled by the Federal Reserve Board, and the short-term money market must be the locus where the board's intentions are carried out. Thus, a sound measure of rates in that market, which

---

[12]Norman G. Fosback, *Stock Market Logic: A Sophisticated Approach to Profits on Wall Street* (Fort Lauderdale, Fla.: Institute for Econometric Research, 1976), pp. 159–63.

our MCI provides, should also reflect those policies if interpreted correctly.

Since Federal Reserve actions have a direct bearing on stock prices, as our 30-year record shows, we have in our MCI a useful tool with which to measure favorable and unfavorable conditions for stocks. With support from the election cycle and the trend change indicators for MCI and the market itself, this measure should be a sound one for low risk investors to track.

Other risk reductions methods for the stock market focus on risk assessment and adjustment for mutual funds and advisors and specific selection criteria for growth mutual funds. We also can time purchases and sales of different types of securities with the Money Cycle stages, such as defensive issues in the first stage and locating undervalued stocks at that and later cyclical stages. When these methods are coupled with the portfolio balancing techniques discussed in earlier chapters, investors should have a valuable overall stock investing strategy that has a high probability for continued validity.

PART FOUR

Getting the Most from
Other Investments

PART FOUR

12

The Shelter Game*

*Why shouldn't the truth be stranger than fiction?
Fiction, after all, has to make sense.*

Mark Twain

John Z. DeLorean knows a lot about tax shelters—now. The folks who invested $18 million in the research and development shelter created for his new auto know even more—in hindsight.

It's a reasonable bet that Esteé Lauder of the cosmetics firm and two of her sons, along with Lawrence and Preston Tisch (the principal officers of Loews Corporation), U.S. Senator John Heinz III of Pennsylvania, Norman Lear, Sidney Poitier, and Andy Warhol all know more about tax shelters than they'd like to know. According to an August 23, 1983, article in *The Wall Street Journal*, all these people were informed that the most they could expect to get back on the shelters in which they'd invested—through a company run by Charles Atkins, the 28-year-old son of the chairman of Ashland Oil—was a sad 30 to 60 cents on each

---

*Because of the now nearly continual changes being made in tax laws and their regulations, the information provided in this chapter and others relating to taxes should be verified by a competent tax professional before making any investment based on it.

193

dollar invested. They were also advised that they might get hit with the very tax bills they had expected to avoid through those investments.

These investors are among the latest to join the long line of well-known people who bought into tax shelters that failed. There's a much larger list of the not-so-well-known folks who have done the same. Unfortunately, there's no practical way of determining how widespread the failed shelter bite has been. In view of the highly publicized problems of the oil and gas drilling business since 1981–82, a field that was abundantly tax sheltered, it's safe to assume that the numbers are large.

Large also are the numbers of dollars still flowing annually through this country's tax-shelter industry. Despite the problems, the total volume of tax-advantaged program sales registered with the SEC in 1983 was estimated to have quadrupled the 1979 level, and it may cross the $15 billion mark when the final figures are in. (At present, that figure may be a bit misleading, due to the inclusion in it of income programs for IRA and Keogh accounts and the exclusion of private shelter partnerships. Even excluding these types of shelters—they about offset each other—there's no doubt the business is booming.)

Given the negative publicity surrounding many famous shelters and the apparent problems of so many others, that burgeoning volume of sales may seem odd. It may seem especially so after 3 years of the Reagan Administration's tax "cuts." It isn't. Not when you consider that the U.S. median family income was nearly $25,000 in 1983 and that married couples whose combined yearly taxable income barely crossed the $45,000 mark still paid more than $10,000 in federal income taxes on it. They were taxed at a 40 percent rate on the next taxable income dollar, too.

Single taxpayers reached that dubious $10,000 federal tax bill at around the $41,000 taxable income level, and they paid the IRS 45 cents of every taxable dollar over that. The Heritage Foundation of Washington estimates that as long ago as 1981 the proportion of taxpayers in 40 percent or higher brackets was 16 percent, *10 times* the 1970 level.

Small wonder that trying to beat taxes with tax shelters is popular, despite the risks (and no small wonder that the underground economy is so widespread).

How Risky Are Tax Shelters?

Of course, trying to shelter and succeeding are two different things, as the DeLorean and Atkins investors can attest. This difference gives rise to the fundamental question about tax shelters: Are they inherently risky? And if so, just how risky are they?

On the scale of risk addressed in this book, most tax shelters fall into the above-average risk category. Some are only moderately risky, and some are outright crap shoots. The trick of course is knowing how to differentiate between the categories.

The general concept of risk in tax shelters requires some elaboration. Tax shelters take on risk in three basic ways:

1. Through the nature of the business with which the shelter is concerned (i.e., the risk in oil and gas drilling, oil production, or research into genetic engineering).
2. Through the way the shelter vehicle is structured—its legal form, its use of cash invested, any debt incurred, the promotion costs, payout to investors, and so on.
3. Certainly through use of the tax laws that have created benefits for investors, such as accelerated depreciation deductions, because of the many gray areas in the tax code.

These sources of shelter risk lead to another—investing knowledge risk. Because the three above risks arise from such diverse and complex sources, investors require a great deal of specialized knowledge about any given shelter in order to evaluate it. Investors may obtain this information and do the comparisons between shelters on their own, or they may rely on others to acquire it and recommend action. Since the average investor needs to acquire quite a bit of basic shelter knowledge, the fact that an investment may be made without it may be the largest risk of all.

To offset the business-side, shelter structure, tax code, and knowledge deficiency sources of risk, Congress has provided just one enticement to shelter investing: the potential tax advantages of deductions, deferrals, and credits. This combination of facts has led most investors in shelters to rely principally on the *apparent* tax benefits and *someone else's* knowledge in making their investments. It's no wonder tax-shelter investing has to be considered above average in risk.

What a Tax Shelter Is

It is important to know that Congress has intentionally created *all* the tax deductions and tax shelters in existence (assuming they're used *validly*). Congress wanted, and still wants, to encourage home ownership, to give a tax break to older people, and to offset personal loan interest expenses just as much as it also wanted to promote so-called low-income housing, oil and gas drilling, and basic research and development—even on the DeLorean auto. One might argue with the wisdom of such encouragement, which is essentially the use of the tax code for social purposes, and make some telling points, but the existence of the inducements are not in doubt. In simplest terms this is why tax deductions and tax shelters exist. Stated another way, Congress wanted to take in partners for its various social and business projects, so it legislated tax incentives to lure individuals to invest in various concepts rather than putting up 100 percent taxpayer money to create them.

However, there is a distinct difference between tax shelters and tax incentives, even though the phrase *tax shelter* is so popular that it has become synonymous with anything that generates a deduction. The following discussion focuses on tax shelters as defined as investments in businesses that are made to acquire something of value with the expectation that they will produce income or a gain on capital invested and also reduce or defer taxes.

Investments in personal retirement plans fall outside this discussion. Whether they are qualified corporate or government plans or IRAs or Keogh plans, it is clear that they provide tax advantages. Yet they don't require investments in business per se, although the investments made under the plan itself may involve a business through buying a common stock, and so on. Since the *plans themselves* generate the tax advantage, not the business investments underlying the plans, investments in such plans will not be discussed here.

Also omitted here are personal tax deductions. Even though Congress may have once thought it wise to provide a deduction on money paid to charity or for home mortgage interest, real estate taxes, medical bills, and for municipal bonds, these uses of income do not constitute true tax-shelter investing. They don't involve making investments in businesses.

However, buying a limited interest in a business partnership that will acquire and lease railroad cars and provide tax benefits for its investors is truly a tax-shelter investment. It meets the above criteria, and Congress believed it was a good idea to encourage that sort of business and created the tax incentives to do so. (No, I don't know why.)

A closer look at tax shelters as business investments reveals that their tax advantages fall into four basic categories, of which one or more are available in varying degrees in most tax shelters. They are the direct answers to the popular tax-shelter question: Where do the tax losses come from? The categories are direct deductions, tax deferral, tax-rate conversion, and investment tax credit.

Direct Deductions.   A tax shelter uses some of the money invested in such a way as to permit the investor to deduct that amount from the gross income on his or her tax return. This includes both cash spent and such noncash expenses as depreciation on property or depletion of a resource, such as oil.

Tax Deferral.   A shelter often allows funds to grow within the business and postpones the tax liability on them, just as earning an investment return on assets in an IRA prevents a tax from becoming due until capital withdrawal. Some shelters pay out cash to investors on a tax-sheltered basis. Others permit funds in the business to be reinvested to gain added tax deductions. All these postpone payment of taxes and thus are advantageous.

Tax-Rate Conversion.   A shelter may convert the tax rate on cash paid out to investors from ordinary income rates to long-term capital gain rates (a maximum of 50 percent and 20 percent rates, respectively). This is done by having the shelter hold a capital asset for more than the long-term gain holding period (six months after July 1984) before selling it and distributing the proceeds.

Investment Tax Credit.   An investment tax credit is a dollar-for-dollar reduction in total taxes due, and it is the high-powered form of tax reduction. It arose because Congress wanted to allow major tax benefits for investment in certain equipment and property.

So Shelters Grew

The existence of these tax incentives was once the most compelling inducement to invest in tax shelters because many investors were able to make big bucks from the incentives alone.

In those good old days (roughly pre-1976), so many multiple-deduction benefits were geared to people in 70 percent top brackets that as long as the deductions kept flowing, it was just fine if the project itself never made money. For example, if an investor put $10,000 into a shelter with a leveraged three-to-one write-off, a deduction of $30,000 was taken, perhaps over two to three years. In a 70 percent top bracket (assuming the full deduction fell into that bracket amount), the tax saving was $21,000, more than twice the cash invested. If the deal made money, part of the deduction was often lost, and so was part of the tax saving.

With the tax reform laws of 1976, 1978, 1981–82, and 1984 (ad nauseum), the top tax bracket was cut to 50 percent (meaning the government would pay at most only half the amount of a deduction) and specific limitations on deductions, called at-risk rules, were instituted for most shelters. The latter action meant an investor had to actually put money at risk in the deal in order to achieve a deduction. Artificial write-offs were largely eliminated. With real money at risk, the quality of the investment project itself became far more important to the investor. (There was one general exception to this rule, the real estate tax shelter. Needless to say, these soared in popularity, aided in part by even faster depreciation deductions than previously allowed.) Therefore, although there are such exceptions as real estate, it is usually true that an investor can lose close to 50 cents of every dollar invested in a tax shelter today if the deal doesn't work. Thus the number one tax shelter-investing rule is: The shelter must make sense as a profit-making business before you choose to invest in it. If it doesn't meet this standard, you're better off giving the money to charity. If you want to send money away with a one-way ticket, at least send it where you think it will do some good. All one-way tickets get the same tax deduction.

As for the exceptions to this rule, a moment's reflection will raise the possibility that some combinations of tax credits, deferrals, and conversion to long-term capital gains will create greater investor advantages than a simple 100 percent deduction and its 50-cents-on-the-dollar maximum loss potential. For example, a 75 percent deduction on capital invested, a 10 percent credit on part of it against other taxes due, and a conversion of any investment proceeds to long-term capital gain tax rates might benefit an investor more than a single 100 percent net deduction for capital invested. So, some deals still attempt to achieve all that, and more. However, if the business flops, the investor is still likely to have a significant real loss whether it's 30, 40, or 50 cents on the dollar. Thus the basic caveat remains paramount: Any worthwhile shelter must make business sense.

How Shelters Work

Tax shelters must have some method of allowing the tax incentives to flow through to investors, and the one legal structure that is almost invariably used to do this is the limited partnership. There are two good reasons for its use. A limited partnership can usually be prevented from becoming a taxable entity itself, and it permits a maximum limitation on the investor's liability equal to the amount of the capital invested.

The limited partnership is structured so that a *general partner* has the key legal role in managing the partnership, and its number of limited partners is determined by the type of partnership offering (public or private) or the amount of capital that's specified to be invested. The general partner must make all management decisions for the partnership. If not, the partnership will risk losing its nontaxable status, a condition that would force the partners to lose their tax advantages (which most partners want to avoid at nearly all costs). Having this responsibility, the general partner can make or break the business and must therefore be both reliable and professionally competent. Naturally, the general partner should be a focal point when studying a tax shelter.

The following section examines risks that are prevalent in any shelter, regardless of type, and includes a checklist designed to aid in that review.

An Overall Tax-Shelter Checklist

April 15 comes and goes, but not without many investors paying the IRS more in taxes than they earned in salary just a few years earlier. Many of them vow that the next year will be different. Somehow more of those tax dollars will be sheltered.

Tax sheltering can, and should, be done by most higher-bracket investors. Unfortunately, most investors wait until too late in the year to do comprehensive tax planning (shelter benefits frequently apply only to the portion of the year remaining *after* the investment is made), and then they invest without adequate information and analysis. All too often a tax shelter is bought simply because a sales representative with a "great deal" catches the taxpayer in a moment of desperation near the close of the tax year. To avoid being caught, remember that it is never too early to start proper tax planning.

Evaluating tax shelters involves almost as much effort as does exploring a new business. In fact, investing in a new business is what most tax shelters do. An investor unwilling to put effort into the job (or to hire someone to do it) can figure that the shelter investment is just a dice roll—except that a tax shelter can lose *more* than all the investment. Losers can be saddled with an investment loss, extra accountant's fees, added tax liability, tax penalties, and even a legal bill. So homework can pay off substantially.

This checklist provides a brief and workable guide for evaluating the range of tax-shelter programs to be discussed. It identifies the most important points in the evaluation of any shelter. Use it in conjunction with the succeeding specific shelter-risk summaries. Because of the enormous variety of details in tax-shelter programs (some of which are probably being created as this is written), don't assume that the following list is all-encompassing. It is simply a detailed guide.

1. Make Sure You Qualify for the Shelter Program.   Almost every limited partnership contains personal financial criteria that must be met before one is permitted to invest. The dealer offering the program will require that you qualify, but checking this point first may save you much effort. The criteria should be clearly spelled out in the offering memorandum. Common conditions include a personal net worth of $100,000 (excluding home and autos) or $50,000 net worth plus an income level that places you in the 50 percent federal income tax bracket.

2. Check the Reliability and Independence of the Salesperson. You'll probably be comparing details on more than one tax shelter, presumably after it's been recommended to you by a shelter salesperson. Therefore, your next consideration should be just how reliable and independent the advice is from that salesperson. Is (s)he paid to *evaluate* the shelter, or just to sell it? If the answer is "sell it," is the salesperson provided with an *independent* evaluation? Is that person's principal compensation paid for recommending good shelters, or is this an adjunct, as with most stock brokers? If the fees are an adjunct, are tax shelters a major source of that person's total compensation? (The more research effort put into shelters, the greater the percentage of total income the salesperson's fees should be and presumably the better the suitability of the program to your circumstances.) The person to look for is one who approaches true expertise in many types of shelters. S(he) should save you evaluation time and provide a viable source of answers to the questions prompted by this analysis.

3. Check Out the General Partner.   The GP is the most important single element in any limited partnership. It is his/her expertise, connections, and business abilities that will spell success or failure of the project. To evaluate this key project aspect, research the following, especially if the broker recommending the partnership can't vouch for each point. These criteria are the most critical for any tax-shelter partnership.

a.   Look at the GP's financial statements for soundness and the ability to finance unforeseen difficulties. Ask for references and check them. Check suppliers to see that the GP is reliable in paying obligations. Check competitors to find out if the GP is well regarded in the business.

b.   Check the GP's track record for length, consistency of performance, and actual results. The facts should be presented clearly in the offering material. If not, query the salesperson. Lack of a stellar record in any of these areas does not necessarily mean the project under consideration is poor, but rather it may indicate a degree of increased risk. Note also whether or not the GP's principal business is one for which this partnership is being developed. Mark a big minus if it isn't.

c.   Evaluate the ability of the GP to analyze prospects in-house. Does the GP have a staff to analyze such things as buildings, leases, and tenants in real estate or to do the geological work and assemble leases in oil/gas projects? If the GP has such a staff and uses it, it means the GP has a solid, comprehensive business. However, it is not necessarily risky for a GP to have some outside analysis done as long as there is staff capability to analyze the prospects brought in.

d.   Look through the offering material for discussions of possible conflicts of interest. Any conflicts should be spelled out and studied carefully to find their possible risk to the partnership.

4. See that the Program Is Presented in an Understandable Form. Use the offering memorandum table of contents to locate the sections that detail what the project involves. Sections having such labels as "Use of Proceeds," "Description of Project," or "Acquisition and Financing" should lay this out clearly. Get a good feel for what will actually occur in the business, when it should occur, and what will happen to your money as it occurs. If you find that this is unclear, ask questions of the salesperson/promoter until it is clear. Be especially careful to locate any wording about a liability on the investors' part to commit added capital by signing nonrecourse notes or through other financing arrangements, such as split down payments in real estate projects.

5. Check the Estimated Tax Write-off.   Verify what the tax write-off has been in previous shelters of the same type involving the same general partner. This information will answer three important early questions:

a.   Will the write-off be appropriate for the tax savings you need (if any)?
b.   Will the write-off be dangerously high (i.e., 3–1, 4–1, or greater), thereby inviting both IRS scrutiny and later efforts by the IRS to recapture the taxes written off?
c.   Does the general partner have a record of similar projects with consistent tax advantages?

The key caution here is that tax write-offs that are considerably more than the amount you've invested usually lead to your paying the piper later.

6. Scrutinize the Front-End Load.   Somewhere near the beginning of the prospectus or offering circular is an expense breakdown for your investment dollar. Obviously, the greater the amount that goes into the actual business, the better off you should be. Sales costs of 8 to 10 percent plus other fees that bring the total to around 15 percent are common in oil and gas shelters, but 25 percent or more has been the norm in real estate syndications when all front-end costs are totaled. I recommend that the total front-end fees not exceed 15 percent in any case. If you're being asked to pay more, expect the sales organization to have done top flight "due diligence" (serious evaluation) of this and competing projects, and to present such detailed comparisons to you.

The flip side to the high front-end cost is the very low load. A low load doesn't automatically mean an investment is good. When you see this apparent advantage, look carefully at the ongoing compensation received by the promoter and the GP, and especially at the payout terms upon the completion of the project. Then compare with similar shelters to ascertain reasonableness.

7. Check the Past Records of the Partnership Team. Compare the team's past records with those of others in the same business. Be sure to compare apples with apples, since types of projects vary considerably under the broad headings of real estate or oil/gas or equipment leasing. The best way to accomplish this is to ask the broker or promoter of the partnership to provide at least three other partnership offerings of the same type and compare their track records. Be alert for differences among oil and gas exploratory, developmental, and combination projects and among real estate equity, mortgage, and combination syndications. Pay particular attention to (a) the total return on investment, (b) how long it took limited partners to be paid their return, and (c) the economic conditions during the track record periods being compared.

8. Compare the Remaining Terms of the Partnership Offering with Similar Offerings. This is the most difficult step because of the nearly infinite variety of terms offered. After comparing the offering costs and the GP compensation mentioned above, compare the following: (a) the ways in which the partnership can be terminated, (b) the limited partners' payout terms (how you get the money and when), (c) transferability of your partnership interest, and (d) assessments of limited partners (calls for added funds). Are assessments voluntary or not? Is there a maximum limit? Under what terms can assessments be made? Look for any special terms that show up in one offering and not others, and determine the real effect of such terms.

9. After Choosing a Possible Tax Shelter, Consider Its Scope. Will it solve more than one financial problem? Will it take care of this year's tax problems or shelter an income stream but leave more complex issues alone? Consider again whether you need a complete financial review and not just a single tax shelter. If you have doubts at this stage, and especially if you have a point or two in your financial affairs left unaddressed by the purchase of a shelter, see a financial planner for an initial discussion before investing. It may well be that (s)he has a more comprehensive plan for you to consider, one you hadn't yet thought of.

10. Address Your Questions to an Independent Professional. The above checklist should have identified a number of important questions about the tax shelters you are considering. Both the clarity and completeness of the answers should give you a full picture of your shelter parameters. When this is completed, one or two shelters should stand above the rest. It will be most useful to have these shelters' offering memoranda reviewed by your accountant or tax attorney for tax relevancy. I don't suggest that you personally analyze the financial projections, accounting footnotes, or tax opinion contained in the shelter's offering memorandum because they are beyond the scope of most investors. These things should be reviewed by experts, and now is the time to have that done.

Tax-Shelter Businesses

The following low-risk evaluation criteria make sense for investors considering the most common types of tax shelters.

Real Estate

Among the principal types of tax-shelter programs an investor will come across, those featuring *real estate* are certainly the most common. Not only are there more property shelters regularly available (partly a result of the tax enhancements created for them in recent years), but they are relatively easy for promoters to sell. Everyone deals with real estate in daily life, whether through home ownership or as a tenant. The availability-familiarity combination makes the real estate shelter the most frequently offered of any type.

There is of course a key tax distinction between the real estate most people are familiar with (their homes) and investment property ownership. The distinction is depreciation, a noncash tax deduction available to income property owners but not to homeowners unless a portion of the home is rented or used in business. It is from this depreciation capability that several important considerations arise, including the rate at which it's taken, possible later income recapture, and whether tax credits are included. More on these in a moment.

Real estate shelters offer ownership of many types of properties, either mixed together in a partnership stew, as it were, or in a single category per partnership. They range from miniwarehouses to hotels; office buildings and apartment complexes are the most common middle-ground choice. Also available to investors in property tax shelters are government-assisted housing programs administered under federal, state, and city auspices. One is a Section 8 Housing and Urban Development project, through which the federal government agency HUD makes up a difference in rent between a fair market value and the amount paid by tenants on either rehabilitated or newly constructed property. A second program, known as Section 221(d)(4), offers benefits from federal subsidies on mortgages. Through this program a developer can obtain larger-than-normal loans, below-market interest rates, and longer payback periods, and all will be funded or guaranteed by a government entity.

Cash versus Amount of Risk.   Real estate tax shelters vary considerably as to the amount of risk and the actual tax shelter provided to investors. Because of the variations in these qualities, real estate shelters can meet a wide range of investor objectives. For example, if the partnership invests relatively large amounts of cash in its properties, perhaps by acquiring mortgages with below-market interest rates, the tax deductions available for mortgage expense will be relatively low, as will be the leverage on the partnership capital. This can reduce the risk, but it also reduces the tax shelter. This kind of project would fit the conservative investor as to risk, but in this case, the investor should not also be seeking high tax write-offs.

Conversely, a high-leverage real estate partnership (utilizing low cash down payments) can increase both risk and tax deductions, and its investors should be so oriented. Therefore, the amount of mortgage leverage on a shelter's properties is the first point a prospective investor should assess in evaluating the program.

Rate of Write-Off.   A second point investors in real estate limited partnerships should be aware of is the *rate* at which depreciation write-offs are being taken on the various properties held. Recent tax law changes have modified the ability of partnerships to generate depreciation deductions. This specifically included a new 18-year write-off on most income properties bought after March 15, 1984 and replaced the 15 percent deductions in effect since 1981. Accelerated depreciation may still be used with a 175 percent of declining balance method, and it still has a "long tail" to it: It may create recaptured income when the properties are sold *after* depreciation has been fully utilized. How this applies to a shelter you are considering is worth discussing with your real estate partnership promoters or accountant.

New Properties.   Potential investors should also note whether newly constructed properties are to be utilized in the shelter program. New properties have relatively high write-off potential compared with other properties, but they generally carry with them higher risks as well. Since new properties must always be leased up from scratch, they run the risk of area overbuilding or other types of cash flow delays before leasing is completed. Overbuilding was a common office-building problem of 1982–84.

Rental Cash Flow.   The matter of rental cash flow is an important fourth point for property shelter investors to consider.

If earning an income from your real estate partnership investment is a key objective, make sure that it is the partnership's key objective, too. Cash flow tends to be a trade-off item with tax advantages: The higher one advantage is, the lower the other in most cases, at least at certain stages in the life of the partnership. Expecting high tax write-offs along with good cash returns is probably an impractical goal, although good initial tax benefits can fit with later sheltered cash flow in many projects.

Rehabilitations.   The Economic Recovery Tax Act of 1982 (ERTA) brought an important older tax incentive to bear in new ways on certain types of properties. Tax credits are now allowed for the rehabilitation of properties 30 years old or older and for certified historic reconstruction. Credits range from 15 to 25 percent of the rehabilitation expense, depending on age of the property. Since tax credits are used to reduce an investor's tax bill directly, they are valuable additions to the standard property deductions. Partnerships directed toward these types of rehabilitations should be sought by investors requiring relatively higher tax-shelter levels.

Management.   A final and important consideration about real estate partnerships is the matter of ongoing property management, which should be specifically discussed in the partnership offering memorandum. A key criteria is finding out whether or not the property management firm is directly affiliated with, or is a part of, the general partner's organization. If so, the general partner can handily oversee and direct that ongoing management, which is desirable if the properties are to be kept in best rental (and salable) condition. This is not to say that third-party management companies can't do the job, but close oversight by the persons responsible for the entire partnership will generally bring best results, assuming they're experienced and qualified. Accordingly, a related question is: How much property management experience do partners possess?

Real Estate Tax-Shelter Risk Evaluation.   When reviewing real estate tax shelters, remember their risk points:

- The higher the average level of mortgage debt in the partnership, the higher the risk and reward potential. That level should always fit your objectives.
- Accelerated depreciation will generally not affect the risks to the investor but may create income recapture at a later date and thereby affect the tax desirability of the partnership.
- Tax advantages may be increased through use of newly constructed properties or property rehabilitation, but they can also increase risks to investors.
- Since real estate partnerships can vary considerably as to risks—with high tax advantages coupled with higher risk on one side and lower tax deductions (especially in early years) joined with lower risk on the other—make sure your personal objectives are being met in the partnership you choose. Evaluate the tax, cash flow, and appreciation potential aspects in this regard.
- Property management is an important aspect of real estate investments and should be most beneficial to investors if it is under direct control of the general partner.

Oil and Gas

The nature of oil and gas tax shelters has taken a dramatic turn since 1981 and the decline in world oil prices. Despite continued favorable profit margins in the price received for oil versus the cost of drilling for it, oil and gas drilling shelters, whether exploratory or developmental (drilling away from or adjacent to known fields, respectively), have declined substantially in popularity. Arising in their stead have been oil and gas *income programs*. In these, the production from a group of wells is packaged by the promoter/oil firm and sold to investors on the expectation of future income from the package. Projected annual rates of return from these income programs have regularly been in the teen percentages, which has made them popular for retirement plans, such as IRAs and Keoghs, and with people requiring some inflation protection on an income stream, such as retirees. A key point to note, however, is that the income from these programs is usually taxable in part. There are few allowable tax deductions in producing oil for these packages, so the investors in turn get fewer. The result is most often a partially tax-exempt, partially taxable income stream. The proportions usually vary over the life of the program.

Oil and gas income programs are not risk-free investments by a long shot, even though events may make them so (i.e., the oil price does not decline and the production amount is adequate for the projected term of the program). It is clear that some risk is involved in future expectations of gas and oil prices. In an industry that was predicting virtually unlimited future oil price increases right up to the moment that world prices collapsed, current projections of any given oil price must be suspect. This is not to say that industry analysts are particularly poor predictors. They may be about as good as those in any industry, but theirs is a business that hangs on world politics to a great degree, especially those in the volatile Mideast. Need I say more?

Accordingly, to evaluate the risk in an oil and gas income shelter, question to what degree the income, and thus the investment returns, are dependent on a particular oil price or price range. Specifically, ask by what percentage the oil price can decline before the projected return is materially affected. (If the price rises, these programs can be very profitable.) If, for example, a 15 percent oil price cut will affect the investor's return by the same amount or more, the risk in expecting a level income from the project is not small. Low-risk investors will require a substantial safety margin in price fluctuations.

Often these programs will also have natural gas production associated with the oil production, and that, too, must be evaluated. This is a highly complex area. Congress is still tinkering with natural gas price decontrol in 1984 (the price situation is complex enough without legislative manipulation). If the partnership relies on given income projections from natural gas, see to it that the figures are conservative and allow room for price fluctuations.

Sometimes these programs also include oil and gas properties that are held for drilling for later production if circumstances and finances are right. They act as "kickers" to the income production and may be calculated into the income stream. The more conservative and risk-reduced programs will rely on these only for potential income increases at later dates, but not to maintain an income level. That's the safest way to use them.

Consider the now out-of-favor oil and gas drilling partnerships, wherein the tax deductions for investors can be substantial—as are the risks. The worry with these programs is that another break in the oil price could cut the production income to a point where the drilling costs make the shelter a loser. That happened to many investors during the oil price cuts of 1981–82. On the other side of that coin, drilling costs have not risen in general anywhere near as fast as the oil price since 1979 (at least worldwide). Therefore, many of the current drilling programs being offered publicly should be viable unless there is a substantial cut in oil prices. Most drilling partnerships have natural gas kickers in them as well, at least to some degree. However, it is the leverage in drilling programs that can be a problem.

A little arithmetic shows how the leverage in oil and gas drilling programs can affect an investor's return. Assume an investor in the 50 percent top tax bracket makes a $10,000 investment in a drilling program that provides an 80 percent tax deduction in the first year and none thereafter. The hard dollars invested would be:

$10,000	Cash invested.
(4,000)	Cash saved in 50 percent bracket with 80 percent deduction.
$6,000	Net aftertax cost.

Now, assume that over seven years (a reasonable payout time) at current oil revenue/production costs, the program *returns double the cash invested*, or $20,000. Allowing for a depletion allowance exemption on the production of 20 percent and the 50 percent income tax on the revenue paid to the investor, here's how the picture would look:

$20,000	Gross income received.
(4,000)	Depletion exemption.
16,000	Taxable income.
(8,000)	Taxes at 50 percent.
$8,000	Net aftertax.
(6,000)	Less aftertax cost above.
$2,000	Net aftertax return.

A $2,000 net return is hardly a whopping return on the cash invested. It is less than 3 percent per year, not compounded, over the seven years, and it required that the program provide an income total of twice the cash invested. Experts in the field say that not one drilling program in three provides that good a return! It is true that the return is aftertax, but tax-exempt money market funds averaged well above that in 1983, which was a low interest rate year relative to the prior five years. If that's the best return to be expected from the shelter over seven years, it would be much better to invest in the money market fund—lower risk, higher return, and instant liquidity for the whole period.

If the oil income fell by 20 percent and drilling/production costs did not rise, the above returns would look like this:

$16,000	Gross income received after 20 percent price cut.
(3,200)	Depletion exemption.
12,800	Taxable income.
(6,400)	Taxes at 50 percent.
(6,000)	Less aftertax cost.
$ 400	Net return aftertax.

Under those conditions the deal would still be profitable, but who would want to take the risk? Perhaps a shortsighted investor who was badly in need of a tax deduction for a given year would try. However, from a pure investment standpoint, it would be a very marginal undertaking, especially with the alternatives available.

Of course, if a rise in the oil price occurred and it looked permanent, and the economics of the shelter in question were based on similar assumptions to those cited above, the risks would drop dramatically. (So would the risks in buying stock in Exxon or Mobil or Standard Oil of Indiana.)

Although evaluating the risk for an oil and gas drilling program certainly involves a good deal more than just the basic numbers in the deal, those figures would be my first concerns in the 1980s. To the figures should be added these risk-reduction questions.

Is the Program a Developmental, an Exploratory One, or Some Mixture of the Two? Developmental programs, you'll recall, are those in which the drilling is to be undertaken adjacent to an existing or known oil field, and they are notably less risky than are exploratory programs in which the drilling is planned for largely new areas.

Where Is the Drilling to Be Done? Geography relates to the developmental versus exploratory question, since certain areas of the United States have relatively lower drilling costs than do others (partly due to shallower wells). Also, certain areas have relatively higher prospects for finding oil because of their many proven fields. The Ohio, Pennsylvania, and West Virginia basin has a relatively lower risk of finding oil and lower production cost for it; the Rocky Mountain West is apt to have a higher risk; and the Gulf Coast should generally fit somewhere between. Area selection will not in itself make or break a project, but it may signal the kind of risk objectives the general partner wishes to undertake.

Evaluating the general partner's record is very important in oil and gas programs because of the amount of expertise required. In addition to the 10 points for general tax shelter evaluation listed earlier, one should seriously investigate the following issues.

Oil and Gas Risk Evaluation

1. How sizable are the GP's programs? Is the driller a major national firm that drills at greater than the $100 million level annually, or does it drill in the $5 million-per-year range? In this business bigger is generally better because of risk spreading and know-how, but size doesn't guarantee results.

2. In the GP's post-1976 programs that are at least three years old, what is the payout amount to investors compared with dollars invested on a pretax basis? Programs earlier than 1976, when the Tax Reform Act of that year changed the at-risk investing rules, are apt to have tax objectives that are different from and not comparable to later programs. Therefore, the results aren't comparable either. On the other hand, partnerships less than three years old probably haven't had time to develop a meaningful payout record. In-between programs should offer investors a good overview of the GP track record.

3. What is the payout record on a year-by-year basis? Compare the first-year payout amount to the latest. Has payout gone up, gone down, or remained level? A drop may signify an early big hit but poor overall results. A moderate, steady rise could identify a developmental program that has succeeded but that would not be comparable to exploratory results. A satisfactory early payout that has been declining, especially if true in the past six months of a multiyear payout, probably signifies a drying up of the income stream.

4. What is the success ratio? Most track records will show the number of wells drilled and the number producing per program and will identify them by exploratory and developmental types. Compare the record with the industry average, which is about 1 producing exploratory well in 10 drilled and 5.5 producing developmental wells per 10 drilled.

5. Is added borrowing involved? As to the terms of the offering, be especially wary of those that involve added borrowing by either you or the GP for the partnership. Look at such leverage as sources of risk in a high-interest rate and flat-oil-price environment. When asked to sign a re-

course note for later payments, the salesperson might say those dollars shouldn't be needed because the production income will fund the need, but the chances are that somehow income probably won't arrive, and you'll be on the line.

6. Oil and gas drilling partnerships are generally high-*business risk* ventures and have moderate to high *structure risk* due to the potential for complex payout terms and advantageous takeouts by the general partner. However, these shelters usually remain on the beaten path through the tax code and are therefore relatively *low-tax risk* programs (assuming, of course, that highly competent tax practitioners structure them).

With all their risks, oil and gas drilling programs could be the sleeper tax shelters of the mid- to later-1980s because the economics are there and, if undisturbed, they could provide substantial returns for some alert investors. Only with a long-term oil price rise, or significant favorable changes in the natural gas price and demand situation can they ever be described as other than *overall* high-risk ventures. Of course, sending tax dollars on a one-way trip to Washington is the ultimate in high risk.

Equipment Leasing

Equipment-leasing tax shelters are probably best described as fast break shelters—those with the best early combination of tax deductions and credits for individuals, *if* the right equipment can be located and *if* they are very carefully structured both in form and for tax compliance. Because of the *ifs*, these shelters are definitely high-risk vehicles from all three principal shelter risk sources. In short, getting the right equipment-leasing "cake" means having that cake and eating it quickly, too. Corporations have munched easily on equipment-leasing shelters since the 1981 tax act, a fact that was greedily eyed by a revenue-hungry Congress in 1984. The problem for the individual investor is getting his/her piece of the cake.

In the simplest terms, an equipment-leasing partnership is rather like an accelerated real estate deal in that it has as its centerpiece a fixed asset(s) that is depreciated for tax purposes over a useful life. That creates tax deductions. Moreover, it has been given *tax credit* advantages similar to the historic rehabilitation form of real property shelters. The speedup comes in the depreciating—which, depending on the type of equipment, can run just 3 to 5 years, versus 15 to 20 years in most real estate deals.

Other features of equipment-leasing partnerships differ notably from either real estate or oil and gas shelters. Equipment deals may involve direct ownership of the property by an investor or investors rather than by a limited partnership structure. Most often, the equipment actually depreciates with use, contrary to real estate, and this represents a significant problem for the investor because *appreciation* in value is often needed to make the equipment-leasing shelter economically sound. If appreciation doesn't occur, there often must be an increase in the lease payments to recover the amount lost by the end of the equipment life. The marketplace will not always cooperate with this need.

Furthermore, because tax law typically requires these shelters to have short-term leases, the income stream is dangerously prone to interruptions. It's much like renting out a two- to four-unit apartment house on six-month leases. Keeping them all rented at the right levels is tricky, and failure produces a real pinch.

The toughest requirements on equipment shelters come from attempts by Congress to make leasing disadvantageous for individuals. Specifically, Congress has made the obtaining of an investment tax credit of 6–10 percent conditional on the equipment's depreciable life and on the above-noted short-term leases, which cannot run longer than half the equipment's depreciable life. It also requires that the leases be "actively run." This provision demands that a minimum of 15 percent of the gross rents from the lease be expended for upkeep, refurbishing, insurance, leasing operations, and so on. This makes equipment leasing the only one of the four shelters discussed here to include a requirement on spending a minimum amount in the business.

As to the kind of equipment that might be leased in a shelter, almost any that address the short-term active lease problem will do. Railroad cars, medical equipment, shipping containers, oil-drilling rigs, barges, smaller aircraft, TV cable systems, and even houseboats are typical objects of an individual's leasing deals.

Probably the greatest disadvantage to equipment leases comes in handling the tax questions at the end of the program. One problem is what happens to the equipment and how that affects the tax situation. Equipment deals do not usually convert any gain on the equipment sales to long-term capital gains: It comes back with its prior tax deductions attached as ordinary income. If there is a loss upon sale, it is a real one affecting the economics of the deal. You can't simply keep the equipment, thanks to the "phantom income" phenomenon. After the depreciable life runs out, the equipment begins to generate taxable income.

Experts in this area believe that these end-of-project "comebacks" really make equipment leasing nothing more than a tax deferral device, albeit a substantial one.[1] This point raises personal considerations on the value of such deferrals to you individually, plus the time value of money discussed in earlier chapters.

Risk Evaluation for Equipment Leasing

- The kind of equipment that might be involved in a leasing shelter has business circumstances peculiar to it. This reemphasizes an earlier point that investors must become familiar with all aspects of the shelter's business or find and rely heavily on an expert. At a minimum, this requires a general partner with extensive experience in the particular equipment's leasing or, in direct ownership situations, a management firm with top-flight qualifications. Ensure that this expertise is present. Note that each business is different: Leasing cable-TV systems has little or nothing to do with leasing containers or aircraft.
- Carefully consider the potential for *phantom income* in long-range tax planning. In most leasing shelters, such income will begin to show up about halfway through the equipment's depreciable life.
- Watch out for costs and potential conflicts of interest in leasing deals. Because of the expertise required, heavy fees are often paid to those experts and to the salespeople who brought the project to your attention. (Naturally.) Often the manager of your lease will have other equipment that could receive priority over yours at a time when that priority might be critical, such as in leasing containers, barges, or rail cars during a recession. Satisfy yourself that there are sufficient management incentives present in your program to give it a high priority or other competitive programs.
- Leasing deals are rife with unfamiliar financing arrangements, and these peculiarities can affect the viability (and your liability) in the deal. Recourse notes are common, and special financing terms may exist. This makes a thorough review by an attorney familiar with such arrangements a highly desirable condition of investment.
- Don't view a leasing shelter as sound just because the numbers in the promoter's projections seem to work out. One tipoff to danger is in the actual, not the tax-depreciated, value assigned to the equipment itself in the program. If the value is above original cost, ensure that it truly

---

[1] See Robert Swanson and Barbara Swanson, *Tax Shelters, A Guide for Investors and Their Advisors* (Homewood, Ill.: Dow Jones-Irwin, 1982).

does have a likelihood for appreciation. If it is lower, determine what
the probability is that the figure will be correct.

Research and Development

Research and development shelters represent the swinging, high-
stakes side of the tax-shelter game. They can be fun, too, where backing a
particular scientific investigation qualifies as fun. As such, they also
make up the riskiest shelter category from the standpoint of the *business
risk*.

Most R&D partnerships are sponsored by advanced technology firms
to investigate product ideas that the firm can't, or won't, back on its
own. The ideas may run the gamut from those that have already been
thoroughly studied scientifically but require commercial proving to
those that are little more than gleams in scientists' eyes. Almost none involves anything close to proven, marketable products. If they did, they
wouldn't fit the R&D category.

Low-risk investors take heed: There's practically no way—not even
through a conservative partnership structure nor through strict adherence to a well-trod path through the tax code—that R&Ds can be low-risk
deals. A sound tipoff to this fact is that most R&D partnerships are now
private placements, that is, partnerships not registered with the SEC or
state regulatory authorities. Instead, investors in them must conform to
certain eligibility and suitability requirements to make the private
grade: Individuals having personal assets of $1 million or more and/or
income of $200,000 annually meet the typical cutoff requirements. The
SEC assumes that level of wherewithal to be able to stand the risks.

With such entry standards, it is common for R&D partnerships to require $25,000 to $50,000 minimum individual investments, which are
then pooled to reach the multimillion dollar goals of many of these ventures. Genentech Corporation, for example, the northern California-
based genetic-engineering company, raised $34 million and $55 million
in two partnerships during 1983. Cetus Corporation, the biotechnology
firm, raised $70 million in R&D deals over a bit more than a year; and
Syntex Corporation raised $23.5 million to investigate five diagnostic
products.

The partnerships are structured so that the limited partners put up
the cash to finance the product from the testing stages to the point of fil-
ing for government marketing approval or beginning actual marketing.

Investors generally receive a payout option upon successful work completion, which may come in the form of royalties paid by the sponsoring firm over 10 to 15 years or as the right to sell one's interest in the product back to the company for stock. Although the partnership must legally own the product and control the licensing and other rights, the fact remains that without a company to "take out" the R&D investors with some form of payment and then to market the product (a capability that some R&D firms demonstrably lack), the partners have at best just an expensive, though proved, idea.

To compensate for their risks, the limited partners in R&D shelters usually obtain sizable tax write-offs (usually 80 to 95 percent of invested capital). They may obtain long-term capital gain tax treatment upon sale of their interests, although this had not been thoroughly tested in the tax courts by year-end 1983.

As to magnitude of projects, at least one large brokerage firm sponsoring these partnerships aims for a goal of 40 to 60 percent gain on the investment. However, that profit may ultimately be taxed as ordinary income—if not entirely lost along with the investment.

Research and Development Risk Evaluation. Since all R&D partnerships qualify as high-risk business ventures, the following points are aimed at identifying the soundest, not the lowest-risk, venture.

- Tax deductions between 80 and 100 percent of capital invested are to be expected, but those offering more than 100 percent write-offs are usually backing a highly "iffy" product.
- Attempt to evaluate the principal market that will develop for the product once it has been proved and approved. If that market isn't truly sizable, there's little point in developing the idea. Most R&D deals will be based on large assumed markets, but then comes the real test: What firm will market the product to that big crowd? Has a company been identified and committed for marketing that has the knowledge and channels to do so, or must this capability be acquired? Can all this be done profitably? Ask that these questions be answered in detail.
- Consider just how good the payout option really is. Not all R&D shelters have similar payout terms. Would you want to own stock in the sponsoring company for a long period if that is to be offered? Is there a cap on the return you can receive, after which all profits revert to the sponsoring firm or others?
- Watch out for the overall tax situation. Are other tax advantages loaded into the deal to make it attractive, such as nonrecourse borrowings or

even tax credits? If so, it might be too good to be true. Note also that effective in 1983 taxpayers must add their R&D shelter deductions onto gross income in figuring a possible tax liability under the alternative minimum tax. This can dramatically alter the value of such deductions.

Cashing In (or Out) of a Shelter

Getting into a tax-shelter limited partnership, even with the study involved, is a snap compared with getting out of one. For one thing, shelters are long-term propositions of rarely less than 5 years, and often of 10 years duration. Aside from annual reports by the general partner and the accountant's yearly K–1 tax-position statements, you won't have much contact with your partnership business during that time. A lot can happen to prospects for your investment in 5, 7, or 10 years.

Also, the investment capital has been out of your hands for that period. Once invested in tax shelters, capital tends to become a case of "out of sight, out of mind." Then one day the notice arrives from the general partner or partnership accountant stating that the business is being wound up, as either a successful or an unsuccessful deal. At that point, one of several things happens.

A shelter that was not highly leveraged and did not provide multiple tax deductions for the capital invested might be wrapped up with no added tax to you, and no significant capital returned or added tax deductions either. The shelter just goes away, taking your capital with it. However, a multiple-deduction partnership or a leveraged program involving recourse notes (you promised to put up additional cash on demand) it not likely to go away. The tax problems will depend on what deductions and leverage were involved in the earlier stages of the deal, but chances are the windup will identify that recaptured, or "phantom," income.

Recaptured income occurs because there's no free lunch at the IRS. If you obtained tax deductions in excess of the amount of capital invested because of borrowed money at risk or due to the partnership's use of accelerated depreciation (as in real estate partnerships), the disposition of the assets owned at the time of partnership dissolution becomes important. Selling a property at a gain will probably mean long-term capital gain income. That's the good deal. Having to foreclose a property could incur phantom income in the amount of deductions claimed in excess of cash invested. In the second case, you would get no cash back (or very little) but would have to report the phantom income—a bad deal.

In other kinds of partnerships, such as equipment leasing, how you'll fare upon wrapup will also depend on the success of the program. If the equipment becomes worthless, you'll get no cash back, and tax experts say that you'll probably have no income recapture as long as multiple write-offs weren't taken on it. However, if the equipment has residual value, you'll most likely have some reportable capital gain; or if the equipment is retained somehow by the partners, there will probably be ordinary income recapture.

Recourse notes involve another problem. Investors in oil and gas partnerships are often asked to agree to put up added capital if it's needed by the partnership. When production flow is less than adequate, the cash may be needed, no matter how unlikely the promoters say that will be at the outset. Investors will probably have taken tax deductions as though that cash had already been invested, and when the capital is required, they'll get no added deductions.

Closing down a partnership is a decision that belongs to the general partner, not the limited partners (you). If you want out before the project is wrapped up, your options are usually very limited, which is why tax shelters are among the most illiquid of investments. Some partnerships provide for a limited number of liquidations on a regular basis and spell this out in the offering memorandum. If no such provision exists, the general partner may be able to locate an additional investor or two to buy your interest. The GP may be legally limited in doing this for tax reasons, so don't count on it; but a buyout is worth asking about. In this situation it's unlikely that you'll get all your cash back; any sale will very probably be at a discount.

Periodically, independent organizations arise that are in the business of buying limited partnership interests in selected programs. They'll also offer a discount buyout, and theirs may be the only offer you get. One firm that has been in business several years and has purchased substantial amounts of selected partnership interests is Liquidity Fund of Emeryville, California.

The other means for disposing of tax-shelter investments require careful planning with a professional tax advisor; they are charity and estate transfer.

To give your interest in a limited partnership to charity, your first need is a sound estimate of the partnership's fair market value, which is a tricky number to obtain. However, once that sum is calculated, tax people say the amount can become a tax deduction for you when the partnership interest is accepted by the charity of your choice. Thus two tax deductions may be obtained for the same investment: one in the initial stages of the program (depending on the type of shelter) and another when the partnership interest is donated. Giving the partnership share to charity is particularly appropriate for those investors expecting to drop from a high tax bracket to a lower one, possibly due to retirement.

Giving the interest to one's children works in a different way, though it can still be tax advantageous. Such a gift will not create an income tax deduction for you, but it does remove the asset from your estate and transfers any taxable income from it to your children's lower (or nonexistent) tax bracket. In either gift situation, remember that proper professional consultation is a must.

Summary

Low-risk investors can best limit the risks in tax shelters through a careful study of the business itself, the partnership structure, and the partnership's use of capital and through a verification of the tax incentives offered. The most manageable of all shelter risks, the investing risk, can be ascertained by a thorough questioning of the points raised in the preceding shelter checklist and risk-evaluation guides for individual shelter categories.

A final word needs to be said about tax shelters that create tax deductions but do little for business viability. The IRS terms these shelters *abusive*, and is going after them with clout provided by new powers in the tax acts of 1981, 1982, and 1984. The IRS defines abusive tax shelters as those formed primarily to evade taxes, without regard to the economic worth of the investment. Assistant IRS Compliance Commissioner Philip Coats calls them "frauds that are euphemistically referred to as tax shelters." "Such frauds," he says, "are characterized by back-dated documents, rigged transactions, forged trading records, and distorted accounting methods."

Whatever may be the last word on defining abusive shelters, the IRS is attacking them with vengeance. Revenue agents were examining in excess of 325,000 tax-shelter cases at the beginning of 1984, up dramatically from the minuscule 400 reviewed in one year a decade earlier. Strengthening their abuse chase, agents have been armed with the power to enjoin sales of a shelter they think is abusive, and they may warn purchasers even before they file tax returns with the shelter deductions included, that "the purported tax deductions aren't allowable." In fact, the 1984 Tax Reform Act requires promoters of tax shelters that offer "substantial" deductions or credits, which are either registered with a regulatory agency or marketed to large investors, to register the shelters with the IRS before offering them to investors.

This adds up to a serious need for greater knowledge about the risks involved in investing in any tax shelter—and the need to exercise real caution, both by you and your tax advisor.

Hedging Your Bets

In futures trading it's usually a race
to see if the rate of adverse price change
will flatten out before the wallet does.

Anonymous

So far this book has discussed essentially direct methods for controlling or reducing risk. The methods have involved approaches to investments, or the timing of them, that are low risk in and of themselves. Balancing short-term and medium-term interest-bearing instruments, using interest rate trends to time the size and type of commitments to stocks, and identifying the higher-risk conditions in tax shelters in order to control or avoid them are all low-risk concepts that work without using hedging instruments.

This chapter will deal briefly with the techniques that utilize *specific* instruments to hedge market positions in *other* instruments. This indirect approach to risk control superimposes one instrument onto another, and it can be just as effective as using the direct, low-risk concepts (indeed even more so, because these instruments can be used to calculate quite accurately the amount of risk in a given market position). These hedges are known as options, futures, options on futures, and convertible securities.

221

Stock Options

Suppose I asked you if you wanted to buy IBM stock and own it for a period of three consecutive months for a cost of $115 per share, a price at which it sold on several occasions during 1983 and 1984. Assume IBM is selling at $116 now and that you said yes to my offer.

If I in turn said, "I'm willing to sell you the *right* to buy 100 shares at $115 each, no matter where the market price goes over the next three months, but selling that right is worth something to me," what would your response be? If you believed IBM would rise some distance above $115 during that period, considering the current cost of $116, you might say, "Maybe—but how much is your fee?"

I'd consult the market and tell you my offer was worth $7 per share. You'd then have to decide whether IBM stock would be worth more than $122 in three months, not $115, or whether someone else would pay more than $7 per share for this right if the stock rose at all. "If I could buy now for $116, why pay, in effect, $122?" you might ask.

I'd answer: "I'm only asking for the $7 per share fee, or $700. Buying the 100 shares now would require $11,600 cash (or half that with the current margin requirement). I'm letting you in cheap." "Done," you'd say of our deal, being the speculator you are, "but I'd like to have the right to sell the agreement we've just made by itself, and at any time during the three months." I'd agree. It's no problem for me whether you or someone else owns this contract.

The above scenario has formed a legitimate option contract. You would have bought from me an *IBM 115 call option with a three-month expiration.*

The deal is very straightforward from your standpoint. You would have risked $7 per share that IBM would rise, preferably above $122, within three months. If it rose to $130, you'd gain $8 per share over your cost, less commissions, or a near-100 percent profit on your $7. Since you would also have retained the right to sell the agreement to someone else, even if IBM didn't rise much above $115, chances are you probably wouldn't lose all of your $7 cost. If the option were allowed to expire, however, you would lose the whole amount. That's all clean and simple. In any case you would know exactly how much you'd risked and that you could lose it all.

From my standpoint, this would have been a much different deal. I would have sold something to you that I might or might not be able to deliver promptly. If I didn't own any IBM stock, I would be speculating against you that IBM would not rise above $122. That's called selling a *naked option*. Since I've got your $7 per share, I could wait to buy the stock until it rose close to $122, which is the point (plus commission) that I'd begin to lose money. If I bought the stock while you still held the option, I'd have a "covered" position.

On the other hand, if I already owned IBM stock, I might only be interested in getting an extra gain on it. If you then asked (called) for the shares and paid me $115 each, combined with your option fee, I'd net around $122 instead of the $115 date-of-sale market price. If you didn't ask for the stock (presumably because it dropped), I'd still be $7 per share ahead of whatever price existed on expiration day. If I already owned the stock, I could let it drop to about $109 before I'd lose money compared with a sale at $116. When your option expired I could write another covered option. (I could speculate anytime with naked options.)

A significant low-risk strategy is involved with this latter "own the stock—sell the option" idea. It's called *covered option writing*. It is not without its own set of problems and pitfalls, but it is a strategy that should be considered by all risk-adverse investors.[1] For those with significant gains in a stock they are considering selling anyway, this is an approach that must be thoughtfully explored.

Covered Call Option Strategies

Promotional brochures always stress that options have "limited risk" because the amount you can lose is fixed by the amount of money you invest in buying them. In truth, the amount that can be lost is all the money you've put up. That is limited, to be sure, but losing all the money invested is not a low-risk investment! For this reason, buying options is a high-risk use of them. Period. However, selling options against a stock previously owned, or just purchased, is not. It's a low-risk strategy and worth considering in some detail.

There are several facets of covered option writing that are important to the writers (sellers). Consider the matter of increased total return. Suppose you bought XYZ stock selling at a price of 40. Also assume that a six-month call option with a 40 call price (known as the "strike" price) was selling in the market for 4. If you then sold that call, waited long enough to collect two dividends of, say, 75 cents each, and had the stock

---

[1]See also L. G. McMillan, *Options as a Strategic Investment*, (New York: New York Institute of Finance, 1980).

called away at 40 six months later, you'd have a $5.50 total return per share, or a 27½ percent annualized gain on the 40 price. Not bad. Of course, if the stock had dropped below about $35 and had not been called by the option holder, you'd have been a loser; but you'd have been worse off without that 4-point option fee. It's also worth noting that if the stock had risen substantially, you'd have forgone that extra profit. That's the risk side of covered option writing.

One way to strive for a greater gain is not to write a call option until (and if) the stock bought reaches a higher level, perhaps a resistance level on the stock's chart. Assume that level is 45 and that you could then write a three-month 45 call for a fee of 3½ points. If the stock later declined to, and remained at, the purchase price of 40 for a couple of months, the call would have lost value in the market. It could then be bought back at a profit, or it could be held until expiration, in which case you'd have a 3½ point profit plus the stock's dividends and be free to write another covered call. Or if the stock rose above 45 and was called away there, you'd have that profit plus the option fee plus the dividends. Of course, this still wouldn't prevent the stock from dropping below your net cost level, but if you'd truly expected that, you wouldn't have bought the stock in the first place. Again, that's the risk.

The sum of these simple covered option writing strategies is that if you wish to buy a stock in anticipation of its price appreciation, or if you already own it at a profit, the covered call option provides an extra return potential while also adding some protection against a modest price decline.

"Rolling"

The next option-writing angle to consider is a bit more complicated. It brings into play the tax factor and is called rolling the option.

The first case involves *rolling up* a call option where you will buy back a call you previously sold and simultaneously sell another call at a higher strike price. Note that all figures below exclude commissions. Take the example of 100 shares of XYZ stock, which in a rising market was bought at 31. At the same time, you sold one six-month call (January expiration) with a strike price of 30 for 3¾ points. A month later, the stock has risen to 35. You now have a couple of alternatives.

1. If you take no action and let the stock get called away at or near the call's expiration, you will collect the dividends until the stock is called, and you will sell the stock, in effect, at 33¾ for a gain of $275 (30 call

strike price + 3¾ option fee, less 31 stock cost = 2¾ × 100 shares = $275). You also will have the use of the funds received from the call sale during that period.

2. Perhaps you believe the stock is going to continue to trade above 35. You then may choose to roll up prior to the call's expiration by buying back the call you sold (for instance, at 6½) and simultaneously selling a longer call (April) at the next strike level of 35, for 4½ points.

The result of the second transaction is a capital *loss* of $275: the difference between what you initially received for the January 30 call and the price you paid for buying it back (6½ January call buy-back cost less 3¾ January call fee = 2¾ net loss × 100 shares = $275). Although that loss is tax deductible,[2] it doesn't look so good—until you see the rest of the trade.

You also have raised from 30 to 35 the level at which the stock can be called from you and, most important, you are still cash ahead $175, the net amount of all your call transactions (4½ April call fee less 2¾ net loss on January call = 1¾ net cash ahead × 100 shares = $175). This is one of the few securities trades that can leave you cash ahead with a tax loss (albeit modified by the 1984 Tax Act).

Here's a tip in executing this strategy. To avoid whipsawing, which occurs when a stock quickly moves up or down after an opposite move, you may want to delay rolling up to the next strike level (35 in this case) by waiting until the stock has moved up close to *two levels* above the first strike price (e.g., from 30 to 40). Such a strategy will accentuate the loss and reduce the cash ahead position, but it is decidedly a less risky approach because it leaves a larger trading cushion below the new current strike price of 40.

One more tip: When placing orders for the simultaneous purchase and sale of different options, do them on a *differential basis*. For example, in the above case, you would place the order by saying, "Buy back

---

[2]The ways in which taxes affect option transactions were notably complicated (as were most investments), by the 1984 Tax Reform Act. For our purposes it is sufficient to know that: (a) A new option type was created, called a "qualified option." It is one whose strike price is not more than two levels, and in some cases one level or closer, to the price of its underlying common stock when written. (b) Such options qualify for tax treatment largely in the way they did prior to the 1984 act, in that short- and long-term capital gain treatment is specified by a holding period. However, that holding period is now six months, and any in-the-money calls (see this section in text) are subject to modified short-sale rules and will have their holding period suspended under specified conditions. (c) Other options and those on broadly based stock index futures contracts have a new tax treatment to avoid "tax straddling" which is similar to other futures contracts in that it calls for a new maximum tax amount.

the XYZ January 30 and sell the April 35 for *a net debit of two points*."
This places an effective limit on the transaction prices, but it also allows
the broker to match those buy and sell prices. If you place specific price
limits on either one or both of the buy and sell sides, the order is much
more difficult to execute.

Rolling Down

A second aspect of rolling a call is one that goes in the opposite direction of that discussed above. It's used to protect capital in *declining* markets and is called rolling down. Before rolling, assume that in August
you purchased 100 shares of XYZ at 34½ and sold one February 35 call at
3⅝ (a realistic value for a call of six months' maturity on a stock of average volatility). Then, if the stock dropped to 30 in two months' time, you
could probably buy back the call at about 1 for a gain of 2⅝ and simultaneously sell the stock for 30. That would result in a *smaller loss* than if
you had not sold the call initially (34½ stock cost less 30 stock selling
price = 4½ loss, plus 2⅝ options profit = 1⅛ net loss, compared with
the 4½ loss in the stock alone).

A roll down is more advantageous. You could buy back the February
35s, hold the stock, and then sell (roll down) to a May 30 call at about 3½.
Under these conditions, even if the stock were later called away at 30,
you would still be cash ahead by virtue of the total net premiums received for the sale of the calls: 3⅝ for the sale of February 35s and 3½ for
the sale of the May 30s, minus 1 for the purchase (buy back) of the February 35s, for a net gain of 6⅛. Subtracting the 4½-point loss on the stock,
you would be net ahead 1⅝ if the stock were called away at 30. You
would also collect any dividends that were paid prior to the stock being
called away and have the use of the call proceeds in the interim.

Make note that the tax situation in this case differs from that of the
rolling-up procedure. With "qualified" options (see footnote 2) you'd
have a short-term capital gain of $262.50 from the profit on the sale and
buy back of the February 35 call, but you would also be obliged to reduce
your cost basis on the stock to 31 by the 3½ points received from the sale
of the May 30 call. The capital loss on the sale of the stock would be $100
and thus would result in a net short-term gain of $162.50.

The striking thing about this qualified option rolling-down strategy is
that even though the stock dropped and was called away at the lower
price, you achieved a capital gain, and that's as rare an animal as achiev-

ing the tax loss while being cash ahead on the rolling-up strategy. Of course, these results assumed that the stock did not reverse its fall and immediately rise after you'd taken the action, which is certainly a possibility to be considered. If it did, though, you'd just consider a later roll up.

This points to the fact that a number of separate decisions were required in each of these situations, a fact that introduces some risk into an equation that otherwise looks very advantageous.

"In The Money"

Consider one more use of the covered call. You've been fortunate enough to achieve a significant profit on a stock, but now believe, for one reason or another, that it could suffer a serious setback. You may wish to protect your profit by selling a call that's known as *in the money*—a call whose strike price is *below* the stock's current price. (An out-of-the-money call has a strike price above the current stock price.) In this situation, you can obtain the greatest amount of protection on your profit by selling the call with the *lowest strike* price available because it sells at the *highest price* among all available calls with that expiration. Here, in particular, watch the tax situation with the new "qualified" option.

Tax considerations aside, let's say an average volatility stock XYZ, which you bought at 30, is trading now at 40. You bought 100 shares, and have a pleasant $1,000 profit. A realistic value for a call of three months' maturity with a strike price of 30 on XYZ would be around 10⅝. If you sold that call while still holding the stock, you'd receive $1,062.50 minus commission. You would thereby protect the $1,000 unrealized stock profit even if the stock dropped to, say, 32 and was called away at 30. Your net profit would be similar to having sold the stock at 40.

On the other hand, if the stock rose to 50 before the call's expiration and was then called away, you'd be paid only 30 but would still have the original option sale proceeds for a net around 40. In effect, you'd have given up the possible extra 10-point gain in return for the downside protection. In sum, even if the stock fell to a price between 30 and 40 and was called away at 30, the sale of the call would leave you no worse off than having sold the stock at 40. For this, however, you'd give up any extra profit above 40 if the stock rose.

Aside from the belief that the stock might drop after you sold the call, why else might you want to make this trade?

1. You might believe that the stock's setback would be temporary and that you'd be able to buy back the call at a lower price when the stock fell, thereby capturing a profit while still holding the stock for a later rise.

2. You might need some current cash, which would be generated by the option sale, and might not mind having the stock called at the lower price, since you wouldn't lose any of the present gain until the stock fell below the strike price.

As you can see, when you're considering the sale of a stock at a significant profit, it makes sense to explore the possible sale of an in-the-money call at that time. Watch for the new tax angles, too.

There are disadvantages, also, to using covered call option strategies on stocks. The most significant is the fact that a number of separate decisions must usually be made in following these tactics. Each decision on the stock's future direction carries with it the risk of error, of course. Errors in these circumstances won't generally result in notable losses because the option writer has the fee in hand and has time on his/her side. Yet, an error can cause the option writer to reverse the position by buying back the option and writing another.

The second disadvantage in call writing is that the commissions in these transactions can become costly. Even using a discount broker, option commissions are larger percentages of cash involved than commissions on the underlying stock. If you trade in only 100 or 200 share lots, thereby trading only one or two option contracts at a time, the costs of several transactions can be prohibitive. The best preventive action to alleviate this problem is not to reverse your option position too quickly but rather to set a mental stop level about 15 percent away from the current transaction level before acting. You should also utilize a service that gives option buy-sell recommendations and helps to set the mental stops at important chart resistance or support levels. This should help minimize transactions and will permit the use of discount brokers for the actual trades because you pay for the advice separately. As an alternative, if your transaction volume is sufficient and you need a broker's tactical advice, you can negotiate with the broker to lower the commission.

Here are some tips on using covered options:

- The question of which month's option to sell constantly faces investors using covered strategies. Each option strike price includes a series of three future expiration months. One series begins with January expirations, another with February, and a third with March, and each group has expirations on each succeeding third month—for example, the first series with January, April, July expirations, followed by the February, May, August series, and then the March, June, September sequence. Only three expiration months are traded at any one time in each series.

When selecting an expiration month, it's a good general rule to try to use the *middle month* in the current trading series. If January, April, and July are trading, the April option should be evaluated first. It should have a sufficiently high price to provide a worthwhile fee to pocket; and if you should buy it back, you'll still have a later month available to roll out to at any time. The first month doesn't usually have a sufficiently high price, and the last month provides no month to roll out to until a new month begins trading. A corollary to this strategy is that if the nearest option month expires within three to four weeks (options always expire on the third Friday of the designated month), selling the *final* month in the series is acceptable. However, selling a *final* month option can badly hamper your alternatives if the stock moves against you and there are two or more months left before a new trading month begins.

- Next, consider which strike price to use, as discussed previously. If a stock is being bought for a short-term run of a month or two, my rule is to wait, if possible, for the stock to reach the option price level that is moderately above your purchase price, and then to sell that covered call. For example, with a stock bought at 40, look for it to reach 44–45 before selling the 45 covered option. With a stock bought at 44, try for a 49–50 stock price to sell a 50 option, and so on. A better profit potential is the advantage in this strategy.

- If a stock is purchased for long-term appreciation potential, then the strike price is of lesser importance, since you'll probably roll up or down once or twice during the holding period. In this case it's all right to use the closest strike price and to sell it at the time of stock purchase.

- A more difficult problem can occur if, while waiting for a short-term run, the stock unexpectedly turns down, creating a loss. There is no firm rule to follow in this situation, but one course of action should be considered: *Do nothing until the stock has dropped about 10 percent from the purchase price* and then sell the next lower strike price option. (Assuming that your reason for buying the stock remains valid.) For example, with a stock bought at 40 and falling, consider waiting until it reaches 36½ and then sell the 35 call. The goal is to receive an option amount that nearly covers the amount of the market loss: 3½ points in the above example. If the middle month of that strike price doesn't do it, consider selling the final month instead, subject to the final month caution already discussed.

An alert, low-risk investor will realize that there are also numerous potential hedging strategies that involve the use of option *spreads*. They require the use of *put options* along with calls, an action that creates something of a standoff between the opposite options and/or a given stock position. An illustration of this strategy occurs with a stock selling at 50, where an investor *sells a call* at 55 and also *buys a put* at 55 in that stock for a given month's expiration. Since investors are usually more optimistic than bearish, the call price will generally be greater than the put, resulting in a net fee gain. Then if the stock drops in price, the put will rise in value as the call falls, providing the investor with gains on both options, which will likely more than offset the loss on the stock itself. The strategy in this case is known as a *bear spread*.

Obviously, the reverse is true for a rising market. By switching the action on the options to a buy call, sell put form, the spread becomes a *bull spread*. Other variations are easy to imagine: different strike prices on the put and the call or different expiration months on the two options.

Unfortunately, the extreme of these possibilities is to arrive, more often than not, at what is known as the *alligator spread*: The point at which the commissions eat you alive! Accordingly, before using any of the spreads, remember that they are very popular with brokers and therefore you should be wary of the costs.

As a last point when considering stock options, remember that for all the effort involved in writing covered options, you're not likely to make significant profits while using them because these are hedging strategies and, as such, offer protection before profits. A reasonable covered option profit goal is 15–20 percent per year. That's consistent with a low-risk strategy, but that goal should be understood before wading into the fray. Besides, what's wrong with a 15–20 percent return per year without much risk?

Futures Contracts

The problem with futures contracts is that they seem to follow a pattern similar to this fictionalized one:

June 15:   An investor buys two Hawaii Macadamia Nut December futures contracts on advice of broker, who says Macadamias will be in short supply by October. Investor deposits $3,000 "good faith" margin per contract, or $6,000, less commissions. He now owns the right to have delivered to him 50,000 pounds of Hawaii Macadamia Nuts in December.

July 12: A severe frost apparently caused by increased sunspot activity sweeps the Hawaiian region where Macadamia nut flowers are in full blossom. December contract price drops 5 cents per pound. Broker requires another $4,000 good faith money to prevent liquidation of the irreparably damaged contract. Investor puts it up.

August 4: Contract price fluctuates in the range of ½ to 1 cent as the reports from the frost-stricken area wax eloquent with pessimistic verbiage about how much of the crop is destroyed and how the quota set by the World Macadamia Nut Cartel cannot be met, alternating with optimistic reports on how much the U.S. Department of Agriculture will subsidize the price.

August 5: A report from a New York-based advisory letter covering Macadamia Nuts assures investors that only 9 percent of the crop will be lost to the frost. Nothing is heard of the frost again. The contract price rises to within ¾ cent of the investor's purchase price. Investor is now out only $2,000.

December 10: Contract price sags to within 1½ cents of the low since June as news reports describe the contract's decline as "profit taking." Investor is now out $4,000 and sells to take tax loss before contract expires.

December 13: Lamumba Dobbs, scion of the family owning a worldwide chain of nut stores bearing his name, discovers an aphrodisiac in Macadamia nuts and places order for 1 million tons preceding a major publicity campaign. Contract prices double in hours.

December 17: December Macadamia Nut Contract expires.

Of course, the contracts don't all work out that way. The example does point up the timing and margin call dangers in futures, however, and those are the greatest risks.

Timing is critical. Not only might the expected event or set of conditions for which a contract was purchased not occur, but it can even happen as forecast *after* another event intervenes and causes a cash loss. The reason is that the small cash amount invested to own the contract creates big leverage. With only 5 to 15 percent of a contract's value invested, which is the typical margin amount, even normal trading ranges can create margin calls. A 10 percent price move against you isn't unusual in a few days time. If you aren't willing or able to put up the added cash, or if the contract expires just after you do so, the loss is realized.

The combination of low-margin and contract-trading rules also function to raise a related risk. You can be required to add more cash and not have the chance to close out the contract even if you wish to. Most futures contracts have daily limit moves. That is, they have specified amounts within which the contract can move on any trading day. When that limit up or down is reached, trading is halted until the next session. However, overnight the margin calls go out to those unfortunate enough to hold the opposite position to the price move and who have been forced below the minimum margin maintenance level by that move. This means more cash up with no chance to cash out. It doesn't take much imagination to see that a severe capital drain can occur if just a few days of limit moves go against your position.

Many other problems can develop on futures contract trading floors that bear little connection to correctly forecasting events and related price changes or to having the cash available to finance the effort. Use of inside information, taking care of personal orders ahead of customers, and manipulating prices are actions by floor traders that some futures traders say occur more often on the nation's 11 commodity exchanges than exchange officials admit.

Among the abuses cited in a 1984 article in *The Wall Street Journal* were the following:[3]

- The federal Commodity Futures Trading Commission (CFTC) alleges that, to create the impression of an active market in certificate of deposit contracts over a two-week period in 1982, as many as 63 floor traders on one exchange created illegal "wash sales"—self-canceling purchases and sales. Another exchange was being investigated for a similar deception in a stock index contract.
- In 1983 a floor trader on another exchange was reprimanded for describing his membership as "a license to steal."

---

[3]"Amateur Speculators Face Pros Holding All the Aces," *The Wall Street Journal*, February 16, 1984.

- One of the nation's principal institutional brokerage firms profited substantially in 1982 from taking positions in bond futures contracts less than two hours before the firm's widely known chief economist publicly issued a highly bullish report on interest rates.
- A study by a congressional committee covering a 16-month period in 1978–79 found that officers of meat and feed companies, trading in large numbers of contracts, took in profits averaging $2.5 million in livestock futures, and smaller investors collectively lost more than $155 million during the same period.
- A Treasury bill-contract trader on one major exchange was censured by the exchange and prohibited from handling customer orders for four years because of a 1980 incident in which customers paid $24,200 more for their contracts than the trader did.
- Late in 1983 the chief internal-policing officer at the same exchange quit after claiming that the exchange's members interfered with his staff's independence.
- In early 1984 the CFTC criticized one of the three largest futures' exchanges for "an almost complete lack of substantive disciplinary action" against members who had violated the exchange's rules.

Exchange officials deny that such practices are widespread. One exchange president flatly stated for the record, "[A]ny indication we're tolerating abuses is erroneous." Yet, problems continue to surface. In April 1984 a sudden late flurry of multimillion-dollar trades occurred in the stocks that make up one of the stock index futures contracts. The event prompted exchange and regulatory agency investigations of price manipulation.

Perhaps amateur futures speculators (85 to 90 percent of whom it is widely agreed lose money) should simply heed the adage "If you can't beat 'em, join 'em." The simplest way to do that, investing in a publicly offered commodity fund run by the biggest names in the business, hasn't, however, been a road to quick riches. In fact, considering the high front-end loads and performance of those funds, it's been a route to the poorhouse lately. According to trackers of these funds' performance, barely more than half these funds were profitable in 1982, and those that had profits averaged only a 3 percent gain in 1981 and in 1982, which were their recent high-water marks.

Of the 64 such funds whose results were reported for the 12 months ended June 30, 1983, the average fund lost 24.5 percent of capital. (The best had a 9.7 percent gain, the worst a 66.7 percent loss.) Possibly that was just a difficult period—despite the fact that it covered one of the best stock and bond market periods in recent years. In a later period, the 12 months ended January 31, 1984, some 52 of 58 funds whose results were reported in *Barron's* lost money for their investors. The average loss for the whole group was 19.1 percent. At least the loss had declined from the prior June year. One might speculate that this was only another difficult period and that the next year would be better, but I suspect there's a greater problem.

In that 1984 report, just less than half, 26 of the 58 funds, reported net profits *during their entire existence*. Some of them dated back to 1978–79. In other words, more than half of them lost money since inception.

It's quite safe to conclude that taking outright positions in futures contracts, no matter who does it for you, is not only speculation but wild speculation and that the odds for long-term success are stacked against you. That probability hasn't prevented futures trading from growing spectacularly. There has been a 162 percent increase in contracts traded in the five years through 1983, largely through the introduction of new contracts in stock index and interest rate futures. Still, the public only accounts for about 25 percent of futures-trading volume. That's quite the opposite of public involvement in another set of money-trading arenas that have grown dramatically despite similar odds, Atlantic City casinos.

The fact of the different levels of public participation in these parallel types of monetary speculation raises an operative question for the low-risk profit seeker: Why should such a high-risk game as futures contracts attract such supposedly conservative players as the professionals and institutions that make up the other 75 percent of the punters? Answer: Most of them aren't betting, they're hedging, and there's a world of difference. Aside from the floor traders and professional speculators, a rapidly growing volume of transactions in futures is arising from institutions that already hold portfolios that are interest rate or stock market sensitive. They're finding low-risk hedges against the vagaries of those markets in futures and options on futures.

Hedging in futures is nothing more than offsetting an existing position in a commodity or index, all or in part, with another contract positioned to capture the opposite market movement. If you owned a diversified portfolio of common stocks, you could sell an S&P Stock Index contract against the portfolio to hedge against a stock market drop. Technically, this differs from creating a spread between two different maturities of the same contract type (e.g., April and December maturities in pork bellies) or between two allegedly related contracts (such as

Treasury bonds and CDs) irrespective of the maturities. In the generic use of the word, both are hedges to some degree. A spread is simply a specialized form.

Among the institutions that are finding futures hedging a potentially profitable way of managing risk are those that traditionally hold sizable long-term bond portfolios, such as insurance companies, and those that make long-term loans in mortgages, such as savings and loans and banks. This trading has often required changes in state laws to allow it.

The technicalities of hedging are complex in most institutional cases and are beyond the scope of this book, but the concept is not. If an insurance company holds a $100 million portfolio of bonds that range in maturities from 1992 to 2002, it does so as part of its investment program for policy premiums and other earnings. Suppose the chief financial officer of the company expects a steady rise in interest rates over an extended period (thereby superseding short-term trading concerns). (S)he may choose to hold the existing bond positions for current income and offset the risk of declining bond prices that rising rates would bring by selling a number of Treasury bond futures contracts against that bond position. If the portfolio bonds happened to be all U.S. Treasuries with the same maturity as the bond contract, and therefore were priced identically to the contract, the financial officer could decide what fraction of the portfolio to hedge and sell contracts up to that amount. However, if corporate bonds are held or maturities differ from the contract, the officer must determine the portfolio risk exposure and a hedge ratio before determining the number of bond contracts to sell. One or more of three mathematical formulas will probably be used: matching maturities and duration, measuring regression of price against rate, or measuring direct variability.[4] In any case, the hedge can be calculated and entered into through bond or commodity brokers.

There are three key facts that anyone wishing to hedge a portfolio of financial instruments in the futures market must evaluate carefully:
1. The leverage risk on the futures contract itself doesn't change because it's hedged by a portfolio position.
2. Additional and potentially difficult decisions are likely to be necessary about the interaction of the existing position and the contract before the latter expires.

---

[4]Further details may be obtained on these calculations and futures hedging generally via mail courses offered by the Center for Futures Education, Inc., P.O. Box 489, Cedar Falls, Iowa, 50613.

3. Hedgers can become speculators quite easily, usually after a successful speculation.

   As to the first point, sizable financial institutions can readily finance
any margin calls arising from adverse contract price movements. It
doesn't matter a great deal that a two-point daily limit rise on a Treasury
bond contract that's been sold against a portfolio position will wipe out
80 percent of an institutional margin of $2,500 per contract (partly be-
cause there's been a gain in the bond's prices). But that doesn't mean the
manager likes it. After all, the loss has been taken and the portfolio has
an *unrealized* gain. This fact is almost certain to matter a great deal to the
smaller investor with less capital. In both cases, it prompts a new decision.
   On that point, consider both sides of the position. If the hedger has
taken a bond contract short position against a bond portfolio as above,
and interest rates do rise after the contract is sold, the hedge is working
nicely for the portfolio manager. Still, (s)he will have a decision to make
prior to expiration as to whether or not to buy back the contract at a profit and sell another to keep the hedge alive. The other side of the coin isn't
so pleasant. If rates begin to fall, contrary to expectations at the time of
the hedge contract sale, losses are being generated on the contract short
sale. On the surface, that doesn't seem bad because they're being offset
to the degree of the hedge by the long-bond portfolio. Recall, though, that
the course of interest rates is rarely steady in one direction, up or down.
Suppose the contract losses begin to generate margin calls, and suppose
at some point the manager decides to cut those losses and rebuy the contract. At that point rates reverse sharply to the manager's original forecast and rise. The whipsaw has happened. A new decision must be made
to sell another contract or wait out the move. The decision stream is in
action, and the brokers are getting the commissions.
   The lesson is that a contract hedge against an already held position is
not a worry-free, no-action hedge. It instead generates the necessity for
more decisions. In this sense it has the same disadvantage as that of
stock option writing discussed earlier: Not all decisions will be correct.
   Finally, when a hedger makes a few correct and profitable decisions
on contracts offsetting existing portfolio positions, thoughts quickly
evolve to increasing the size of the hedge. Where 100 contracts offset
half a portfolio, 200 will fully offset it next time; 250 the time after that
will leave a little extra profit for still another time, and so on. Without

much effort, the hedger has become a speculator with at least part of his/her position. Can disaster be far behind?

Withall, the smaller investor should remember these pitfalls in considering futures hedging—be it in stocks or bonds or gold. That investor might note that one way much of the sting has been taken out of the pure futures contract market is through combination of the two hedging instruments, options and futures.

Options on Futures

The latest wrinkle in the hedging game has developed in what appears to be an impossibly complex interaction of the technicalities of options, such as those on stocks, and futures contracts. As a result, the use of options on futures involves more math in calculating risk exposure and hedge ratios than that required for futures contracts alone. The effect of the pairing is to shift the operative considerations to options criteria from futures. The option becomes the action vehicle. For all intents and purposes, the discussion above on stock options applies here. The principal difference is that the underlying vehicles for these options are contracts instead of securities. In general, that difference increases potential price volatility when compared with options on stocks, but it changes little else.

An investor with a good-size stock, bond, or gold portfolio can hedge against a price decline in those three markets by selling (writing) an option at a specific strike price for the applicable futures contract. Using 1984 contracts as examples (excluding commissions), an investor could hedge approximately an $82,000 diversified stock portfolio by selling an S&P 500 futures Sept. 165 call option for $1,725 on the Friday shown in Table 13–1. (S)he could take similar action on a $60,000 bond portfolio via a Treasury bond futures September 60 call option sale for $2,109 per Table 13–2. With about $38,000 worth of gold, an investor could hedge that amount via a sale of a gold futures August 360 call option for $2,250, per Table 13–3. Similar hedges could be obtained in buying applicable put options.

In each case the criteria for future action are essentially the same as if the investor had sold a call option or bought a put option on a stock, with one significant difference: The option on futures is settled, if called, by delivery of the futures contract in all cases, whereas a stock option is set-

TABLE 13–1

CHICAGO MERCANTILE EXCHANGE
FUTURES AND OPTIONS WORLDWIDE

Options on S&P 500 Futures
Most Active Series
(Price = $500 times premium)
For the week ended May 25, 1984

Contract Month	Strike Price	Friday's Close	Change From Last Friday	Thursday's Open Interest	Weekly Volume*
CALLS					
Jun	155	0.70	−2.00	1,639	1,170
Jun	160	0.10	−0.65	4,731	3,602
Jun	165	0.05	−0.10	3,885	2,776
Jun	170	0.002	−0.048	1,187	20
Jun	175	0.002	....	385	....
Jun	180	0.002	....	182	3
Sep	155	3.85	−2.45	109	126
Sep	160	2.00	−1.90	2,753	3,257
Sep	165	1.00	−1.10	851	506
Sep	170	0.40	−0.70	106	47
PUTS					
Jun	145	0.20	+0.15	864	373
Jun	150	1.05	+0.70	2,085	1,601
Jun	155	3.85	+2.35	2,532	2,765
Jun	160	8.25	+3.70	3,205	2,042
Jun	165	13.20	+4.25	3,151	128
Jun	170	18.15	+4.30	5	10
Sep	150	2.40	+1.05	320	334
Sep	155	4.45	+1.70	767	442
Sep	160	7.50	+2.40	1,281	782
Sep	165	11.45	+3.05	81	8

Weekly Volume Calls* 11,572   Weekly Volume Puts* 8,543
*Includes Friday's estimated volume

tled by delivery of the underlying stock. Thus if the S&P 500 September 165 call option hedge is called away by the buyer, the hedger doesn't deliver a portfolio of stocks that comprises the S&P 500, but must buy a September S&P 500 futures contract for delivery. This necessitates another transaction, the market price of which can fluctuate at some variance with the option premium received on the original sale.

Needless to say, institutions and individual investors alike are treading lightly and rather slowly into this options on futures arena. Still, these vehicles have the same advantage that any option has over any futures contract: The amount of dollar risk to the buyer is limited to the amount paid for the option and limited for the seller to that amount involved with a subsequent decision. There are no margin calls directly associated with any options. That's at least one relief.

Traders Criteria

Most experienced professionals in the futures trading business believe certain criteria lead to success for both hedgers and speculators—

TABLE 13–2

⊚ Chicago Board of Trade

OPTIONS ON U.S. TREASURY BOND FUTURES
CHICAGO BOARD OF TRADE
($100,000; pts. and 64th of 100%)
For the week ended May 25, 1984

CALLS

Contract Month	Strike Price	Friday's Close	Change From Last Friday	Open Interest As of Thursday	Volume (5/18-24/84)
June84	62	....	....	....	3,819
June84	64	....	....	....	159
June84	66	....	....	....	125
June84	68	....	....	....	3
June84	72	....	....	....	3
Sept84	58	2.52	− 58	212	18
Sept84	60	1-44	− 40	5,400	2,726
Sept84	62	60	− 22	18,328	24,630
Sept84	64	28	− 15	20,796	22,734
Sept84	66	12	− 07	15,981	10,144
Sept84	68	04	− 04	13,988	4,589
Sept84	70	02	− 02	13,217	432
Sept84	72	01	....	11,356	182
Sept84	74	01	....	10,248	20
Sept84	76	01	....	4,840	0
Sept84	78	01	....	1,350	0
Sept84	80	01	....	1,874	0
Dec84	58	....	0	....	0
Dec84	60	2-05	− 38	188	176
Dec84	62	1-20	− 27	1,614	531
Dec84	64	52	− 18	1,712	1,398
Dec84	66	29	− 14	5,420	1,664
Dec84	68	.15	− 09	2,845	1,450
Dec84	70	08	− 05	3,708	297
Dec84	72	05	− 02	2,674	270
Dec84	74	03	− 01	2,649	268
Dec84	76	01	....	1,611	109
Dec84	78	01	....	102	2
Dec84	80	....	....	0	0
Mar84	60	2-30	....	0	0
Mar84	62	1-50	....	0	0
Mar84	64	1-10	....	0	0
....	....	....	Total:	140,121	75,757

PUTS

Contract Month	Strike Price	Friday's Close	Change From Last Friday	Open Interest As of Thursday	Volume (5/18-24/84)
June84	62	....	....	....	2,962
June84	64	....	....	....	523
June84	66	....	....	....	298
June84	70	....	....	....	10
Sept84	54	08	....	560	617
Sept84	58	52	+ 23	5,481	6,204
Sept84	60	1-36	+ 38	12,922	11,210
Sept84	62	2-49	+ 57	7,149	4,244
Sept84	64	4-17	+ 1-03	8,548	2,552
Sept84	66	5-62	+ 1-12	3,491	2,811
Sept84	68	7-62	+ 1-20	1,061	70
Sept84	70	9-62	+ 1-20	1	11
Sept84	72	11-62	+. 1-20	0	0
Sept84	74	13-62	+ 1-20	0	0
Sept84	76	....	....	0	0
Sept84	78	....	....	0	0
Sept84	80	....	....	0	0
Dec84	54	....	....	0	0
Dec84	58	1-36	+ 32	1,423	1,297
Dec84	60	2-31	+ 45	1,764	533
Dec84	62	3-42	+ 55	1,929	522
Dec84	64	5-01	+ 1-01	1,316	271
Dec84	66	6-43	+ 1-11	677	288
Dec84	68	8-29	+ 1-21	23	3
Dec84	70	....	....	0	0
Dec84	72	....	....	0	0
Dec84	74	14-27	+ 1-19	0	0
Dec84	76	....	....	0	0
Dec84	78	....	....	0	0
Dec84	80	....	....	0	0
Mar84	54	54	....	0	0
Mar84	58	....	....	0	0
....	....	....	Total:	46,345	35,426

Volume: 186,940; Open Interest as of 5/24; 326,587.
Price reported as a premium.

TABLE 13–3

COMEX Gold Futures Options

Four World Trade Center, New York, NY 10048
For more information call (212) 938-2993
100 troy oz: $ per troy oz

May 25, 1984

CALLS

MNTH/STRKE		VOL.#	OPEN INT.†	WEEK'S HIGH	WEEK'S LOW	CLOSE	NET CHANGE	FUTRS. CLOSE
Aug84	360	780	1414	34.00	26.80	38.00	+ 10.50	397.10
Aug84	380	4174	3213	20.00	9.00	20.00	+ 8.20	397.10
Aug	400	4614	6538	8.20	2.30	8.00	+ 4.20	397.10
Aug	420	2440	5839	3.30	.60	3.20	+ 2.10	397.10
Aug	440	392	2761	1.20	.30	1.10	+ .60	397.10
Oct84	360	40	40	....	....	44.50	+ 9.00	405.30
Oct	380	110	203	23.00	18.00	28.00	+ 7.50	405.30
Oct	400	1357	1020	15.00	7.50	14.40	+ 4.90	405.30
Oct	420	813	864	7.30	3.00	7.10	+ 2.50	405.30
Oct	440	173	155	3.40	1.50	3.20	+ 1.20	405.30
Dec84	380	118	175	32.50	25.00	35.00	+ 6.50	413.80
Dec	400	661	2161	19.70	13.50	22.30	+ 6.30	413.80
Dec	420	1907	1836	13.50	6.50	12.80	+ 4.20	413.80
Dec	440	1105	1571	8.00	3.10	7.80	+ 3.40	413.80
Dec	460	407	1382	4.00	1.60	3.80	+ 1.50	413.80

PUTS

MNTH/STRKE		VOL.#	OPEN INT.†	WEEK'S HIGH	WEEK'S LOW	CLOSE	NET CHANGE	FUTRS. CLOSE
Aug84	360	2984	5368	1.40	.70	.70	− .50	397.10
Aug84	380	4374	5100	6.60	3.00	3.10	− 1.90	397.10
Aug	400	676	1491	19.00	10.00	10.80	− 6.20	397.10
Aug	420	473	1554	34.60	31.50	25.00	− 8.50	397.10
Aug	440	0	11	....	....	44.00	− 9.00	397.10
Oct84	360	299	300	2.80	1.70	1.70	− .80	405.30
Oct	380	400	367	6.80	4.80	4.30	− 2.30	405.30
Oct	400	109	193	16.00	11.80	10.00	− 5.00	405.30
Oct	420	40	140	....	....	21.50	− 7.00	405.30
Oct	440	0	0	....	....	36.00	− 9.50	405.30
Dec84	380	934	1331	7.00	4.70	4.50	− 2.00	413.80
Dec	400	195	732	14.50	9.50	9.00	− 5.00	413.80
Dec	420	133	306	25.00	19.00	19.00	− 6.00	413.80
Dec	440	0	65	....	....	31.00	− 9.00	413.80
Dec	460	2	32	....	....	47.00	− 10.50	413.80

#Volume figures reflect Friday through Thursday trading.
†Open interest figures as of the close of business on Thursday.

COMEX. The World's Metals Market.

although importance of the qualifications varies for each. Successful futures traders usually are:[5]

1. Well capitalized with long-term reserves. Losses can be readily absorbed and are taken at moderate levels, and profits develop from a wide range of markets.
2. Able to trade in many markets at once, preferably 15–20, and have less than 20 percent of capital in any one market at a time.
3. Able to spend full time following market prices and trends as part of a long-term plan to reach predetermined goals.
4. Familiar with technical trading actions, such as price alerts, protective stops, and equity loss limits. Successful traders always cut losses

[5]These qualities include several noted by commodities trader Stanley Angrist in *Forbes*, July 1983.

and recognize wrong positions by not averaging down. They react automatically to preset buy and sell signals.

5. Familiar with "local conditions," for example, the times of day when few people are working the trading pits and the prices therefore become less competitive. They also recognize that in the usual choppy markets (such as those of late 1983 and early 1984), two out of three trades lose money.

6. Able to recognize that the mechanics of futures trading by the public tend to work against the individual investor's success.

If you can meet all those criteria, you might have a chance of success in futures trading.

Meanwhile, two reasons that the publicly offered commodity funds don't have better performance are that those run by the major brokerage firms make their money on commissions and fees and are therefore not as willing to let positions ride as traders do, which reduces chances for big gains. Also, the successful funds become very large very fast, which runs them into legal limits on position size. This leads to investing capital in less promising markets. Finally, commodities require longer-term trends of several months to develop significant profits. When markets aren't providing that ingredient, profit odds are against both the trader and the investor.

Convertible Securities

Convertible bonds and preferred stocks are in themselves potentially good vehicles for achieving low-risk profits. They are simply securities that can be exchanged for another security, usually the common stock of the issuing company. The right to convert usually lasts for the life of the convertible, although its terms may change over that time. Convertibles are issued in most instances because the issuing company wishes to add a kicker to the offering that will persuade investors to accept a lower interest or dividend return. When this kicker takes the form of a conversion right into the company's common stock, the investor is given hope the stock will increase in price, thereby making the convertible more valuable.

There are several criteria that are important in selecting a convertible bond or preferred for low-risk profits. Right off, the investor needs to know the *conversion value* and the *investment value* of the convertible. The conversion value of the convertible equals the number of common shares into which it can be converted multiplied by the market price per share. The investment value is the estimated price at which the convertible should sell if it had no conversion value. This value is figured by taking the quality rating of the convertible and its interest coupon/dividend and calculating the price at which it must sell to match the yield similar nonconvertibles.

From these two figures arise several evaluation criteria. For example, if the convertible currently sells at a price well above its conversion value, investors are paying a substantial premium for that conversion privilege, and the risk in the current convertible price is relatively high. If it is also selling well above its investment value as a nonconvertible, important risk is also present from this source. If the underlying common stock should become less attractive in the market for any reason, the current convertible price will not be supported by its value as a straight bond or preferred of similar quality.

Next comes the question of leverage. Most convertibles will move in one direction or the other more rapidly than will their underlying common stock. Thus they have leverage on the common. If a convertible is close to its investment value, it will move down more slowly than the common because it's approaching the point where it's trading as a pure bond/preferred, where the conversion right is available free.

On the other hand, there is the possibility that the convertible may be overlooked in the market as the prospects for the common improve while a significant yield differential in favor of the convertible exists. Where these conditions are present, the convertible should move almost as rapidly on the upside as the common, at least for a time. The convertible price at which these conditions are useful is calculated based on the relative market risks and conversion/investment values of each convertible.

Another calculable value of great importance to low-risk investors is the *relative volatility* of the convertible. As we know, volatility is the investment measure of risk. If you can determine how volatile a given convertible will be in relation to other investment vehicles, you'll be able to fit it nicely into your own level of acceptable risk. Relative volatility becomes the measure of safety of the convertible compared with both bonds and stocks.

A number of other factors must also be taken into account when evaluating convertibles. These include (1) size of the issue to determine liquidity, (2) call date and call terms, if any, (3) most obvious, the yields on both a current and to-maturity basis, and (4) the investment quality of the issue.

Fortunately for the average low-risk investor, the foregoing criteria are presented in publications of the convertible evaluation services, principal among which are *Value Line Options and Convertibles* and *RHM Convertible and Warrant Survey.* No serious investor in convertibles should be without the data they provide.

Selecting a Convertible

First and foremost low-risk investors should evaluate growth prospects for the underlying common stock (not necessarily high growth because that may equate with high risk). You'll also want relative value in the underlying stock, per the discussion in Chapter 11. Without growth prospects and value underneath the convertible, one might as well buy a straight bond or preferred.

Next should be found a relative volatility level compared with the average stock that fits with your investment criteria. If you wish to take less risk than that of the average stock (as shown by a stock beta of 1.0), the relative volatility of the convertible should be below 100 percent of the average stock.

From this point on, seek the best combination of the following criteria on a *relative basis* among the convertibles being considered: (1) lower premium over conversion and investment values, (2) better upside movement potential and lower downside risk for a given price change in the common than that of comparable convertibles, and (3) the best relative current yield compared with both the underlying common and other convertibles.

Here's an example of a brief convertible bond analysis, based on the low-risk criteria above, as of early May 1984.

> Eastern Gas & Fuel Associates
> 9.75% Cv. Bond due 2008 (Traded OTC)
>
> Price: 92, Current yield 10.6%
> Convertible into 33.003 shares common.
>
> Common price: 24.25, yield 5.4% (Traded NYSE)

Evaluation:

1. This common stock is expected to show a 28 percent gain in per-share earnings this year and a tentative 40 percent gain above that in 1985, according to *Daily Graphs* estimates. The chart pattern is favorable, having recently moved above its 200 day MA, but a *negative triple top* has formed in the 26 area—an important caution.

2. The conversion value is 80; the convertible thus sells at a moderate 15 percent above conversion. The investment value is 72, a relatively high 22 percent below the current bond price.
3. The relative volatility is 75 percent according to *Value Line*, certainly a modest risk compared with the common, which is rated at 105 percent of the average common stock.
4. The leverage is very favorable: the convertible bond should move about 60 percent as fast as the common on the upside but only about 33 percent as fast on the downside, according to *Value Line*.
5. The convertible offers nearly double the yield of the common.
6. The convertible is not callable until August 1986 and was issued in moderate size of $50 million. The OTC trading of the bond is a distinct disadvantage for purchases in size.

An investor favorably disposed to the overall stock market climate and the common stock of Eastern Gas & Fuel under these circumstances would find the convertible bond an attractive, low-risk alternative to Eastern common stock. Suppose circumstances didn't develop so well in the months following purchase. Suppose the overall stock market took a turn for the worse in the face of rising interest rates. What could be done then? Riding through with the convertible and better than a 10 percent yield isn't a bad idea, but perhaps that could be improved. Convertibles can be hedged.

Hedging Convertibles

There are two direct methods for hedging existing convertible securities positions. One is via a short sale of the common stock; the other is by sale of call options against the convertible. To fully hedge via the short sale of common shares, the nearest round number of shares into which the convertible could be converted would be shorted. (Any fraction thereof could also be used.) This hedge is particularly useful when the downside leverage of the common is notably greater than the convertible, as in the Eastern Gas & Fuel example above. A downward move in the common will generate greater profits on the short sale than the loss on the convertible. One might even reduce the number of shares shorted to allow for this and thus reduce the exposure if the stock moves up.

The stock-shorting hedge has one distinct disadvantage compared with the option hedge. Proceeds of a short sale are not available to the seller, but proceeds of option sales are. This means that a hedge of the same number of call options as common shares that would be shorted will generate income to the seller for a notable improvement in return potential. In fact, the most operative criteria for deciding between a common short hedge and a call option hedge will be the relative valuations of the convertible itself and the option premiums. If the convertible is undervalued and the option premium is relatively high, the option hedge will work most effectively.

Note that the convertible and option services carry evaluations of the relative values of each hedge plus the number of shares to be shorted/call options to be sold in hedging. They also rank the relative attractiveness of the convertible for hedging. In the case of Eastern Gas & Fuel, Value Line gave it a C ranking, compared with the A the service considers minimal for a good hedge.

As a final caveat to all hedging, Value Line's comment on convertible hedges could well apply: "Caution. Hedging is exceedingly complex and should only be attempted by very experienced investors."

Summary

Investors should realize that, while hedging investment positions can now readily create low risk conditions, understanding the nature of the vehicles to be used and the tax treatment of the transactions is a relatively complicated task. Nevertheless, creation of new hedging vehicles is on the front burner for the securities industry, whether the average investor likes them or not.

Among the hedging vehicles, the use of covered stock options is still the most practical in that the hedge involved is a straightforward one and they are widely available and actively traded. The 1984 Tax Reform Act significantly altered the tax advantages in them, however.

Futures contracts continue to be the fastest way to make or lose money this side of Atlantic City games, and where stock index futures are concerned, their *raison d'etre* appears the same. Options on these and other financial futures do offer a way to specify the amount of money to be risked, but also provide good reward opportunities for the successful speculator/hedger, if the number of consecutive decisions necessary to succeed doesn't exceed the ability to make them.

Foreign Trades

14

*Do not do unto others as you would
they should do unto you. Their
tastes may not be the same.*

George Bernard Shaw

For the majority of American investors, the idea of buying securities in foreign countries is akin to trading fur skins with the Russians. They see it as remote, unfamiliar, and vaguely unpatriotic. They have a point, but not a realistic one.

Certainly there can be some bother when dealing over multithousand-mile distances in buying stock or notes, but that ceased to be a significant deterrent with the advent of satellite communications. The London gold fixings are still the world's benchmark until trading ceases around 11:30 A.M., New York time. A phone call from San Francisco to London now costs about the same as one to San Diego. What's more, any product unfamiliarity problems can be overcome with a little study, and patriotism is hardly a factor when U.S. banks have fallen over each other rushing to make foreign loans.

However, this latter fact raises the matter of fear that somehow a foreign market is "too foreign" and might disappear overnight. (The bank-

247

ers must wonder about that.) There is fear that something mysterious will happen to one's money in a distant land. But this would hardly happen in London, Toronto, or Tokyo if one dealt with a known and reputable firm, and such firms are easy to find.

The greatest problems we face when dealing abroad include none of the above. Instead, they are lack of unique investment products and, to some degree, the lack of *daily* information about those that are of interest. The latter problem is more a function of habit than true difficulty. A broker or dealer who can buy the security abroad can also provide information as frequently as you'll need it. However, such information doesn't just pop out of *The Wall Street Journal* every morning as does General Motors close.

The lack of unique investment products is probably the individual investor's main drawback to investing abroad. This arises because of the size and competitiveness of U.S. markets and U.S. securities firms. Wall Street can invent great numbers of new investment vehicles because the market is so large that it can absorb the best the Street's brains have to offer, and cerebral competition keeps the ideas flowing. The concept of options, for instance, dates back to 16th-century Dutch tulip traders who used options as hedges on their shipments. However, it was the U.S. markets in the early 1970s that developed them into instantly tradable vehicles for the public. Forward contracts on gold and silver and currencies have existed for decades around the world (principally in Europe), but it took New York's COMEX and Chicago's IMM to bring them into popularity. They are now called futures contracts in the United States.

Occasionally the U.S. markets leave ideas alone or don't develop them to the same degree as foreign experts, usually for good reasons. However, two of these foreign ideas are particularly worth considering because they've grown up in London—a market that closely resembles and is easily accessible to the United States. The two vehicles, which can also meet specific investor objectives that are important these days, are Eurodollar floating-rate notes (FRNs) and currency funds.

Eurodollar Floating-Rate Notes (FRNs)

FRNs and currency funds aren't foreign stepchildren that Wall Street has ignored. FRNs are available in the United States, but they developed in Europe faster than in the United States because of the wide financial product needs of many international borrowers. As the market grew it was dominated by institutions for two reasons: In Europe the general public is not a major force in the securities markets, and in the United States the prime advantage of FRNs to individual investors, their inflation immunization, became less valuable as inflation rates fell soon after the FRN market got rolling. Institutions have noninflation reasons for buying FRN's, and thus forged the market and have largely had it to themselves. However, since major U.S. brokerage firms have the capability to trade in the London FRN market with smaller American investors, this need not remain the case if inflation rates rise dramatically again.

The Eurodollar floating-rate note is a relatively unfamiliar beast to most American investors. The market for them is large and diverse, totaling $billions. (The Kingdom of Sweden floated a single $1 billion issue in late 1983, the largest on record.) The market involves issuers from banks and sovereign states to a range of corporations. The U.S. dollar is the currency denomination, and the notes are usually issued in bearer form.

FRNs differ from one another in four important ways:

Maturity.   They range up to 15 years, but most are issued with 7- to 10-year maturities.

Current Interest Rate/Term.   Interest rates change at either three-month or six-month intervals and are based on a specified market reference rate.

Reference Rate.   The most common base is London interbank offered rate (LIBOR), which is the Eurodollar rate quoted constantly for borrowings between banks. It's similar to the federal funds rate in the United States. The coupons are set a fraction above the reference rate according to terms specified at time of issue. In addition, most FRNs have a minimum coupon rate below which the rate may not be fixed.

Prices.   Prices change within relatively narrow ranges for similar quality issues and are market determined. A study of 37 FRN issues showed that the average difference between high and low prices during a period of sharply fluctuating interest rates (1979–81) was only 3.7

points.[1] Compare this with 15-point average fluctuations on domestic U.S. "floaters" during the same period.

Table 14–1 shows a daily quote for FRNs in 1983. The arrow points to the listing for the National Westminster Bank 10½ percent note due June 1990. Reading that line from left to right, this note's minimum coupon is shown to be 5½ percent (the lowest rate to which the interest coupon can fall). Next given are the maturity year, '90, and the current coupon, 10½ percent. The next coupon change date is June 25, 1984. The quoted price is 100.93 bid, 101.13 offered, including commissions.

Data provided by a broker would show that this note's coupon changes every six months and is set ¼ percent over LIBOR when changed. It was issued in an amount of $150 million ($50 million being a substantial institutional size) and has been callable since June 1982 at par (100). It also has been putable at 100 since 6/82, which means that the buyer can sell it back to the issuer at 100. Finally, its minimum coupon rate is 5½ percent.

The greatest value of any FRN is its use as a hedge against rising interest rates. Whereas a fixed-rate issue of the same maturity would be forced down in price as rates rose, an FRN will remain relatively constant in price, but its coupon will rise. Obviously, the reverse is true in falling-rate periods. If one expected rising rates, a choice of the notes with three-month coupon changes would be best, since the coupon would reflect the rise more quickly than with six-month changes. However, during declining rates one could switch to the six-month-change notes to cushion the falling-rate impact and ultimately would be protected by the minimum coupon found on some FRNs.[2]

Of course, if a falling-rate environment were expected, *fixed-rate* notes would be more advantageous in maintaining a high yield and offering price appreciation. As noted earlier, forecasting short-term interest rate movements is a highly conjectural occupation. FRNs thus offer at least a viable means for protecting capital in all rate environments.

Timing

Two facts are worth noting about timing FRN purchases. The first is the price stability around coupon-fix dates. Figure 14–1 shows a typical

---

[1]"Eurodollar Floating-Rate Notes: Determinants of Price Behavior," (New York: Salomon Bros., Henna and Niculescu, 1981).

[2]Sophisticated investors use a variety of techniques to establish points at which swaps into other issues should be made, depending on market forecasts, but these are beyond the scope of this book. Interested investors should review the four-part Salomon Bros. study, one part of which is identified in the previous footnote.

TABLE 14–1

Floating Rate Notes — Dec. 30

Banks

Issuer/Min cpn/Mat.	Coupon	Next	Bid	Askd
Allied Irish 5¼-95	10 1/16	6-8	98.10	98¼
Allied Irish 6¾-84	10	3-30	99.95	100.15
Allied Irish 5¼-87	10 3/16	1-6	99.95	100.15
Allied Irish 5¼-92	10 1/16	4-17	99.16	99.36
Andelsbanken 7-84	10 1/16	6-6	99.90	100.15
Banco Serfin 7¼-86	10	4-5	84	89
Bco de la Nacion 6-86	10 5/16	3-26	94	98
Bco de la Nacion 6-87	10	4-23	93½	95½
Bco Exterior 1996	10 7/16	6-21	98.03	98.23
Buenos Aires 7¾-86	10½	6-7	94	98
Bco di Roma 6-87/91	10 1/16	4-30	99.85	100.05
Bco Hisp Amer 1995	10	4-20	97.96	98.16
Bco Desarollo 9½-87	10¾	6-13	91½	96½
Bco Nl Mexico 6¼-87	10¼	5-17	85	90
Bcp Nl Mexico 5¾-92	11⅛	2-8	78	83
Bco Pinto 6¾-85	10 5/16	5-18	97	—
Bangkok Bk 6½-84	10⅜	12-29	99¾	100
BFG Fin 5½-89/94	10 9/16	1-13	99⅝	100
Bkers Trust 5¼-94	10 11/16	3-22	100.55	100¾
BK Ireland 5⅛-89	10¼	2-29	99¾	99.95
BK Ireland 5¼-92	10⅝	1-25	98⅞	—
BK Montreal 5¼-90	10⅞	6-20	100.90	101.10
BK Montreal 5¼-91	9 15/16	4-30	99.95	100.15
BK New York 5¼-96	—	1-10	99¼	99.45
BK N. Scotia 5¼-88/93	9 15/16	4-30	99.97	100.17
BK Nova Scotia 5¼-94	10 7/16	1-11	100.26	100.46
BOT (Sterling) 5¼-90	9½	11-21	98.80	100
BOT Hdg 1987	10 11/16	1-26	100.40	100.60
BOT Hdg Feb 5¼-88/91	11¼	2-6	100.63	100.83
BOT Hdg Dec 5¼-88/91	10½	6-12	100.18	100.38
BOT Hdg 5½-93	9 15/16	4-24	100.55	100¾
BOT Hdg 5¼-89	9⅞	1-27	100.10	100.30
BBL Intl 5-86	10⅜	5-23	100.20	100.40
BBL Intl 3-95	10¾	6-15	100.35	100.55
Bq Indosuez 5½-85	11	1-27	—	—
Bq Indosuez 5¼-89	10 9/16	1-13	99.80	100
BQ Ext Algerie 8⅜-84	11 9/16	2-9	100	100½
BUE 5¼-89	10⅜	3-20	99.46	99.66
Bk Arab Int'l Inv	10	3-30	97⅞	98⅜
BK Worms 5¾-85	11	6-19	100.35	100.55
BK Worms 5¼-94	11¼	2-6	99.27	99.47
BFCE 6⅜-84	10 9/16	2-29	99.95	—
BFCE 5¼-87	10⅞	1-27	99.90	100.10
BFCE 5¼-88	10	4-30	99.54	99.74
BFCE 5¼-Jan.88	10 9/16	1-20	99.76	99.96
BNP 1982/84	10 11/16	2-22	99.85	—
BNP 5¼-85/88	9 15/16	1-31	99.95	100.10
BNP 5¼-89	10 3/16	5-9	99.17	99.37
BNP 5¼-87	10 1/16	3-22	99.85	100.05
BNP 5¼	10 9/16	3-1	99.97	100.12
BNP 5½-91	10 11/16	2-22	99½	99.65
BNP 7½-96	10½	6-13	99.73	99.93
Barclays O'seas 5-90	10¾	6-15	100.98	101.18
Barclays O'seas 5-95	10 9/16	1-31	100.93	101.13
Bergen Bank 6-89	10 3/16	2-29	100¼	100.45
Bergen Bank 5½-88/91	10	1-18	99.95	100.15
Chemical 5¼-94	10 5/16	3-23	100.57	100.77
Citicorp 1984-RRN	10⅛	1-30	100	100½
Citicorp 3-94	10⅝	3-12	101.10	101.30
Citicorp undtd	9 7/16	1-13	100.40	—
Citicorp 5¼-84 ex w	9¾	3-2	99.98	100.13
Contil 5¼-94	10	12-28	99.67	99.87
Chase 5¼-93	10 9/16	1-31	100.17	100.37
CIBC 5¼-94	10 9/16	1-18	99.95	100.20
Christiana Bk 5¼-91	10 3/16	2-9	100.05	100¼
CCCE 5¼-98	11 5/16	2-9	99½	99.70
CCCE 5¼-02	10 5/16	3-14	99.27	99.47
CNCA 5¼-95	10½	6-7	99.80	99.95
CNCA 5¼-97	10 5/16	3-26	99.70	99.90
CCF 5¾-85	10 5/16	5-9	100	100.20
CCF 5¼-90/95	9 15/16	4-9	99½	99.70
CCF 1989/96	10⅜	5-31	99.78	99.98
CCF 5¼-86/98	10 9/16	3-26	99.94	100.14
Creditanst 5¾-84	10¼	5-25	100	100.20
Creditanst 5½-91/97	10 11/16	3-16	100½	100.70
Creditanst 1994	—	1-11	99.73	99.93
Credit Lyon 1994	—	1-18	98.73	98.93
Credit Lyon 5¼-87	10⅜	3-21	99.85	100.10
Credit Lyon 5¼-89/94	10 3/16	1-5	99.80	100
Credit Lyon 5¼-97	10	4-5	99.53	99.73
Credit Lyon 5¼-91/95	10¼	5-29	99.65	99.80
Credit Nat'l(ster.)95	9 13/16	3-15	98.55	98.80
Credit Nat'l 5¼-88	10⅞	1-18	99.80	100
Credit Nat'l 5¼-94	10¾	3-9	99.65	99.85
Credit Nord 5¼-89/92	10 11/16	6-23	99.44	99.64
Den Norsk 6-Nov90	10 5/16	2-9	99.90	—
Den Norsk 6-Dec90	10 9/16	6-19	100	100.20
Dresdner Fin 1993	9 15/16	4-19	100	100.10
EAB 5¼-90	10 3/16	3-26	100.22	100.42
EAB 5-93	10 9/16	6-15	100.05	100¼
Eula 8-89	10⅝	6-25	75	80
First Interstate 1995	9 15/16	3-6	99.35	99½
First Chicago 5¼-94	10⅛	2-21	100.40	100.60
Fuji 1996	—	1-12	98.67	99.77
Genfinance 1992/94	—	1-19	99.62	99.78
Genfinance 5¼-87	10 1/16	4-30	100.08	100.28
Genfinance 5¼-89/92	10⅜	6-30	100.30	100½
Girozentrale 5¼-91	10⅝	3-23	100½	100.70
Gotabanken 6-88	10 3/16	5-18	99.92	100.12
Grindlays 5¼-92	10 1/16	3-29	100.15	100.35
GZB 5¼-96	10 3/16	5-29	99.55	99.70
GZB 5½-89	10⅛	2-9	100	100.20
GZB 5¼-92	10 3/16	3-8	100	100.20
IBJ 5½-85	10 3/16	6-5	100.23	100.43
IBJ 5¼-87	10⅛	4-17	100.45	100.65
IBJ 5¼-Oct 88	10 1/16	4-13	100.58	100.78
IBJ 5¼-Nov 88	9 3/16	5-18	100	100.20
KOP 5½-92	10 3/16	5-9	100¼	100.45
Kleinwort Ben 5¾-91	10⅛	2-17	100.05	100.30
Korea Ex Bk 7½-85/88	10 1/16	4-5	98¼	—
Korea D.Bk 7½-86/89	10 3/16	6-5	98	—
LTCB 5¼-85	10 3/16	5-14	100.18	100.38
LTCB 5¼-86	10¼	6-15	100.62	100.82
LTCB 5½-89	10½	6-11	100.78	100.98
LTCB 5½-Jly 89	10⅜	1-19	100¼	100.45
LTCB 5¼-92	10 1/16	5-31	100.09	100.27
Lloyds Eurofin 5¼-92	10	6-6	100.42	100.62
Lloyds Eurofin 5¼-93	10	4-30	100.42	100.62
ManHan O'seas 5¼-94	10⅛	2-29	100.08	100.28
Marine Midland 5¼-94	9 15/16	1-6	100.04	100.24
Midland Intl 6-87	10 1/16	5-25	100.62	100.82
Midland Intl 5-89	10 9/16	6-22	100.93	101.13
Midland Intl 9-91	10	4-30	100.81	101.01
Midland Intl 5¼-92	10½	6-7	100.80	101
Midland Intl 5½-93	10¾	1-26	100.80	101
Morgan Grenfell	—	1-11	99.64	99.78
Mort Denmark 5¼-92	11	6-19	99⅝	99¾
Mort Denmark	10 9/16	3-8	99.68	99.88
Morgan 5¼-97	10 1/16	2-16	100.54	100.74
Natl Westmin 5½-90	10¾	6-25	100.93	101.13
Natl Westmin 5¼-91	10 9/16	1-18	100.67	100.87
Natl Westmin 5¼-92	9 15/16	4-25	100.70	100.95
Natl Westmin 5¼-94	10⅛	4-16	100.38	100.58
Nippon Credit 5½-85	10 7/16	12-28	100	—
Nippon Credit 6½-86	10 11/16	1-16	100.05	100¼
Nippon Credit 5¼-90	11¼	2-10	100.24	100.44
Nedfibra Fin 5½-88	10¼	7-3	93	98
Nacional Fin 5½-86	10⅜	12-28	83	88
Nacional Fin 5¼-88/91	9 15/16	3-28	82	87
Nacional Fin 1985/93	11⅜	1-9	89	94
Nordic Intl 5½-91	10¼	5-9	99.80	100
O.L.B. 5¼-94	10 1/16	5-25	100	100.20
Oesterreisch Bk 5¼-86	10 5/16	5-18	100	100.20
Pk Banken 5-88/91	10 9/16	6-19	100.28	100.48
Bk Scotland 5¼-86/94	10	1-16	100.18	100.38
Sanwa Intl Fin 5¼-88	10 3/16	3-26	100.12	100.32
Saitama 5¼ 1993	10 5/16	6-5	99.92	100.12
Scand. Fin. 5¼-93	10 1/16	4-13	98⅞	—
Scand. Fin. 1993	10 9/16	6-21	98.80	99
Scotld Intl 5¼-92	10⅛	3-23	99.93	100.10
Ste Generale 5¼-90/95	10 9/16	3-1	99.86	100.06
Ste Generale 5¼-90	10 1/16	5-9	99.70	99.90
S.G. Alsac 5¾-89/91	10 9/16	1-18	99.30	99½
Stand & Chart 1994 5¼	—	1-5	99.95	100.15
Stand & Chart 6¼-84	10 7/16	5-31	99.95	—
Stand & Chart 5½-90	11 1/16	2-16	100¾	100.95
Stand & Chart 5¼-90	10 9/16	3-9	100.73	100.93
Stand & Chart 5¼-91	10 3/16	5-18	99.97	100.17
State Bk India 6¾-87	10 7/16	5-31	98½	—
Sumitomo Fin 5½-88	11 3/16	2-9	100.12	100.32
Svenska Handels 5-87	10⅞	1-18	100¼	100.45
Sparebanken 6-87	10 9/16	6-21	99	99½
Ste Fin Europ 5½-88	10⅜	5-21	98⅝	99
Ste Fin Europ 5¼-89	10⅜	6-1	98½	99
Ste Cent Bque 6½-87	10	4-5	99	99¼
Sundsvallsbken 6-85	9⅞	4-11	99.76	99.96
Toronto Dom 5¼-92	11 1/16	2-14	100.12	100.32
Thai Farmers 7¼-84	10¾	6-25	99⅝	100
Union Norway 6-89	10½	1-11	99⅝	100
United O'seas 6-89	9 15/16	12-30	99.90	100¼
Urquijo Intl 6-86	10¼	3-23	99	99¾
Wil. Glyn's Bk 5¼-91	10½	3-16	100.62	100.82
Zentralspark. 5¼-91	10¾	1-12	100¼	100.45

Non Banks

Issuer/Min cpn/Mat.	Coupon	Next	Bid	Askd
Azienda 5¼-90	11⅛	2-17	99¾	100¾
Alfa 10-88	11¼	3-21	50	60
Kindom Belgium 5-2004	—	1-9	99	99.20
CEPME 5½-88	10⅛	3-6	99.82	100.02
CEPME 5¼-89/92	10⅝	6-12	100	100.20
CNT 5¼-91	10 3/16	5-8	99.60	99.80
CNT 5¼-90	10	4-24	99.58	99.78
C.F. De Electr.5¾-88	10 7/16	5-10	83	88
Credit Foncier 5¼-93	10	4-6	99.78	99.85
Denmark(ster.) 98-5¼	9 3/16	2-22	98.35	98.60
Denmark 5¼-88/90	10⅝	1-9	99.87	100.07
Denmark 5¼ Oct.88/90	10	4-13	99.45	99.57
EEC 1988/90	10 3/16	1-5	99.96	100
Enpetrol 7-86	10½	12-23	99¾	100¾
EDF 5¼-90/92/95	11⅜	2-10	99.90	100.05
Hydro Quebec 1994	—	1-19	99.56	99.66
Ind. Penoles 10-86/89	10⅜	1-19	80	85
Eurofima 5¼-89	10 1/16	3-27	99.88	100.08
Ireland, Rep. of	—	1-11	97.95	98.10
IC Industries 1991	11⅛	1-15	98.85	—
ICO 5½-89/92	10½	1-11	99	99½
IHI 5¾-85	10⅛	4-27	100.18	100.38
C.Itoh 5¼-87	10 7/16	3-21	100.38	100.58
InvCp India 6½-91	10 9/16	6-18	97	98
Indonesia 1993	10	4-6	97	97½
Malaysia 1988/93	10 9/16	2-27	98.57	98.77
Malaysia 5¼-89/92 Dec	10 1/16	6-5	98¼	98.45
Malaysia 5¼-89/92 Apr	10	4-6	98¼	98.45
New Zealand 5¼-87	9⅞	4-9	99.95	100.10
New Zealand 5¼-92	10¾	6-22	100¼	100.45
RENFE 88/90/93	10¼	3-27	98.55	98¾
Rep Philippines 6½-86	10	4-24	91	93
SEAT	10¾	6-22	98.05	98¼
SNCF 5¼-88	9 13/16	1-30	98.92	99.12
SNCF Sterling 90/93	9⅝	1-20	99.45	99.65
Spain 88/90/93	10⅞	2-29	99.55	99¾
Sumi Heavy 5½-84	10½	3-13	100	—
Sweden 93/98/03	10 5/16	5-17	99.60	99.65
Sweden 5¼-87/89	10 11/16	2-29	100.10	100.30
Sweden 9lock-90/91	9 15/16	1-23	99.72	99.92
Sweden 5¼-88/90/93	11 3/16	2-3	100¼	100.30
TVO lock-1991	10 1/16	5-31	92	94
Offshore Min. 1986	10⅞	1-23	100¼	100.45
Offshore Min. 5¼-91	10¼	6-4	100.20	100.40
Private I.C. Asia 7-86	11⅝	2-10	99⅜	99⅞
Pemex 7-84	11	1-27	93	98
Pemex 6-88/91	9⅞	4-11	83	88
Vitro 1988/91	11 1/16	1-23	77	82
Kingdom of Thai 7-84	10 5/16	3-15	99⅞	100¼

Prices supplied by Credit Suisse-First Boston Ltd., London

Source: *The International Herald Tribune,* December 30, 1983.

FIGURE 14–1
DEVIATIONS OF SEMIANNUAL FRN PRICES OVER THE COUPON CYCLE (based on average price movement of five selected issues)

At fix date, coupons are reset to market levels, and fix date prices of individual FRNs will tend to the "normal" (average) price for each issue. After one to two months, coupons may no longer be in line with market rates. Hence, FRN prices will begin to move away from rollover-date levels. Then as the next fix date approaches, the market will begin to focus on the next coupon, and prices will again move back toward "normal" levels.

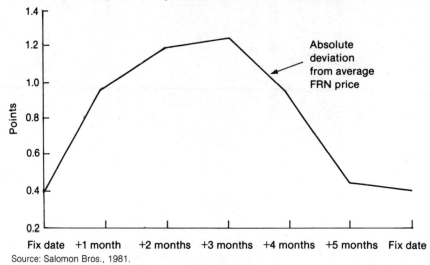

Source: Salomon Bros., 1981.

price pattern for six-month coupon-change FRNs between coupon-fix dates. Naturally, market conditions may alter this pattern somewhat. The key point is that as the note approaches its coupon-fix date, it will return to a "normal" price for that issue (which can be determined from its price history), and in the two- to three-month period following the fix date, it will be at a maximum deviation from that normal price. This implies that under usual conditions the best time to purchase an FRN will be just prior to its coupon-fix date, and the best selling time (if one wishes to swap) in a flat- or falling-rate market, will be two to three months after a fix date. In a rising-rate period, a swap sale will maximize price around the fix date. It also should be noted that three-month change notes have a similar, but smaller magnitude, price pattern.

Buying Criteria

A second point to consider is how to determine which note to buy on any given day. To do this, one must first narrow the range of FRNs to consider on the basis of (1) credit quality, (2) coupon term versus interest rate forecast, (3) size of issue, (4) callability and putability, and (5) final maturity, plus any other criteria the buyer deems important for purchase. Once this is done, you'll have a list of several FRNs that meet your general objectives and that you can check for price.

Having done the above culling, calculate the *simple spread*, or common denominator for each note on that list. The spreads will reveal which note is priced best. Suppose an FRN had these characteristics as of December 31, 1983: Current coupon—11 3/16 percent; fixed 1/4 percent over LIBOR; next coupon change date 2/3/84; callable at 100 on 2/3/88; current offered price 100 1/4. You can proceed as follows:

1. Change the fixed coupon reference rate (¼ percent) to basis points (100 per one percentage point) = 25.
2. Take the current price above or below the call price and amortize it per year to call date in basis points. In this case, ¼ percent over a call price of 100 will be amortized over 4 years and 34 days, giving 4.093 years to divide by 25 = 6.11 basis points (b.p.).
3. Since this amount will be lost per year until the call date, *subtract* it from the 25 basis points in the coupon reference rate difference, leaving 18.89 basis points. (The amount of change to call date would be *added* to the amortization if the price were *below* 100.)
4. Now take the difference between the current coupon (11 3/16 percent) and the current *LIBOR* (10 3/8 percent on the date), which is 13/16 percent. This will be earned above current LIBOR until the next coupon-fix date of February 3, which is 34 days days away. Converting to basis points, 13/16 = 81.25 per year, to be earned in 34 days (.093 of a year) = 7.55 basis points. Divide this by the number of years to call (4.093 in this example) = 1.845 b.p.
5. That figure is then combined with the result in step 3 to become 20.935 basis points. This is the "simple spread" for the note, and it can now be compared with the simple spreads for each of the notes under consideration. The *largest* spread is the more favorable one, and it should be the note bought after prior culling.[3]

These same general characteristics apply to U.S. domestic floaters, although individual issue and market characteristics should be studied before purchase.

---

[3]A more sophisticated spread analysis would take into account the cost of financing this purchase over the period until coupon change.

Investors interested in the Eurodollar FRN market should look to any of the major U.S. national brokerage firms for current data. Nearly all have London offices with adequate expertise, if your local representative doesn't. At least two investment firms, Merrill Lynch and Bache, have said they will do 10-note ($10,000 face amount) minimum FRN transactions. For institutional expertise, Salomon Bros., Goldman Sachs, and Shearson Lehman Kuhn Loeb are active in the FRN market in London.

Currency Funds

As for currency funds, they have been a United Kingdom speciality for a very short time; meaningful growth dates only from 1982. They grew up because European investors are far more foreign currency-conscious than are Americans. Since these funds permit an investor of modest means to invest either singly or in a basket of foreign currencies or (for more money) to have capital managed among the currencies, they've become a popular way to diversify assets. During the 1982–84 heyday of the dollar, currency funds provided an easy means for foreigners to invest in U.S. currency. Because Americans don't need to go offshore to invest in dollars, they've largely ignored these funds. In days of a weaker dollar, the reverse will probably be true, although some American mutual fund groups will likely start their own currency funds if they see a sufficiently large market. Additionally, there's a tax peculiarity to the funds that's somewhat murky at the moment, although it should be clarified soon.

The most often asked question I get when discussing foreign currencies versus the U.S. dollar is: What's the best way to invest in foreign money? It may not be topic A on everyone's lips, especially with a strong dollar, but there is enough interest to warrant a good "think." The problem has been the lack of a really good answer.

An investor can always buy travelers checks in any foreign currency denomination, but they earn no interest and usually have either a purchase fee or redemption charge. Some organizations in the United States have offered CDs that are denominated in foreign currencies; the major foreign exchange firm of Deak-Perera, through its Deak National Bank arm in New York, is the most notable. Theirs has been a satisfactory method, since the deposits are insured by the FDIC as to capital integrity at the bank (though not against market fluctuations). However, there is a 2 to 3 percent spread between the bid and the offered side of the currency quotation to offset during the holding time.

The fact is, in the United States you just can't go to a local bank and arrange for a time deposit in the foreign currency of your choice, although there are some indications that this may be changing at the major international banks. This was also true in the United Kingdom until several of the major London merchant banks began offering foreign currency funds in the early 1980s. The funds have been successful, although they are commonly administered in the Channel Islands, not in London for tax reasons. For investors with a true international bent, they represent a sensible way to play the foreign currency market.

The investor is offered a single fund and allowed to choose one of a variety of currencies or has available a different fund for each currency. N. M. Rothschild & Sons purveys 11 different currencies within one fund, and you select one or more of them. Guiness Mahon has 5. In addition, most merchant banks have a fully *managed fund* in which they select what they believe to be the best total return currencies. The investor in such a fund buys the banks' selection and expertise. (Rothschild's only undertakes individual direct-advisory relationships with clients who wish to invest a substantial amount and does not operate a "managed fund.")

The individual currency funds are not registered with the SEC in the United States, although at least one fund was undertaking that registration at the beginning of 1984. This means that the funds cannot solicit American buyers, but most will accept American deposits with the acknowledgement that they were not solicited. This also means that no SEC regulations involving disclosure, insider dealings, promotion, or other restrictions are applicable to the funds, which may not necessarily be a disadvantage. However, it does create something of a "behind closed doors" atmosphere for them compared with American investment vehicles. Nevertheless, share prices are readily available from the fund managers in London and the managed funds prices are quoted daily in the *Financial Times*. The risk of currency declines is yours to bear, but so is any appreciation.

A second important point to be aware of is that these funds retain all income and currency appreciation generated by the fund, less management fees and expenses, and any gain is reinvested in the fund. This means the funds cannot be used as income-generating vehicles, unless you sell shares regularly. It means, too, that the *share price* reflects both the income and any profits or losses generated. No provision has been made to pay out the income earned on a regular basis to share holders.[4]

---

[4]Recent changes in U.K. tax laws are prompting the fund groups to bring out income-distributing funds.

These circumstances have created an anomoly in U.S. income tax laws, which is under request for a ruling by the IRS. The problem is that any income or gains on capital earned by any U.S. citizen worldwide is taxable when earned, whether the money is paid to the investor or not. But there is an exception in the tax code when income is generated by a foreign-owned corporation and held in the corporation, as long as that corporation is owned 50 percent or more by five or more foreign citizens. The currency funds discussed here fall into that category, at least at this writing.

It would seem that the reinvested income and gains in these funds would *not* be taxable to U.S. holders until actually paid out to the holder. And it also makes sense that they should qualify for long-term capital gain treatment if the shares are held for more than one year. That's a big advantage.

Alas, nothing is simple in taxation. My conversations with a tax lawyer at a Big Eight accounting firm and the fact that one of the major currency funds is attempting to obtain an IRS ruling on this subject suggest that there is a gray area here. The lawyer and the fund believe the income and gains in these funds when held by U.S. shareholders may be subject to current U.S. income tax. On the other hand, a member of one of the most prestigious currency-management firms in London advised me that the firm has opinions from three U.S. tax counsel that the U.S. exemption is valid. In any case, holdings in these funds must be declared to the IRS under the foreign accounts section of Form 1040.

As mentioned above, currency fund groups usually have a fully managed fund under their aegis that covers a spectrum of currencies. In their performance chase, some are also permitted to invest in instruments other than the staples of such funds, which are bank CDs and government paper. (Check the allowable investments for each fund before investing.) One of these firms, Guiness Mahon, achieved notable results in 1982–83 by investing in *bonds* denominated in foreign currencies. Although these investments significantly increased the risk profile of the fund, Table 14–2 shows that they paid off. The results have been left in pounds sterling, as they were originally reported, to show how the firms performed against one foreign currency. To calculate how they would have fared against the U.S. dollar, *reduce* the results as follows: for one year, 11.3 percent; for two years, 20.7 percent.

As you can see, those adjustments would wipe out most of the managed currency funds' gains, except for the higher-risk Guines Mahon unit. Still, remember that this was calculated in a rising-dollar period.

TABLE 14–2
FULLY MANAGED CURRENCY FUNDS*

			Results of £1000 Invested and Held for:†	
Fund Manager and Fund	**Value of Fund (millions)**	**Date of Launch**	**One Year**	**Two Years**
BRITANNIA INTERNATIONAL INVESTMENT MANAGEMENT				
Britannia Managed Currency Fund	£24.7	9/80	£1137	£1339
BROWN SHIPLEY TRUST COMPANY (JERSEY)				
Brown Shipley International Currency Fund	£0.8	4/82	1161.24	—
GUINNESS MAHON FUND MANAGERS (GUERNSEY)				
Guinness Mahon International	£16.9	5/80	1403.5	1623.7
HILL SAMUEL INVESTMENT MANAGEMENT INTL.				
Hill Samuel Managed Currency Fund	£42.4	6/82	1257	—
SCHRODER UNIT TRUST MANAGERS INTL.				
Schroder Managed Currency	£3.4	12/81	1161.48	1310.42
VANBRUGH FUND MANAGERS				
Vanbrugh Currency Fund	£65.0	5/81	1103	1329
RBC INVESTMENT MANAGERS				
RBC International Currency	U.S. $14.7	12/82	1181	—

*Year is to November 1.
†On an offer-to-offer basis, with income accumulated.
Source: *Financial Times* (London), December 1983.

Another type of foreign fund, known by its 60s heyday nickname, the "offshore" fund, is worthy of mention. It offers potential U.S. tax advantages similar to the above currency funds by reflecting income and capital gains in the share price instead of paying them out to investors. But the funds in this category invest in the whole range of securities—from stocks to bonds. What's intriguing about these funds is that they can invest in U.S. securities from their offshore bases, thereby allowing a U.S. investor to own U.S. stocks on a potentially tax-advantaged basis. The bad news is that most won't accept U.S. investors as a general rule, which they say is necessitated by their need to keep the fund 50 percent or more foreign owned. The following table, published in the November 7, 1983, issue of *Forbes* under the heading "Look, but Don't Touch," shows that the gains from these "offshore" funds have been quite satisfactory, albeit the period selected coincided with a bear market low rising to a bull market high.

Fund	Portfolio Emphasis	Assets as of 6/30/83 ($ millions)	Average Annual Return 1/1/75 to 6/30/83 (percent)
Berry Pacific Fund Ltd.	Far East	$200.4	19.6%
Delta Investment Co.	U.S.	113.7	29.3
Fidelity American Assets NV	U.S.	87.5	25.9
GT Dollar Fund Ltd.	U.S.	112.5	18.6
Quantum Fund	Intl.	351.2	41.1
Worldwide Special Fund NV	Intl.	92.5	24.2
Wilshire 5000 index	U.S.	—	19.4

Of course, many other foreign investments can and, for some people, should make great sense. One example is options on gold and silver bullion, which for several years enjoyed an important plus in the foreign arena because the options were traded heavily in Amsterdam, Montreal, and Vancouver, in contrast to the relatively narrow market offered in the United States by Mocatta Metals. However, with the advent of options on gold futures contracts on the COMEX beginning in the summer of 1983, the majority of this foreign investment boon was lost. As a result, the volume in metals options in Amsterdam dried up, according to brokers in London. On top of that, Canadian brokers won't accept option orders from Americans.

Another foreign market has been preempted by American capability: the foreign currency "forward" market. This market allows you to buy Japanese yen, Swiss francs, German marks and other key currencies in the form of forward or futures contracts from international banks. (The Swiss specialize in them.) You can also buy these futures contracts on the London International Futures Exchange (LIFFE) and the International Monetary Market in Chicago. You can also purchase *options* on these monies through the Philadelphia Stock Exchange.

In the case of the futures, you face significant risk in that a market which moves against you may require additional funds in order to hold a position. However, with the currency options offered in Philadelphia, the most that can be lost is the amount paid for the option. You can best measure your investment risk by dealing in the options on the Philadelphia Exchange, while buying or selling unhedged currency futures or options contracts is definitely a crapshooter's game wherever played.

Hedging is certainly possible with any of these contracts. The individual or company that must often hold sizable cash positions in key foreign currencies can offset or "immunize" the risks in those positions with currency futures or options. Again, the options will offer a greater degree of risk control. Suffice it to say here that hedging, for instance, 12,500 British pounds or 62,500 Swiss francs, which are the minimum option contracts, is not a common individual investor occupation. We'll leave that to the professionals.

Summary

When all is said and done about investing abroad with low-risk constraints, the alert and serious investor should keep in touch with foreign markets as potential money-making arenas in this world of instant communications and rigorous competition. American investment firms may create the lion's share of new investing vehicles, but it's the special-purpose new idea, wherever it arises, that may best fit your situation.

The best vehicles to arise in recent years and to remain largely in foreign waters are, (1) the Eurodollar floating rate note, which is the center of a very large market, but is largely unknown to American investors, and (2) the foreign currency fund, which has not been popular in the United States due to weakness in recent years of foreign currencies against the dollar. Both deserve serious thought by Americans interested in their long-range future.

PART FIVE

Tricks
of the
Trade

This part of the book contains a series of comments, tips, and discussions on two investment areas that all investors eventually deal with, taxes and real estate.* Each subject is massive enough to be the topic of an entire book, and many have been written about both topics.

For the purposes of this discussion, however, taxes and real estate will be dealt with in terms of hands-on ideas that can be applied to your personal investments right now. The tips were compiled with the assistance of our CPAs and attorneys, and especially through the extensive knowledge of my business partner, attorney Jack Padrick. But be sure to check with your tax or real estate professional before using them, because no tax-related idea (and most property-planning concepts quickly involve taxes) is totally safe in these days of annual congressional tinkering with the tax code.

---

*The discussions are adapted from articles that appeared in my *Low Risk Advisory Letter* or related publications and that have stood the ultimate investment test, time.

With Taxes

15

*"Taxes are what we pay
for a civilized society."*
Justice Oliver Wendell Holmes

"The tax system we've got is lousy."
Former Treasury Undersecretary Charls E. Walker

In the middle 1980s it's difficult to conceive of the fact that for nearly two thirds of U.S. history the federal government had no power to directly tax individual incomes. How strange that seems in an era when more than 96 million individual tax returns are filed per year (up from 350,000 in the first payment year, 1914), but perhaps as many as one sixth of the work force evades, underreports, or just plain cheats on its income taxes. Noncompliance isn't so surprising when you consider that in 1972 the New York State Bar Association told Congress that the Internal Revenue Code's then "Byzantine complexity" could cause a "breakdown in compliance." That was before the code itself had increased in size by nearly one third to more than 5,100 pages at year-end 1983 and about 1,000 new pages were added by the 1984 Tax Reform Act.

A book titled *The Dictionary of 1040 Deductions for 1982* listed more than 1,800 separate deductions, credits, exclusions, deferrals, and so on, that individuals could use just on Schedules A through F of their tax returns. Any bets on the size of a new edition of that volume by the end of 1985?

Of course, this massive mess has not gone unnoticed. It's just gone unreformed. In the past few years virtually every national news and information periodical has featured cover stories on the problems and some potential solutions to the tax imbroglio, usually around tax-deadline day. To wit: "Cheating by the Millions,"[1] "The Tax Maze: Time to Start over?"[2] ad infinitum. Just as regularly, Congress makes its pilgrimages to the shrine of Tax Reform and Simplification, there to deposit another 1,000 or so pages of law under one half-baked title or another. Economic Recovery, Tax Equity and Fiscal Responsibility, and Deficit Reduction are three recent calamities.

The reasons for the apparent hypocrisy are simple:

1. The government (any government) always perceives a need for more money.
2. There is always an excuse to raise the money, especially in recent times of economic stress.
3. All new broadly based taxes are unpopular.
4. All major revenue limiters in the forms of deductions, credits, exclusions, and exemptions have powerful constituencies supporting the status quo.
5. Ergo, the excusable revenue need must be filled from the backwaters, nooks and crannies, and newly discovered streams in the revenue code.
6. This harvesting requires new complexity and convolution, plus a new swipe at the tax "avoision" and cheating crowd (those persons who either (1) see no difference between tax cheating and allowable legal gambits or (2) those who consciously cheat).

While waiting for an unforeseen series of events or a clutch of inspired leaders with great followings to attack the inconsistencies, taxpayers are left to cope as best they can. The best practical solution to the problem for investors is to recognize the situation the revenue code presents and to use all legal gambits possible to preserve one's personal revenue streams.

The situation was succinctly put by Susan Lee, an editorial writer for *The Wall Street Journal*, a couple of years ago. She wrote: "After all, a

[1]*Time*, March 28, 1983.
[2]*Newsweek*, April 16, 1984.

penny earned is a penny taxed; a penny saved is a penny taxed twice; but a penny spent or borrowed, ah, now that's a penny. In fact, it's pretty close to a nickel." I would add to the phrase "a penny spent or borrowed," the words or *sheltered*, where sheltered is used in the broad sense of tax protected.

To aid in this legitimate, if unarguably irritating, pursuit of tax-protected income, the following practical solutions to common problems are offered.

Best Buys for Your IRA

The best tax saver around for the average (and above average) working person is an IRA.

Probably the most frequently asked question about IRAs, now that they've become popular, is what to invest them in. Unfortunately, there's no single best answer to that because the answer depends on what is already held in the IRA (or in other IRAs), how long one has until retirement, and one's temperament relating to investment risk. The following points are therefore generic to all types of IRAs and are given with the low-risk concept foremost in mind.

The best general-purpose IRA investments are clearly interest-bearing vehicles with high rates of return and top safety, such as Treasury notes. Good short-term interest rate protection from money market funds is also desirable. The reason is that the tax-deferred nature of the plans' earnings means that you can compound interest without a tax bite until withdrawal. Over several years, that's an enormous advantage.

This group includes zero-coupon notes. They have tax disadvantages outside retirement plans, since taxable interest is imputed to them when held by individuals, but they are excellent vehicles within IRAs and other retirement plans.

Investments that do not bear interest have a distinct *disadvantage* when you are looking for capital growth within such plans. You not only lose the tax-deferred compounding of interest, but you may also be converting long-term capital gains into ordinary income. That's the opposite of what you should be doing. Growth assets should be held outside the plan where possible.

Here's an example. Assume that your average federal tax bracket just prior to retirement was 40 percent and that it dropped to 32 percent after retirement. (Most people would be lucky to get that big a cut.) Also assume that you held a growth asset in your plan and an equal amount of the same asset outside the plan. The year before retirement you sold those assets to capture the gains. Within the plan the gain would be tax deferred, but only until you began withdrawing the money upon retirement. At that point, the proceeds of the gain would be taxed at our assumed 32 percent ordinary tax rate.

However, the same asset held outside the plan would be subject to a long-term capital gain tax upon sale, which would be only 40 percent of your normal rate. Thus you'd pay only a 16 percent tax (40 percent times 40 percent bracket) on that gain the year before retirement. That's a significant (one half) tax saving over your tax rate after retirement.

Then there's the matter of losses. If forced by market conditions or other concerns to take a loss on an investment, would you rather have the loss in the IRA or outside it? Since the loss is of no use for tax purposes in the IRA because it's not tax deductible, you'd naturally rather take the loss outside your IRA or other retirement plan. Accordingly, you'll want investments that have the least chance of developing losses held inside the IRA, and vice versa. High-risk investments therefore generally belong outside the plan, and the idea of holding the most secure investments within the plan is further strengthened.

Thus the rule for retirement plan investments is: Compound in the plan and grow outside it. You'll be tax dollars ahead by doing so. Of course, if you can't accumulate investment assets outside your plan because your contributions and required income leave little excess, you'll probably be forced to violate the rule. Many self-employed people, especially those with one-person corporations, fall into this category, but the attempt should still be made.

Cash Your Savings Certificate?

A hot question of the day is: How do you figure whether it's worth cashing in a bank or S&L savings certificate and paying a withdrawal penalty in order to capture those high yields available in money market funds or Treasury notes?

First, don't make a yield comparison between money market funds and savings certificates. You can't correctly compare a varying MMF rate with a fixed certificate rate. A good yield comparison is between your certificate yield and that of a Treasury note that has about the same maturity date as the certificate. If your certificate has more than two years to maturity, use a maximum note maturity of 36 months as the basis for the alternative yield. Then follow the steps given below.

1. Ask your bank or S&L to figure your exact penalty for early withdrawal from the certificate.
2. Meanwhile, find the highest yield shown in your newspaper for the Treasury note with a maturity within a month or two of the maturity of your savings certificate (3 years maximum from today, remember). Subtract your certificate interest rate from the T note yield. The result is the interest rate advantage in percent per year from switching.
3. Now subtract your early withdrawal penalty before tax (step 1) from the amount of dollars presently in your certificate account. Then multiply this result by the percent in step 2 (the interest rate advantage in switching). This is the net dollar gain per year from the interest rate differential.
4. Multiply this number by the total number of years, including fractions, to certificate maturity. This is the total interest-rate-derived dollar gain before tax.
5. Now take your early withdrawal penalty and find your actual aftertax cost of paying the penalty. Since the penalty is deductible on IRS Form 1040, even if you don't itemize deductions (on line 26), you'll need to find your true dollar cost. To do this, add up your top federal and state tax bracket percentages and subtract that number from 100 percent. This gives you the percentage of your interest penalty that is not saved by the deduction on your 1040. Multiply this percentage by the dollar penalty from step 1. This is your aftertax cost of withdrawing your funds.
6. Finally, subtract this aftertax cost of withdrawal from the result of step 4 (the dollar gain before taxes). This is a good approximation of the gain (or loss) you'll have in making the switch. If the gain is small, remember that the T note has an advantage in that you pay no state income tax on its interest, but unless you're in a nonincome-tax state, you do pay on the certificate interest.

Now you can make the switch decision.

A Rolls in Your Future?

When someone wants to discuss the merits of some income tax-cut proposal and what folks in the upper tax brackets will do with their extra

dollars, remember the "Parable of the Rolls-Royce."[3] The parable surfaced a few years ago when it was noted that Britain, with all its economic
woes, was seeing an upsurge in its Rolls-Royce population. How could
things be bad when people were buying more luxury cars? Especially,
how could one criticize the high (then 98 percent) tax rate on unearned
income in Britain when the well-off folks still had plenty in hand to buy
those fine motor cars? Simple. It was a better "investment" to buy a Rolls
than almost any income-producing security. Taking the recent (until
1981) U.S. 70 percent top tax on investment income as an example (it
was obviously worse at 98 percent in Britain) and a $50,000 auto as the
investment, the problem becomes clear. If you put the $50,000 in a secu-
rity paying, say, 15 percent, the income would be $7,500 per year, of
which you as the wealthy taxpayer could keep $2,250. If you instead
bought a fine, previously owned Rolls for the same money, then you
would have the pleasure of driving luxury for no out-of-pocket cost and
an income loss of less than $200 a month. What's more, the Rolls might
well appreciate in value, and the government would get zero tax revenue
from that gain. How do you beat that?

Next time someone suggests soaking the rich with taxes you might
ask whether (s)he is on retainer by Rolls-Royce, Ltd.

Keep Your Income Home?

When deciding whether or not a negative cash flow from a rented
home is advantageous, this simple financial test will help: Remember,
this is a financial test only. You may have personal or other reasons for
overriding its results.

Start with the approximate market value of the home and a conservative assumption as to the expected annual rate of appreciation over the
next couple of years. For example, use $100,000 and 8 percent, respec-
tively, and assume the equity in the home is $50,000. Let's also figure that
there's a negative cash flow (out-of-pocket cost of owning it) of $250 per
month, or $3,000 per year before tax.

Take the negative cash flow and subtract from that amount your tax
savings as a result of deducting that cost on your tax return. With a 40
percent top federal bracket for the example, the annual tax savings on a

[3]Mentioned here with thanks to Daniel Seligman, who writes the excellent "Keeping
Up" column in *Fortune*.

$3,000 deductible cost would be $1,200. Subtracting this from the $3,000 would leave a $1,800 real net negative cash flow from owning the house now.

Next, look at the appreciation potential. The assumed 8 percent of the $100,000 market value would equal an $8,000 tax-deferred gain per year. Subtract the real negative cash flow from it to get the net tax-deferred gain or loss. In this case it would be a $6,200 net gain, which looks good so far.

There's one more step. Compare this figure with the amount you could earn, aftertax in a high-grade security of a few years' maturity. This is done to approximate the alternative cost of reinvesting the proceeds of selling the house.

In early 1984 an aftertax five-year Treasury note yield to maturity in a 40 percent tax bracket was about 8 percent. To use this with the aftertax equity you'd have to invest after sale of the home, the capital gain tax on $50,000 in the assumed tax bracket would be 16 percent, or $8,000. That would leave $42,000 to invest (ignoring the home sales costs), which multiplied by 8 percent is $3,360. This is your alternative return.

Now compare that return with your present return. If the present return ($6,200) is larger than or about equal to the alternative return ($3,360), you're better off keeping the home. If not, you should consider selling it and reinvesting the proceeds. Incidentally, it's not safe in 1984 to use an annual appreciation factor of more than the 8 percent example above. It should probably be less.

Selling Worthless Stock

Somewhere in the course of a lifetime, most investors will find themselves with a stock or bond that worked out badly and collapsed instead of soaring as anticipated. It occurs far more frequently than most private investors (or professionals) care to admit. If you ever find yourself in this unhappy circumstance, take solace in the fact that you can do something constructive about it, while still nurturing the hope that the cursed security will rise again.

You could make a bona fide sale in the open market to establish the loss, of course. However, this doesn't offer you the benefit of any future climb. Internal Revenue Code Section 267 prohibits you from making the sale to a related party, such as a spouse, child, parent, brother, or grandchild, but it does not forbid a sale to an *in-law*. Therefore, keep the stock/bond in the family by obtaining a current quote on the security in the open market and selling it to an in-law to establish your tax loss in a given year (perhaps to offset other gains). Then you can still have the family benefit from any upturn.

Be sure that you get a full record of the transaction and that you can establish the sale price as fair and realistic. In fact, the same procedure applies to any security where you have a loss.

Although your brother-in-law might not be thrilled to put up hard cash for a "worthless" security, his outlay should be minimal under these circumstances.

Saving around the House

The do-it-yourself idea in home repairs or remodeling has become highly popular with homeowners over the past decade for the obvious reasons of soaring costs, unreliable outside workers, and pride in personal accomplishment. The tax aspect is considered less often. Such fixings aren't deductible on a private residence (though some can be used to increase your cost basis in the home).

A second tax angle is well worth noting: The higher your tax bracket, the more advantageous it is for you to take hammer, saw, or paint brush in hand. A family in a 50 percent bracket, for example, considering $1,000 worth of remodeling through an outside contractor, might find the actual cost of materials to be $350. To have a contractor do the work, they'd need $2,000 worth of before-tax income. To do it themselves would require only $700 of before-tax income. Thus the higher your tax bracket and the greater the contractor's profit, the more it is to your advantage to do work yourself. Utilizing paid vacation time to pound and paint gives the most attractive time/tax advantage. Note, however, that the reverse is true for deductible work on income property.

Gaining on the IRS

There are at least two ways to accept a short-term gain within your family and still avoid paying tax on it simply by taking advantage of your children. An easy way to let your child's (or grandchild's) tax bracket avoid a tax bill on your profit is either to give or to sell to the child the asset carrying the gain. Probably the simplest way is to give the asset away.

Assume that you have 1,000 shares of stock purchased at $2 per share, and its current market value is $4 per share. Also assume that your unwillingness to take the short-term gain this year (perhaps because it will push you into a higher bracket) piques your interest in this form of disposal. By making a gift of the stock to your child at your cost of $2,000—possibly through another adult as custodian for the minor, depending on your state's Gifts to Minors Law—the potential gain would be transferred from you to the child.

If the child (through the custodian) immediately sold the stock, the realized gain of $2,000 would be the child's and would thus stay in the family. The child would pay no tax, assuming his/her total income for the year didn't exceed $3,300, and there would be no gift tax because the amount is less than the annual exclusion you have for gifts ($10,000 per spouse). The custodian could then invest the proceeds for the future benefit of the child. Remember that the asset, and any proceeds from it, would be the child's property—not yours.

A sale of the stock to the child/custodian would accomplish the same thing, except that the child would pay you for your cost of $2,000 and then sell the stock to realize the profit. This would leave the gift exclusion untouched, permitting you to give an additional amount up to the annual maximum to the child if you so wished.

Whichever method you choose, these transfers may be important ideas for any investor to consider when a short-term gain is nagging as year end approaches.

Tax Odds

Suppose the investment world has been kind this year, and you are holding a significant capital gain at this moment. It is still a short-term gain, and it won't become long term until mid-January next year. Two problems face you: Do the prospects for this marvelous investment justify holding it any longer? Are the tax advantages of a long-term capital gain sufficient for you to offset all or part of the holding risk?

Conveniently, the difference between tax rates for short-term gains and long-term gains in your tax bracket offers a way to determine the percentage risk in holding a short-term gain to make it long term. Here's how. Suppose your top federal tax bracket is 40 percent. (Use your own bracket in figuring your actual odds.) This means that taking the gain before the end of the new 6-month holding period will donate 40 percent or more of the gain to the government (depending on the size of the gain), leaving you 60 percent. By waiting the full 6 months and a day to sell, you can have your gain taxed at only a 16 percent rate (40 percent long-term rate times 40 percent bracket), thus leaving you with 84 percent of the gain.

To calculate your waiting risk, take the aftertax fraction for the amount kept, short/long term, 60/84, or 71.4 percent in this case, and multiply it by the dollar amount of the present gain. This will provide the amount to which the current gain can decline before you lose by waiting for the long-term gain. In this example, if the gain were $10,000 now, 71.4 percent of it, or $7,140, would be the tax break-even point. Proof: If taxed as a short-term gain, you'd have $6,000 aftertax. If taxed as a long-term gain at 16 percent, $7,140 would be the gross taxable amount, which would leave you with the same $6,000 aftertax. So your present investment could decline to $7,140 from $10,000 at the time it became long term and still leave you net as well off as if you had sold now. Note that these figures are approximations.

This little piece of arithmetic may add important information to your holding decision. In the above example, if your investment were in a nonvolatile stock with continuing good prospects, the likelihood of its declining 28.6 percent to 71.4 percent of present value within a few months might be small. Holding for long-term gain might then make sense. Note also that if the investment were to gain from present levels, you would be even better off waiting. On the other hand, if yours were a highly volatile investment with unclear prospects, the possibility that a 28 percent decline might occur quickly and thereby wipe out your holding advantage might make an early sale useful.

Capital Gains Worksheet

The simplified worksheet below gives instructions for calculating one's annual capital gains position. Make use of it to figure net tax-deductible capital items. Before using the worksheet, calculate total short-term and long-term gains/losses separately to enter as indicated.

I. Short-term capital gains/losses (*less than* 6 $ _____
    months and one day after purchase if
    bought after 7/15/84)[4]

---

[4]The long-term holding period was 1 year and 1 day since 1969.

Previous year's carryover	$ _____
Short-term total	$ _____
Long-term capital gains/losses (*more* than 6 months after purchase if bought after 7/15/84)[5]	$ _____
Previous year's carryover	$ _____
Long-term total	$ _____

II. Depending upon what is shown above, follow *either* step A or B below. Read each step first to see which one is applicable to your situation.

    A. If *both* short term and long-term amounts show *gains*, they are reportable as such and are taxed: short term at your ordinary income rate, long term at 40 percent of the ordinary rate.

    B. If *one* of the two totals shows a *gain* and *the other a loss*, net one against the other.

Short-term total	$ _____
Long-term total	$ _____
Net gain/loss	$ _____

III. Does the net arise because the short-term or long-term total was larger?

    Short _____ Long _____

    1. If the net shows a *gain*, it is reportable and taxed at ordinary or long-term rates, depending on whether it arose from a short- or long-term gain, respectively.

    2. If the net shows a *loss* and it arose from the *short-term* total being larger, up to $3,000 can be deducted this year. The balance is applied to future years.

        a. If the *loss* results from the *long-term* total being larger, the amount deductible is 50 percent of the net loss, but up to a maximum deductible of $3,000 this year. Any balance is applied to future years.

        b. If *both* short-term *and* long-term totals show *losses*, deduct the full amount of the *short-term loss* up to $3,000 this year, and carry any excess forward to next year. If the full $3,000 short-term loss is deducted, any *long-term loss* is carried

---

[5]The long-term holding period was 1 year and 1 day since 1969.

forward to next year. If the *short-term loss* is less than $3,000, you can deduct 50 percent of the long-term loss that is sufficient to bring the total deduction to $3,000. Carry forward to next year the unused balance of the long-term loss.

Finally, total any potential short-term and long-term gains separately, and refigure the above worksheet with a view to taking the maximum short-term loss this year and offsetting as much of any long-term loss as possible with capital gains. Obviously, market conditions will be taken into account in taking these gains or losses.

Summary

This chapter provided some tips for finding your way through the tax-code maze. The right interest-bearing IRA investments can be a big help. Sometimes it's a good idea to cash in a bank or S&L savings certificate to take advantage of high-yielding money market funds and T notes. Some investors have even found a Rolls-Royce to be a better tax saver than securities. Other possibilities are using negative cash flow from rental property by figuring your total return on income property, selling stock to in-laws, making do-it-yourself repairs, and giving stocks to your children. Calculating your tax odds in holding a security to the new 6 month long-term gain date will certainly make the hold or sell decision easier.

16

On Your Property

*Property exists by grace of
the law. It is not a
fact but a legal fiction.*

             Stirner

Real estate, even back as far as the purchase of Manhattan for $24 in trinkets, has been the number one path to financial success in this country. More wealth has been built on property than on any other industry. Even the currently advanced value of the broadest measure of industrial wealth in the nation, the Wilshire 5000 Stock Index, is arguably worth less (about $1.5 trillion) than the property in a half dozen of our largest cities.

But these are not the inflation days of the '60s and '70s, upon which so much recent property wealth was built. Is real estate still a good investment? In my opinion, the answer is a strong, although qualified, yes. Real estate still favorably combines three important qualities not found in any other *single* investment: appreciation/inflation hedge, tax shelter, and cash flow. However, the relative strength and importance of each of these qualities compared with other investments is changing. That fact is critical to what you must know about real estate investing now.

As one example, take the common assumption about real estate leverage. For a $100,000 down payment, John Buyer purchased a $500,000 apartment building and agreed to pay the $400,000 balance as a mortgage over a period of 10 years. Assuming an annual inflation rate of 7 percent over this 10-year period and an increase in the price of the property at the same rate, it appears that John's real estate investment merely kept pace with inflation. Wrong. Real estate offers leverage. Specifically, inflation was increasing the value of John's *entire* $500,000 investment, not just the $100,000 down payment. Thus the value of the total property in one year would be $535,000. That is only a 7 percent increase in the total property valuation, but it represents a 35 percent return on John's $100,000 invested capital. In 10 years this inflation-compounded value of the total property would be around $1 million, which is 10 times John's original cash investment.

The story sounds great, but it's not the whole story. What if the inflation rate averaged only 4 percent and the original purchase price discounted that a couple of years into the future? In other words, what if there could be no appreciation expectation for a few years? Not only does the original price paid take on great importance, but so do the other two qualities, tax shelter and cash flow.

Since the house is investment property, it is assumed to be generating income to pay for itself in whole or in part. John will normally be able to shelter from the IRS any cash flow from the property plus some portion of his income from other sources. This income sheltering is due primarily to depreciation that may be taken for tax purposes on the building and other improvements whether the property goes down or up in value. If the depreciable real property improvements in the example were initially valued at $450,000, under the Tax Act of 1984, John could depreciate this amount on a straight-line basis over an 18-year period at $25,000 per year. In 10 years, John would have benefited by $250,000 in depreciation-generated tax shelter alone, plus any profits or losses on the operation of the property. Finally, under the current tax laws, John could then sell the property and pay tax on any resulting gain at or below the maximum long-term capital gain rate of 20 percent.

Those are fine advantages, but John can't ignore the possibility that a high-interest rate mortgage, vacancies, or unforeseen problems could cause the operating expenses to begin to absorb more than all the cash flow for an extended period. If so, tax losses could become real dollar losses and not just depreciation-created paper deductions. This is when cash reserves begin to play an important part in the investment equation; otherwise, the investor could be faced with foreclosure or an unfavorable sale.

To these problems add the other real disadvantages of real estate: illiquidity, management headaches, changing market conditions, and complex tax laws. Some people don't sleep well with a million dollar mortgage over their heads. The sum of this is that real estate is not for everyone, especially now. That leads to the first item in a list of points you must know to survive in today's tougher real estate environment.

Know Yourself

Real estate investing normally means large financial commitments, including debt. If you are by nature a worrier, then real estate is probably not your cup of tea. Even for a homeowner, the purchase of a house is usually the single largest financial transaction of a lifetime. For the successful real estate investor, transactions in the hundreds of thousands—if not millions—of dollars are not unusual after only several years of investment activity.

So, don't invest in real estate just because your friends do or because it has been great. Also, if you are considering real estate only as a way to make money, you'll probably find it requires too much time compared with other investments. But if you view it as an opportunity to use your imagination (e.g., visualize a property for what it can be, not just what it now is), your communication and negotiation skills (buying and selling property and dealing with tenants), and your organizational abilities (managing the property effectively and efficiently), you will probably find real estate investing personally challenging, fulfilling, and financially rewarding, too.

Success in real estate is like success in athletics, music, or any other field. It requires a commitment of time and effort commensurate with the results to be achieved. Its advantage is that it does not require the degree of physical or mental superiority often necessary for a corresponding degree of financial success in most other endeavors. Hard work and perseverance are the great equalizers in real estate.

For the beginner, real estate offers one true advantage: You can participate while continuing your regular job. In fact, part-time real estate investors have been far more common than full-time professionals. However, this is changing because of the growing complexity of tax laws, financing, and economic conditions and the sheer magnitude of the dollars involved. Because of these and other factors, the part-timer of yesteryear who bought a duplex or similar real estate investment alone is now more likely to join with other small investors in a syndicated limited partnership run by full-time professionals.

Whether to invest on your own in real estate or let others lead by participating in a limited partnership should depend primarily on the amount of personal satisfaction and challenge you want out of your investment, apart from any monetary return. Needless to say, individual investing offers greater rewards but also greater risks and time commitments; thus the importance of knowing yourself.

Conclusion: Invest in real estate only if it is right for you. Otherwise try the stock market, Las Vegas, or whatever else interests *you*.

Know Your Goals

Knowing your goals is another common investment criterion. It has just become very important to real estate because of the tighter operating climate. After deciding to invest in real estate, define your goals and specific objectives. These will vary by investor and even during the lifetime of a particular investor.

A young person of considerable ambition but few financial resources may have as a primary objective the building of an investment worth as rapidly as possible. This young person has little to lose and a lifetime to recover from failure. (S)he may risk much or all (s)he owns by buying with the minimum possible down payment and borrowing as much as possible (leverage). If the project fails, the young person has a long time to try again, but if foresight, inflation, or the real estate cycle favors the investment, (s)he could be on the way to fortune.

On the other hand, such a high-risk/reward relationship should not be the objective of a midcareer person who is already reasonably successful in his/her job. For this person the objective is more likely to be the tax sheltering of income from the investor's principal occupation, plus the appreciation/inflation hedge benefits of real estate. Risk and mangement time should be minimized by investing via limited partnerships (no personal liability or management responsibilities) or in properties with triple-net-type tenant leases, wherein the down payment is substantial and the leverage moderate. Since one of the objectives for this type of investor is to build up an estate with before-tax, not aftertax, dollars, the investment properties should probably be exchanged (not sold) on a tax-deferred basis for larger properties as the years go by. Thus the government helps build the real estate portfolio by permitting one to put into real estate the income tax dollars that would have otherwise gone to the IRS. In addition, the investor can construct tax-deferred exchanges so that capital gains taxes are also postponed indefinitely.

For older or retired people, safety and income are the usual objectives. In that case, the real estate investment should be structured to reduce risk greatly and to increase certainty. For example, any properties in the portfolio with substantial mortgages may be exchanged for properties that have little or no debt or are otherwise risk-free (say, property triple-net leased by a major firm for 30 years with annual rent increases tied to the full consumer price index). Finally, when the investor dies, the tax laws bequeath one last benefit—the heirs receive all properties based on the then-full-market value. If the heirs sell the properties at that price, *no capital gains tax is paid by either the heirs or the investor's estate.*

Conclusion: Tailor your real estate investments to your net worth-building, tax-shelter, or income goals, and you may still find some salvation in today's unheavenly property market.

Know the Cycles

Real estate, like the stock market or gold and silver, moves in cycles. So, most investors try to buy when real estate is at the bottom of its cycle and to sell when it's at the top. Although that sounds like a good rule, it's virtually impossible to follow because the absolute low or high cannot be definitely determined until *after* the fact. However, absolute observance of the concept "buy low, sell high" is not essential. In fact, attempting to follow it too closely is risky because there can be false bottoms and tops in the market.

I recommend that low-risk real estate investors avoid trying to pick the absolute top or bottom and instead give the market time to solidly establish its new direction up or down. They should be prepared to act quickly before the trend becomes so obvious that less sophisticated investors make their move en masse. You can afford to miss the top and bottom 10 percent (or even 25 percent) of the cycle if you are consistently able—with little risk—to take advantage of the 50 percent to 80 percent remaining. In short, don't be greedy. As an old friend said, "Bulls can make money and bears can make money, but hogs get slaughtered."

The obvious question is, What can we learn from the cycles themselves? History never exactly repeats itself, but a study of real estate cycles reveals some interesting facets. First, cycles tend to last five to nine years. Second, the longest part of the cycle has been the up portion. These two factors need to be considered by any real estate investor who wants to benefit from the up portion of the cycle as well as to be protected from the subsequent downside risk.

Up Markets

For example, in 1984 the broad real estate market was bouncing along the bottom of its cycle and starting on the up leg. Under normal conditions, this upward trend would last about three to five years before a new high was reached.

Because of the longer length of the normal uptrend portion of the cylce, you should have adequate time to ensure that the market is truly rising before you have to commit your dollars. Waiting until the upward trend is clearly established can cut risks substantially and still give the opportunity to participate in most of the price rise in a typical upward real estate cycle.

Down Markets

The same situation does *not* apply, however, when the market starts to go down. The top of a market can be wiped out in a much shorter time span than it took to form the bottom of the market at the start of the cycle. Also, in contrast to the considerable amount of time buyers have to enter a typical rising market, sellers may have almost no time to get out after the market has turned down. Accordingly, I strongly recommend that you do not try to catch the very top of the real estate market as a seller; instead take your profits earlier, and simply wait for the next cycle.

A further fact of interest is that most sellers tend to lag the market. They continue to try to sell too high after the market has topped out and has started down. Then, after being forced to hold during the down and bottom portion of the cycle, they again lag the market and sell too low and too soon as the market starts back up. This fault gives smart buyers time to note the uptrend and still buy at low prices. If you don't have funds available or if the upturn is still in doubt, use options or a delayed closing to lower your risk while increasing leverage.

A Tip-Off

Often a leading indicator of an approaching top or bottom is the "herd" mentality. When most people are rushing to buy, the top is probably near; conversely, when no one wants to buy, the bottom has probably been reached or is close. So, when the herd goes rushing by, it's time to start preparing to move in the opposite direction.

As a final point, remember that the overall real estate cycle can encompass differing cycles for different types of property. For example, apartment projects were definitely starting their up cycle in early 1983, and office buildings were still in a down cycle. Shopping centers and industrial projects were in the process of forming the bottom to their particular cycles.

Know the Product

Every piece of real estate is unique—no two properties are alike. This important principle is recognized and deeply ingrained in our common law heritage, which permits a purchaser to demand "specific performance" on a real estate sales contract because money damages alone are considered insufficient. Since properties vary so much, the law will not attempt to equate two seemingly similar ones.

This legal principle highlights an important difference between real estate and some of the other forms of investments such as the stock market. Because the stocks of various companies can be professionally compared by trained analysts, the stock market is considered an efficient market; real estate is an inefficient market, partly because of the difficulty in comparing properties. This very inefficiency can make real estate profitable for you as an investor if you will take the time and effort to know a particular property or properties better than anyone else—even the owner.

Knowing property better than the owner may seem unusual, if not impossible, but it isn't that difficult. Many owners are absentee investors—dentists, widows, heirs, or people who simply have little or no understanding of, or interest in, their properties for whatever reason.

Rules of Thumb

Therefore, look for the seller (or buyer) who knows little about the property and real estate in general. If you then become totally knowledgeable about that property, you will have a substantial advantage in buying (or selling). Thus, a good rule is always to *know more* about the property than does the other party, or you are likely to end up with the short end of the deal. By the way, since you can never "steal" a property from a true professional, save your time and energy by looking elsewhere if you run into a professional seller and you want a bargain that's going to make you rich.

An important part of knowing a particular property is to learn all you can about *similar* properties. That's where hard work and perseverance give you an advantage over others, even if they have more financial resources or a higher IQ. What counts is how you use what you have. If you have studied many similar properties, you will know—as well or better than anyone else—just what a particular property is worth in a particular location at a particular time.

In this regard use the "rule of 100"; that is, look at 100 properties before buying 1. Of course, the more knowledgeable you are of a particular type of property or location, the less comparison shopping is necessary; but the concept is valid and should not be ignored, especially by the beginning investor. You can reduce the amount of time necessary for such comparisons (sellers should also do a similar type of comparison before pricing their products for sale) by specializing in a particular type of property or location. Also use brokers, accountants, lenders, and other experts knowledgeable of the desired product, such as a 20- to 40-unit apartment complex with condo conversion potential located within two miles of the center of "old town."

Conclusion: Use the inefficiency of the real estate market to your advantage. Seek out and find those deals that are underpriced for whatever reason. Remember that you need to know the product better than only one seller (or buyer); the rest do not matter.

Know the Location

For the typical real estate investor, the most important rule to remember is an old one: "location, location, location." Other rules have changed or can be violated with little adverse effect, but location remains as important today as it was when the early settlers located their towns and homes near water or railroad junctions. Today the focus is on proximity to mass transit, freeways, even sewer lines. The factors that make a particular location desirable will change, but the importance of location will not. For example, even if you paid too much for a property initially, that may not matter if your choice of location was good (or if you're lucky and a new IBM plant is built nearby). Even if you bought the property for a song, you could still lose your investment if the area becomes a slum.

Don't be led astray where location is concerned. Certain real estate agents love to lead a novice buyer to one bargain property after another—and it's no coincidence that none of these bargains is in a strong or improving location. There is usually a good reason the property is bargain priced. If the real estate salesperson looks around anxiously while walking across the parking lot or through the building, then you *know* it's not the best location.

Unless you're a knowledgeable real estate investor intimately familiar with the particular location, buy only the best location—and one that is obviously getting better, not worse.

There are many ways to become an expert on location. Some are costly, such as hiring site experts. If you are willing and able to put the time in yourself, the job can be done without spending a lot of money. A great deal of free, but very valuable, information on the future of an area can be obtained by simply talking to government officials, especially those concerned with proposed sewer and highway construction or building permits; to telephone and gas utility employees; and to local realtors who are knowledgeable in the activities of major firms, such as shopping center developers. If your investment is sizable, rent a small plane and fly over areas of key interest. From the air, the direction of growth and how much growth might be affected by artificial boundaries (highways) or natural boundaries (hills) often becomes more readily apparent.

An example of how natural boundaries can affect growth and permit the astute observer to predict growth occurred over the past two decades in the San Francisco area. The city is confined on three sides by water; growth could only occur down the peninsula toward San Jose, which was already growing rapidly itself. With Stanford University located between the two cities, the development of Silicon Valley, and an extremely desirable living environment, the growth of the entire peninsula was assured. As a result real estate fortunes were made in the area that exceeded even the unbelievable success stories of Hewlett-Packard, Apple Computer, and other new companies spawned by high technology.

This was an example of the effect of location over a relatively large area and a long period of time, but changes in location can occur far more rapidly and in smaller areas. Generally, it is in these more limited areas that the small investor can, and should, become expert (e.g., a six-block area of "old town" that is coming back).

The important elements of location are twofold: First, find a changing area; second, learn all you can about the area to become the expert. Most other investors, especially those from outside the area, simply won't take the time or have the opportunity to know your backyard as well as you do. Thus you can force that investor to compete on your turf, and you will gain the advantage by turning location to your benefit. You'll be on par or above it with the locals, besides.

Know How to Buy, Hold, and Sell

Assuming you've found the right property in the right location, there is a tendency to think the hardest work is over: Once you agree on a price with the seller, you simply close the deal, hold for a period of time, sell, and count your profits. If it were that easy, we'd all be rich. The actual buying, managing, and selling is where things get tough.

Look at the process itself for the most important criteria. First, acquire and use the best legal, financial, and technical experts available. Buying and selling property is now very complicated and requires use of these experts from the beginning. For example, if you were to buy and lease back a small commercial building from a person who had owned it prior to January 1, 1981, you would be unable to obtain the benefit of the 15-year depreciation schedule provided by the Economic Recovery Tax Act of 1981. A good property accountant would bring this factor to your attention. Similarly, buying a property could be an unwise decision if you did not have it inspected by a structural engineer: you might buy a building with major roofing or foundation problems.

Second, "falling in love with the property" before or after buying it will result in paying too much on purchase or holding the property too long before selling. Always remember you are investing to make money—not to develop emotional ties to the property.

Buying

After developing the proper emotionless state of mind toward the property, analyze it without regard to the asking price. Look at the property as a buyer, manager, and seller, and then decide what it's worth to you as part of your investment portfolio and game plan.

This approach will set a ceiling on the price and terms you will pay independent of the offered price. Then you can concern yourself with the asking price. If after your best efforts the seller will still not agree to price and terms within your preset parameters, walk away! There is always another day and another property. If you weaken and pay too much, you'll have to live with that mistake during the entire time you own the property, including when you sell it. "You make your profit when you buy, not when you sell" is one of the truisms in real estate.

Since how you buy is so important, work hard at it. Learn all the analytical tools the professionals use, including statistical ratios, capitalization rate, gross rent multiplier, price per square foot (gross and rental), cost per unit, rent per square foot, and replacement cost. Also learn how these tools can be misleading and how they can differ by area, type and age of building, financing, and much more. For example, the gross rent multiplier is considered to be a fairly important price indicator for apartment investments, but it's not nearly as important for office buildings or shopping centers, for which the capitalization rate or price per square foot are of much greater significance. In another case, two apartment buildings may have the same gross rent multiplier, but in one instance the tenant pays for utilities, and in the other apartment complex the landlord pays, thus distorting the value of the gross rent multiplier. This is why all facets have to be analyzed in depth.

A common analytical mistake made by buyers is to look at today's rents but at last year's expenses in determining what the property will do in the coming year. This is combining oranges and apples. When using future rent estimates, also use future expenses. With even modest inflation, expenses will go up; rents may, or may not.

Last, do comparison shopping. Even if the figures and indices look good on paper, always compare with similar properties located in the same area. For example, to a Californian almost any out-of-state property looks good on paper. However, when actually compared with other property in the same out-of-state location, the property is often not a bargain at all. Never, never buy at more than replacement costs for a location. If someone can build for less next door, you'll be the one hurting, but if it costs them more to build, you'll normally be well protected.

Holding

The term *holding* for real estate investors is a misnomer. One should never simply hold income property. It should be managed and managed actively during ownership. Granted, it takes time and effort to manage property, but how you manage determines your operating profit or loss.

How you select tenants, price rentals, set up replacement or maintenance schedules, upgrade the property, change services or activities—all these variables and more constitute managing a property. It's not simply a matter of watching your pennies. Sometimes paying more for a good on-site manager or buying a higher quality carpet can be most cost effective.

It's best for every serious real estate investor to manage his/her own properties at first. Only when one knows how to manage property will (s)he be able to manage property managers. Only experience will tell you when, and whether, it will be more cost effective to continue management or to use the services of a professional manager. Then, when using a manager (on-site or professional), make sure (s)he knows exactly what your goals and objectives are for the property—and for the manager. Then keep in regular contact by receiving timely reports from the manager and giving your comments and instructions. If the manager handles a number of properties for various owners, remember that the "squeaky wheel gets the grease." Squeak often enough to be remembered. By the same token, if the manager is doing a good job, let him/her know it by words and deeds (dollars).

Selling

Planning the sale of property should begin even before it is bought and should continue during the entire period of ownership. Buying and managing should be part of one's overall investment sales plan.

For example, one might look for property whose seller or lender would carry back 10-year (or longer) financing at a favorable fixed interest rate without a "due on sale" clause. As the economy improved, or if inflation heated up, the buyer would be in a position to sell the property in three to five years, with the buyer being assured of five to seven more years of good financing. The higher the interest rates at resale time, the better off one would be. Thus the importance of planning for the future sale, even as you are in the process of purchasing the property.

Use brokers, but reserve the right to find buyers yourself. Remember, no broker is going to be as committed to the proper sale of the property as are you, the owner. Also look for a broker as you would any other expert. There are good and bad ones. Work only with the best one(s) you can find. A good broker can make a sale and can also save time and frustrations by separating the lookers from the serious prospects.

When a prospective buyer is brought to your attention, meet with that person before putting much extra time and effort into the possible sale. Size up the purchaser yourself, and also seek outside input on the type and character of the buyer. If (s)he has a poor reputation in property dealings, don't waste your time and energy. You may end up in a lawsuit instead of selling the property.

Added Cautions

As the seller, don't guarantee anything unless the guarantee is carefully written because you will no longer control the property after sale. For example, a seller recently guaranteed for a one-year period no more than a 7 percent vacancy rate in the apartment complex he was selling. Since the complex had been averaging less than a 2 percent vacancy, he felt little concern. The buyer immediately increased rents by 40 percent, most of the tenants left, and the seller was stuck with the guarantee. The buyer used this free (to him) opportunity to renovate and upgrade all the vacated apartments.

Be aware that many sellers increase rents just before putting the property on the market to make the income and expense figures look better (even if this will mean a higher future vacancy factor for the new owner). They may also classify as improvements many of the repair expenses from the preceding year. For the buyer, either of these approaches can distort estimates of operating income and expenses, and the result can be an operating loss instead of the projected comfortable cash flow.

As a seller, actively manage the property to increase net income well before sale, and then present the true figures accurately. Remember that a sale doesn't necessarily end your contact with the property, especially if the property was sold on an installment basis or you carried back any form of seller financing.

Last, and most obviously important, never allow yourself, as a seller, to get into the situation where you must sell. If so, all negotiating advantages tilt in favor of the buyer, and it will cost you dearly.

Know the "Kicker"

In the latter part of the 1970s, real estate was so hot that many investors made money regardless of how they bought, managed, or sold property. This may happen again in the late 1980s, but to invest on that basis is mere speculation, and your odds are as good (or bad) as gambling in Las Vegas.

To profit consistently in the tough investment climate of the 1980s, it's important to structure real estate investments so that the odds are in your favor. One good way to do this it to acquire a kicker that will pay off over and above any normal appreciation from inflation or an upturn in the real estate cycle. A *kicker* is anything that will add value to a property when you sell or rent it, but for which you don't have to pay full value when you purchase the property initially. A familiar example of an investment kicker in the past decade was the *condominium conversion potential* in many apartment buildings. When the concept was new, attractive apartment complexes could be purchased for their rental value only; but when converted to condos, they were worth 50 percent to 200 percent more. Of course, as the condominium conversion process became commonplace, the premium for such apartments became so great that the conversion feature as a kicker all but disappeared.

By finding the right kicker you benefit in two ways. First, there is the personal satisfaction of knowing you have searched and found what others did not have the vision to see. Second, the property will be enhanced in value to the extent that you are able to develop (or simply make known to others) the new, added, or alternative use for the property.

Finding the Kicker

The investor's task, therefore, is to discover the special value in a property that has been overlooked by others or to find a way of creating value in a property where it had not previously existed. Some of the special situations that investors in the 1980s should look for or try to create are:

- Condominium conversions—not just of apartments, but also of office buildings, mobile home parks, marinas, and parking garages.
- Rehabilitations of older or certified historic buildings where very favorable tax benefits and incentives are offered by the federal government.

- Distressed or foreclosed properties, which may be acquired at below-market prices.
- Properties with favorable financing at long-term fixed interest rates that can be passed on to a subsequent buyer, especially if interest rates rise.
- Properties that can be purchased with heavily discounted paper. For example, you buy a $100,000 mortgage note at a substantial discount and then find a seller of property who will accept the note at its face value for all or part of the purchase price of the property. The result—if the discount on the paper was 40 percent—is that you just purchased property for up to a 40 percent reduction in price.
- Resort-type properties that can be resold on a time-sharing or shared-ownership basis. With shared ownership, which is becoming popular in some parts of the country, investors own a piece of the whole operation and not just one unit for a few weeks a year as in time-sharing.
- Well-located and constructed HUD or other government-subsidized properties where rents are now controlled but where the government will, at a specific date in the future, allow private financing and freedom from all rent or other controls.
- Surplus schools, old warehouses, churches, and other buildings that can be converted to more valuable uses as apartments, office space, or miniwarehouses.
- Properties with unused land that can be made suitable for additional buildings or uses due to rezoning, sewer construction, or other factors.

Looking for special or changing values requires a degree of imagination and plain hard work, but investments without such pluses will probably do no better or worse than real estate in general. In the 1980s that may not be enough.

Know How to Negotiate

After much hard work, you finally find a property you want. You then analyze it thoroughly, compare it with similar properties, and decide how much it should be worth. Your actions up to this point have been logical and analytical—in short, an objective, professional appraisal of the property based on mathematical formulas, ratios, capitalization rates, internal rates of return, and so on. This is equally valid for all properties.

When you actually buy (or sell) the property, a new and unscientific element is introduced into the equation: the human factor. As two individuals, the buyer and seller, start talking, greed, suspicion, fear, pride, and all the other human emotions rise to the surface. More often than not, emotions dictate whether the purchase or sale will be made.

An Art

During this phase, the key to success is the ability to negotiate the human factor to one's advantage. For example, you determine during the negotiation process that the critical factor for the sellers is the price (perhaps so they can tell the neighbors how much profit they made on their house or other property). You might then offer to give them their price if you can get terms (interest rate, down payment, etc.) that more than make up for their asking price.

Successful negotiating is an art, not a science, and it can be learned and practiced in everyday life with business associates and friends. Whether it's a real estate deal or just hoping to talk a police officer out of a traffic ticket, practice the techniques of negotiating every chance you get. In addition to the suggestions below, books on various facets of the subject include: *You Can Negotiate Anything, Power Negotiating*, and *Winning through Intimidation*.[1]

Do's and Don'ts

The more you practice the art of negotiation, the better you'll get, and this can mean the difference between success and failure in your next deal. There are no absolute rules in negotiating because every buyer and seller is unique, but here are a few helpful tips:

- Learn all you can about the other party, and then establish a positive feeling or "body chemistry" with that person (or persons).
- Never argue personalities; instead, maintain a professional and friendly relationship.
- Accentuate the positive points and benefits in the negotiation; avoid or eliminate the negative.
- Find ways to meet the needs of all parties and seldom say no without offering an alternative approach.

---

[1]Herb Cohen, *You Can Negotiate Anything* (New York: Bantam Books, 1982); John Ilich, *Power Negotiating* (New York: Playboy Paperbacks, 1982); Robert Ringer, *Winning through Intimidation* (New York: Fawcett Book Group, 1979).

- Don't mislead the other party on even minor points; it's not ethical and can blow the whole deal.
- Don't be too greedy; leave something on the table for the other party, or they'll probably back out or cause problems even after agreeing to the deal.
- Practice patience. Henry Kissinger once wrote: "The side which is willing to outwait its opponent—which is less eager for a settlement— can tip the psychological balance."
- Learn when to speak, when to listen, and above all, when to stop talking once the other party has agreed to your deal.
- Last, remember that the most successful negotiation is the one in which both parties come out ahead.

Know Your Exposure

No matter how good an investment in real estate may be, (and I think it's one of the best), it's not perfect. Those who wish to be investors in real estate must educate themselves as to the risks that exist or that may occur. Don't expect the real estate broker to warn you of these perils— that's not how they make sales.

Risks to Avoid

Of the many dangers inherent in real estate investing, the following are the more common risks.

Property Is Illiquid.   The average person who thinks about purchasing real estate too often thinks only of the potential profit when the economy and prices go up. Alas, the economy can also recess, as all property investors have realized in the past few years. This is when real estate's illiquidity becomes an issue.

Face it. Real estate simply cannot be sold as fast or as easily as a stock or gold. If through fear or necessity you have to sell property quickly in a down market, you will be making money—for someone else. To protect yourself, remember that real estate moves in cycles, usually concurrent with major movements in the economy. Therefore, concentrate your purchases during the period the real estate cycle is bottoming out and starting back up. Restrict purchases during boom periods.

Since there is always the risk of a false bottom in the economy, it's wise to maintain a strong cash reserve to help see you through rough economic times or unexpected heavy expenditures, such as having to replace the roof when it should have lasted another five years.

Also, don't overleverage a property—for example, no cash down or only 10 to 15 percent down. Contrary to the popular book, "nothing down" is for crap shooters, and not all dice rollers are around for the next game. Putting at least 25 percent cash down at closing should, in sound properties, start you off with a positive cash flow. By maintaining a strong cash reserve as recommended, you will be in a relatively low-risk posture if the economy falters and in a very good position to leverage profit substantially when the economy does recover.

The Mortgage Comes Back to Bite.   Mortgages can be major risks if bought at the wrong point in the real estate cycle without adequate reserves or if property is purchased with a short-term balloon mortgage that one couldn't refinance in time. Regardless of the reason, the major concern is to avoid personal liability on that mortgage. For example, it's one thing to lose a $15,000 cash investment in a duplex. It is a totally different thing to also be liable for an $85,000 mortgage on the property. It's even worse for the larger investor whose mortgage is $1 million or more. Losing a down payment can make you bleed, but paying off a large mortgage in default may cause a hemorrhage so acute the financial fall could be permanent.

Property can and should be purchased on a *nonrecourse* basis; in other words, the lenders may foreclose and recover the property, but they cannot pursue you for any deficiency. Always include in a purchase offer a clause to the effect that recourse will be to the property *only* in case of default. If you offer a substantial cash down payment, the seller and lender are far more inclined to acquiesce to this condition. Also, now that a majority of all real estate investment purchases are made by syndicators, the sellers and lenders are more likely to agree to the nonrecourse provision because this is the way real estate syndicators buy properties. Syndicators do this for a technical reason: their limited partners can then add a proportionate share of the mortgage to their cost basis for tax-shelter purposes. It may even help in this regard to syndicate yourself. It takes only one general partner (you) and one limited partner (your spouse or child) to form a limited partnership.

Last, various states have laws that limit mortgage default actions to the property only. In California, for example, a purchaser who buys a fourplex or less has no personal liability on the mortgage. Similarly, some HUD-insured mortgages on subsidized housing limit the recourse of the lender to the property itself.

The Law or Tax Regulations Change. There can be no absolute protection against a community, state, or the federal government enacting laws adverse to real estate investors, but some preventive steps can be taken. Rent controls, for example, are normally enacted in university towns or in communities where tenants constitute 40 percent or more of the electorate. Therefore, risk-adverse investors often avoid the purchase of any residential rental properties in these areas. However, with little risk one can acquire commercial buildings in these same areas, such as office buildings, warehouses, and shopping centers. IBM, U.S. Steel, local attorneys, or other business tenants don't get the same sympathy from legislators, and thus the rent control threat to such investments is minimal.

Probably the most difficult action to protect against is a future change in the tax laws (which are currently favorable to real estate). As previously indicated, the 1984 tax act extended the depreciation schedule for income-producing real estate from 15 to 18 years. Prior to the Economic Recovery Tax Act of 1981, properties often had to be depreciated over a 25- to 50-year period. That's three different schedules in as many years.

One way to protect against such a risk is to buy before the law changes again (and it may have changed by the time this book is in print). The other protection method, which should be followed as a normal practice, is to buy real estate for economic reasons first, not for tax reasons. If the property makes sense as an investment without regard to its tax benefits, then the effect of adverse changes in the tax laws will have been minimized. Real estate is so well favored under the current tax laws that one must assume some of the benefits will be taken away. However, real estate will probably continue to be blessed more than any other form of investment because so many voters have a piece of the real estate pie.

The Neighborhood Changes. This risk of neighborhood change can easily be avoided. Unless you are a specialist in distressed and decaying areas, simply restrict investments to areas that are obviously improving (e.g., in the direction of good growth). Don't take unnecessary chances by buying in unstable areas; the return does not justify the risks in most instances, except for professional property improvers.

Diversify Out of Risk

Probably the most fundamental approach to reducing property risks is to simply limit the proportion of investments in real estate. A properly diversified portfolio should not have more than 25 to 30 percent of its investments in real estate (excluding the investor's home). This limitation should not be exceeded unless the investor is well experienced in real estate and has structured the remainder of his/her portfolio with a good percentage of liquid assets, such as Treasury bills or money market funds, to offset the illiquidity of the real estate portion. With such a balanced and diversified portfolio, one can protect and profit at the same time—truly the goal of low-risk investors.

Know Your Profits

Telling you to know your profits may seem superfluous. The typical real estate investor will say, "Show me a profit and I'll know it." However, profits can come in many forms if one just broadens the definition. Owning real estate, for example, can offer peace of mind for many investors because it can provide an inflation hedge, or retirement capital, or a job-loss security blanket.

Some owners of real estate find benefits in making their investments a family endeavor. They buy homes or small apartments, and then the entire family works together to paint, repair, maintain, keep records, and seek tenants or buyers. When the kids go away to college, the parents buy or trade for a small apartment building in the college town, which can be maintained and managed by the children. The parents then pay the children the going rate for such services, and thus some, or all, costs of college can become a *before-tax* cost to the parents. Also, the parents' expenses for traveling to inspect, oversee, and discuss their real estate investment with their children are tax deductible.

Other real estate investors carry this type of tax benefit (profit) even further. They buy investment property in whatever geographical area is of interest to them or their family—Hawaii, the Caribbean, a ski area, by a lake, or in the towns where their children, parents, or friends live. Then when the investor(s) travels to these areas, some, or all, of their expenses can be written off and shared with the government. Remember, if you are in the 50 percent tax bracket, the IRS is your 50/50 partner in most profits or expenses.

If management freedom is important, the investor can acquire buildings with strong long-term tenants under a triple-net lease whereby the tenant is responsible for all repairs, maintenance, taxes, or other problems. The investor's work can then be limited to depositing the lease payments—almost.

If you want profit in cash but don't want to pay taxes on it, simply refinance the mortgage on the property and pocket the cash, tax free. In fact, proper planning can make real estate the ultimate tax shelter. You can spend a lifetime investing in real estate without ever paying any ordinary income or capital gains tax on the dollars taken out of the properties by way of cash flow, refinancing, appreciation in values, or "sale." This all can be accomplished by steadily exchanging up for larger properties, thus avoiding any capital gains or other taxes that normally arise from a sale. If this pattern is continued until your death, the new tax basis for your beneficiaries will be the value of the properties at the time of death. This means that all capital gains (as well as recapture of any accelerated depreciation), which would normally be payable on the increase in value of the properties over the years, will have been forgiven. This savings could be worth thousands, or even millions, of dollars.

Of course, you don't have to wait for death to reap your profits! You can always sell some, or all, of your properties while alive and thus enjoy the full profits yourself. Assuming the properties have been held for at least one year, gains will be taxed at the maximum capital gains rate of 20 percent if no property exchange is involved.

It's Your Choice

As you look at the various "profits" that can be realized through real estate investments, review the first two tips in this series: Know yourself and know your goals. They are the keys that will permit you to truly know your profits, whether in the form of freedom from a nine-to-five job, security in your golden years, or simply tax sheltering your other income.

Fat, Dumb, and?

All too many real estate investors can be categorized as "misled" today. How so, you ask, if the market value of their investment property is going up with inflation (albeit slowly), their cash flow is increasing, and their tax benefits leave them among the very few still smiling on April 15 each year? The answer becomes evident if investors analyze their investments not on the basis of return on original investment, as is commonly done, but rather on the more revealing basis of return on equity. The return on original investment approach compares current returns (or cash flow) with the original investment. This really tells little about a property's current performance and seriously misleads the investor as to the best use of equity as potential investment capital.

Investment Example

To illustrate, assume that an investor purchased a $250,000 fourplex apartment seven years ago with a 20 percent down payment ($50,000). (Use of such high leverage in today's marketplace usually results in negative cash flow and undue risk.) His/her equity in the property at that time, therefore, was the $50,000 invested. Also assume, for simplicity, that (s)he obtained a 25-year mortgage at 10 percent interest for the balance of the purchase price. Finally, assume that in the first year of ownership, the units achieved a cash flow return of $5,000 and that, because of inflation and management, the investor experienced an appreciation rate of 10 percent per year for both cash flow return and property value for the five-year period to date.

As shown in Table 16–1, the investor's cash return would have increased from $5,000 to $7,320 during the five years. As a return on original investment, the annual cash return would have increased from 10 percent to 14.6 percent ($7,320 divided by $50,000).

Viewed only from the standpoint of a return on investment, this result appears to be fine. Actually, the investor's situation would have been deteriorating in terms of alternative or best usage of increased equity.

Return on Equity

Whereas the original investment is a static figure, equity is a constantly changing variable and should be viewed broadly as the amount of dollars or value an investor has available for any investment. The figures in Table 16–1 show that at the end of five years the value of the investor's equity would have grown even faster than the cash flow return. Using the new equity ($214,227) to compute current return as a percentage of current equity (instead of as a percentage of the original $50,000 invest-

TABLE 16-1
EXAMPLE OF RETURN ON INVESTMENT

End of Year	Property Value	Mortgage Balance*	Equity	Cash Return
0	$250,000	$200,000	$ 50,000	$ 0
1	275,000	198,200	76,800	5,000
2	302,500	196,000	106,500	5,500
3	332,750	193,800	138,950	6,050
4	366,025	191,200	174,825	6,655
5	402,627	188,400	214,227	7,320

*From standard mortgage-payment table.

ment), a dramatically different perspective is revealed, as shown in Table 16-2. Analyzed in this fashion, the results show that the investor would have obtained a very poor return on his/her investment equity.

Alternatives

If, after the five years, that investor were offered an investment property that required a 53 percent down payment, (s)he would probably decline by pointing out that the first property had been purchased with only a 20 percent down payment and that (s)he fully intended to invest only when similar leverage could be obtained to take maximum advantage of today's inflation. Yet, the actual equity in the example's fourplex represents the same 53 percent ($214,227 divided by $402,627) that would probably be scorned.

What would happen if the investor made an IRS Section 1031 tax-deferred exchange of the current $214,227 equity for a much larger apartment complex? Assuming $200,000 of such equity was applied as a conservative 33 percent down payment, the investor could own $600,000 of investment property. Assuming again the same initial 10 percent cash

TABLE 16-2
RETURN ON INVESTMENT VERSUS RETURN ON EQUITY

Year	Return on Original Investment (percent)	Return on Current Equity (percent)
1	10.0%	10.0%
2	11.0	7.2
3	12.1	5.7
4	13.3	4.8
5	14.6	4.2

flow return, the investor would be earning more than $20,000 per year versus $7,320 in the first example. Add to this the additional tax shelter and appreciation buildup on the new property's overall value (10 percent in one year equals nearly a one-third equity gain), and it becomes clear why the total equity in any investment property must be frequently evaluated. It must remain the best use of the investor's resources. In the final analysis, an investor's equity in any property is nothing more or less than an investment resource—to be managed properly or wasted.

An Interest-Free Loan from Uncle

One morning several years ago, John Freebie awoke to the tough reality that he wasn't going to achieve anything approaching financial independence on his salary alone, even though it had increased by one third in three years. The spurting cost of living and higher tax brackets he faced annually had cut his net gain to practically nothing. As Freebie reflected, it became obvious that what he needed was an investment return that exceeded inflation, was tax sheltered, and could be pursued part time.

A quick answer was real estate. It had generally appreciated faster than inflation and had definite tax advantages. How should he get started? His only real asset was his $30,000 home equity. The problem was how to convert it into a tax-sheltered investment. Freebie had several routes open, including three that are discussed here:

1. Sell his present home and buy another at an equal or higher price (to defer taxes on the profit) and making a minimal down payment on the second one to free up as much cash as possible for an income property purchase.
2. Refinance his present home, using the new cash to buy a second property for income production.
3. Find a tax-free (technically, tax-deferred) way in which to sell his present home, buy a lower-priced one (or rent), and use his remaining equity to finance the purchase of another investment property.

Using a concrete example clarifies the alternatives:

Present Value	Amount
Home	$100,000
Mortgage	70,000
Equity	30,000
Maximum mortgage	80,000

Under option 1 Freebie would be distinctly limited. He'd have to buy a second home at $100,000 or more, probably using $20,000, less closing costs, as a down payment on his new home. This would leave less than $10,000 free cash to buy an income property. Perhaps he'd get a condominium worth $50,000 as income property. He would then quickly discover he'd be paying high interest costs on his new home but getting little depreciation (shelter) from the income property. The total value of properties under this option would be $150,000 (if the new home had cost $100,000 even), of which only $50,000 would be depreciable (less land value), since only investment property, not personal residences, can be depreciated for tax purposes.

Option 2 is another way of accomplishing the same thing. In fact, it's the one that most beginners on the real estate ladder favor because it's the simplest. By refinancing the present home at $80,000 plus fees (or by taking a second mortgage), Freebie would again free nearly $10,000 from his $30,000 equity, thus providing the opportunity to buy the condominium to turn into rental property. Yet, he'd still be limited: The high interest costs on the refinancing could be prohibitive, and the tax-shelter potential would not be great because of the low value of the condo. The value of the properties and their depreciable portion would be exactly the same as under option 1 above.

Under option 3, more work would be required, but the results would be dramatically different. Freebie could immediately rent out his present home and, by so doing, qualify it as income property. If he then refinanced it for $80,000 (some lenders might offer only $75,000; a few might offer more), he would have put himself into an interesting situation. High refinancing costs could still be a problem; but, if they were overcome, he would have $20,000 equity in his rented home income property, which he could later use in acquiring a larger income property. Also, he would still have about $10,000 cash available to purchase a new residence, such as a $50,000 condominium.

Here, the tax law would be in his favor. Since his original home would then be income property, Freebie could downgrade to a less expensive home, such as the condominium, without tax liability. The cost of his original home would then become the cost basis of any later swap in income properties. As long as he continued to trade up with other investment properties, the tax due on any capital gain would be deferred under Section 1031 of the Internal Revenue Code. It's the key to this option.

Now, Freebie would be ready to take a final step. He would locate a real estate specialist in tax-deferred income property exchanges (swaps) and would offer the $20,000 equity in his rented home in exchange for a small duplex. The specialist could then locate an available duplex, and a tax-free exchange under Section 1031 could be worked out, perhaps by having Freebie take out a second mortgage on the duplex. If the duplex were valued at $150,000 in the deal, the numbers might be as depicted in Table 16–3.

Thus, Freebie could have turned his unfriendly Uncle Sam's tax restriction on primary residence downgrading into an interest-free loan equal to the capital gain taxes saved. Also, that loan would have continued to build up value indefinitely if he continued to trade up his investment properties. More simply, he could have significantly increased his use of leverage (borrowed money) to accomplish his purposes. After completion of the swap and purchase of his residence condominium, he would have had $200,000 worth of property potentially appreciating for him, plus depreciation write-offs on $150,000 worth of income property (less the income and land value), plus a deduction for the interest on his condominium residence. These are the fundamental reasons tax-exempt property exchanges are so widely used by knowledgeable investors in an inflationary climate.

Word of caution: The disinflationary period that began in 1980 has increased the risk of high leverage. The foregoing example will work in

TABLE 16–3
EXAMPLE OF OPTION 3

Item	Amount
Total duplex price	$150,000
Equity in rented home exchanged for duplex	20,000
Mortgage on duplex at 80 percent	120,000
Subtotal	140,000
Second mortgage required	10,000
Total	$150,000
Total mortgages	
Duplex (income property)	$130,000
Condo (residence)	40,000
Subtotal	170,000
Total equity	
Duplex	20,000
Condo	10,000
Subtotal	30,000
Total value of property	$200,000
Depreciable portion (value of duplex minus land value, e.g., $10,000)	$140,000

such a climate, but more care must be taken as to the amount of borrowing, adequate cash flow, and adequate reserves for staying power.

The Ins and Outs of Trading Properties

As we look at real estate and the 1970s inflation we find a fine perspective in the advice given by President George Washington in a letter to his stepson, J. P. Custis:

> Reflection must convince you of two things: first, that lands are of permanent value; that there is scarcely a possibility of their falling in price, but almost a certainty of their rising exceedingly in value; and secondly, that our paper currency has depreciated considerably, and that no human foresight can tell how low it may get.
>
> By parting from your lands, you give a certainty for an uncertainty. The advice I give you is not to convert the lands you now hold into cash faster than a certain prospect of vesting it in other lands more convenient requires of you.
>
> This will, in effect, exchange land for land, it being of no concern to you how much the money depreciates if you can get land of equal value to that you sell. It may be said that our money may receive a proper tone again. I shall only observe that this is a lottery. If it should happen, you have lost nothing. If it should not, you have saved your estate.

This was wise advice 200 years ago, and it is still so today as the dollar continues to depreciate (even if more slowly than a couple of years ago). However, the old-time solution of selling and then buying no longer makes sense in most instances because of the impact of the current U.S. tax structure. If Washington were to sell real estate today, he would have to pay a maximum 20 percent capital gains tax on the ostensible profit, whether it was due to good management, inflation, or the recapture of previous depreciation. As every investor knows, a dollar paid as taxes is a dollar lost.

Code 1031

To update Washington's advice is to add to his recommendation the use of the tax-deferral benefits noted earlier from section 1031 of the Internal Revenue Code. This IRS section permits the deferral of capital gains taxes where investment property is traded—not sold—for other investment property of a "like kind." Fortunately, the definition is broadly construed. For example, all of the following are considered "like kind": raw land, apartment houses, office buildings, shopping centers, a leasehold interest where the term is 30 years or more, and even mineral rights if certain conditions are met. Property that is not exchangeable under section 1031 includes personal residences (unless converted to rental units) and real estate owned and held by a broker for sale (stock in trade). Also, personal property exchanged for real property will not qualify for favorable tax treatment.

In calculating the possible tax effect of any exchange, consider the tax status of each party separately. The trade can therefore be tax-free (deferred) to one participant, taxable in full to another, and partially tax-free and partially taxable to other parties. What normally determines the tax consequences of a trade is the "boot" received or given. (Boot is anything of value that is transferred that doesn't qualify as "like kind" property. It can be cash, notes, stocks, bonds, or other forms of personal property.) Since the property values differ in most trades, a balancing of the equity of each participant through the transfer of boot is required.

A Trap

A trap for the unwary is that boot received does not have to be actual. It can be in what is known as "constructive receipt," such as in the form of relief from a mortgage. If your mortgage is assumed by the other party (unless offset by your assumption of that party's mortgage), such mortgage relief is considered boot and is treated as though you had received cash. The law provides that you will be taxed on a capital gain or net boot received, whichever is smaller. Beware of boot: Always have the full tax consequences calculated before you enter into any exchange.

There is a general rule of thumb for achieving a nontaxable exchange: Acquire property in trade with an equal or greater equity and a larger market value (sales price) than what you relinquish. Here are a couple of examples.

The Two-Party Exchange

Suppose John Freebie owned a duplex with a market value of $120,000, which he wanted to exchange for a 12-unit apartment owned by Jane Green valued at $350,000. Assume that Freebie's current mortgage balance on the duplex was $80,000, and thus his equity was

$40,000. In turn, assume that Green's 12-unit apartment had a mortgage of $290,000 and her equity was $60,000. A tabulation of the exchange would show:

Item	Freebie Duplex	Green Apartment
Market value	$120,000	$350,000
Mortgage	80,000	290,000
Equity	40,000	60,000
Equity difference	20,000	0

Since the equity has to be balanced for each party to be willing to trade, Freebie would balance the equities by giving boot to Green in the amount of $20,000. This is usually accomplished by having Freebie give Green $20,000 in cash or by having Green accept a second trust note or mortgage in payment. The net effect for Freebie would be that he could acquire a much more valuable piece of investment property through an exchange, without having to pay any capital gains tax at that time. Additionally, Freebie's new 12-unit apartment would provide substantially more tax-shelter benefits because of its greater value and thus increased depreciable basis. Any inflationary increase in property values would benefit Freebie on a multiplier basis. Used as a tax-free pyramiding device, trading up through exchange is probably the most effective estate-building technique available to the investor.

Now, suppose Green didn't want Freebie's duplex. What then? If exchanges were limited only to two individuals who wanted the property of the other, there would be few exchanges indeed. However, such is not the case, since there is no limit to the number of parties and pieces of property that can be involved in any given trade. Freebie and Green, or more specifically their brokers, would simply structure the trade so as to involve a third party.

Multiparty Exchanges

Using the previous example, suppose a buyer (Brown) was found for Freebie's duplex. Suppose further that Brown agreed to pay $40,000 down in cash and to assume the $80,000 mortgage. As part of the multiparty exchange agreement, Brown's $40,000 would then become part of the down payment (along with Freebie's $20,000 note) on Green's 12-unit apartment. The end result might be as shown in Table 16–4.

TABLE 16–4
EXAMPLE OF A MULTIPARTY EXCHANGE

Party	Item	Amount
Green (seller of 12-unit apartment)	Cash	$ 40,000
	Note	20,000
	Subtotal	$ 60,000
Brown (buyer of duplex)	Market value	$120,000
	Mortgage	80,000
	Equity	$ 40,000
Freebie (buyer of 12-unit apartment)	Market value	$350,000
	Mortgage	290,000
	Green note	20,000
	Equity	$ 40,000

In summary, there are several things to remember about property exchanges:

1. Property traded must be "like kind" property.
2. Internal Revenue Code Section 1031 merely defers taxes until the final disposal of your property or properties; but in the interim, the effect can be substantial.
3. Any property exchange should be structured and documented by a competent broker, lawyer, or accountant so that the IRS cannot claim it was really a sale—for example, of the duplex from Freebie to Brown and then a separate purchase by Freebie of Green's 12-unit apartment.
4. Multiparty exchanges are relatively easy to set up. So if you want to trade for a certain property, it doesn't really matter whether the owner wants your property or cash.
5. Watch out for constructive or actual receipt of boot in any form that could cause you unnecessary and undesirable tax consequences.

Starker Exchanges

When recession talk gets serious and interest rates have soared, the real estate crash idea is hauled out and promoted. It happened in 1974 and again in 1981–1982. Whatever the validity of the arguments, the thought that low-risk real estate investors should take a cautious approach is worth discussing. In this vein, the paramount question is how the low-risk investor can protect against, and profit from, whatever uncertainties lie ahead.

From the pure profit side, the worrier's approach is to sell real estate investments first and wait out the near term. If prices go down, (s)he will be in an excellent position to buy back into the market at a lower price and thus to be well postured to ride the next economic wave. The obvious disadvantage is that prices may not go down as inflation continues—recession or no recession—and therefore, some potential profit would be lost.

A second disadvantage of selling investment property is that the investor would be liable for a maximum 20 percent federal capital gains tax on the profit of the sale. The sale of such investment property on an installment basis would defer proportionately some of the capital gains tax, but if inflation continued or even accelerated, the installment sale would also be disadvantageous as the value of the dollar declined over the installment period. It thus may look like real estate worriers have no practical way to go.

The Starker Reality

Not so. On August 24, 1979, the U.S. Court of Appeals, Ninth Circuit, held for a taxpayer named Starker against the Internal Revenue Service in a landmark case of true significance to real estate investors: (*T. J. Starker v. United States*, 602 F 2d 1341, 1979). The decision could be most timely for current owners of investment property who are concerned with the vagaries of the real estate market over the next couple of years. The court held that an exchange of "like kind" investment property does not require a simultaneous exchange of title or beneficial ownership and that the possibility of receiving cash does not preclude the applicability of section 1031 of the Internal Revenue Code and its tax-deferral benefits. Income property investors know that section 1031 permits the deferral of capital gains taxes where investment property is exchanged for other investment property of a like kind.

The Facts

The importance of Starker requires a look at the facts of the case to permit a better understanding of its ramifications. On April 1, 1967, T. J. Starker and his son Bruce entered into a "land exchange agreement" with the Crown Zellerbach Corporation to convey 1,843 acres of timberland to Crown. In turn, Crown agreed to provide the Starkers with suitable real property within five years in exchange or to pay any outstanding balance in cash. A specific dollar "exchange value" was entered on the books of Crown to the credit of the Starkers. The Starkers deeded their land to Crown, and over the next two years they located property of the correct dollar value, which Crown then purchased and conveyed to the Starkers.

The Starkers paid no capital gains taxes, claiming they were entitled to deferment of such taxes because the transaction had been an exchange under section 1031 and not a sale, even though there was a time lag in the actual transfer of certain of the properties, and they could have received cash if property acceptable to them was not located within the five-year contract period. The IRS challenged this contention, and eventually two cases were tried: one involving the son's interest, which was decided by a lower District Court in 1975 in favor of the son and not appealed by the U.S. Government; and one involving the father, which was decided by the same lower District Court in 1977, but in favor of the government. The father, T. J. Starker, then appealed to the Ninth Circuit U.S. Court of Appeals (western United States), which reversed the lower District Court's decision. In both cases, therefore, the Starkers ultimately prevailed over the IRS on those issues discussed here.

Using Starker

The significance of Starker is directly related to a growing uncertainty in the real estate market and the opportunity presented by the decision to lock in today's prices legally without immediate tax consequences while awaiting more certainty in tomorrow's market. For example, if Starker's principles were applied by an investor who sold investment property anticipating a 1031 swap, and if a real estate price decline did occur, the investor would be in an ideal position to acquire new property at a reduced price, deferring capital gains taxes. If, on the other hand, prices did not go down, the investor could still select other investment property as rapidly as possible to close the transaction and still defer taxes. In this case, the investor would suffer some loss in price appreciation in the interim, but (s)he would be protected from a major drop in price. (After all, peace of mind should have some value.) Finally, the investor could have the option of taking cash at any time. Here, of course, the capital gains taxes would be applicable, and section 1031 would not.

The combination of hedges arising from Starker clearly should be intriguing to those concerned about any price declines in investment real estate. If any real decline becomes evident, this alternative will be even more interesting even though the 1984 tax act adjusts the time frames within which a Starker (nonsimultaneous) like-kind exchange can be made.

Under the new law, a Starker exchange must be completed within 180 days of the first property transfer or the due date of the taxpayer's tax return, whichever is later, in order to defer tax on any gain. Moreover, the property to be received as part of the exchange will have to be identified within 45 days of the first transfer. The IRS may have lost the court battle, but apparently not the war, here.

Warning

Because of the tax and other technicalities involved here, *investors should call on competent, professional assistance* before attempting to structure any section 1031 tax-deferral exchange, especially of the Starker variety.

Additionally, the Economic Recovery Tax Act of 1981 lessened and complicated the tax depreciation aspects of exchanging properties in providing for a new and more favorable 15-year depreciation schedule under the "Accelerated Cost Recovery System" (ACRS). (That was raised to 18 years in the 1984 act.) However, to prevent existing property owners from simply trading properties back and forth to become eligible for the shorter depreciation schedule, Congress adopted "antichurning" rules. To prevent such "churning," Congress effectively said, if an investor exchanges a property that was owned prior to 1981, ACRS cannot be used on the carried-over portion of the new property's basis.

What this means to you as an investor is that when you exchange, your basis in the new property is made up of three components:

1. Your basis in the old property.
2. Any cash you add.
3. Any additional debt you take on.

In a typical exchange deal, most of the basis in the new property is made up of the last two components. Under the new tax law, if you exchange a property you owned prior to 1981, you must continue to depreciate the carried-over basis (item 1 above) under the old and less beneficial depreciation system. The rest of the basis in the new property must be depreciated using ACRS. In essence, the antichurning provision of the new law creates a two-track system, which will be an accounting headache, since there will be two types of depreciation schedules on your tax return.

Notwithstanding the disadvantages cited, an investor still is advised to consider an exchange. Selling instead of exchanging means paying the capital gains tax, which reduces the amount of cash available as a down payment on another property. Normally, the less cash available, the smaller the property that can be purchased. In turn, the smaller property means less (1) depreciation, (2) potential appreciation, (3) cash flow, and (4) mortgage amortization. Thus exchanging can still pay off for the investor.[2]

Summary

The cardinal rules of low-risk real estate investing are to know:

1. Yourself.
2. Your goals.
3. The cycles.
4. The product.
5. The location.
6. How to buy, hold, and sell.
7. The kicker.
8. How to negotiate.
9. Your exposure.
10. Your profits.

To maximize profits, use the tax laws to get the greatest deductions and to defer taxes as long as possible. Knowing these laws and being familiar with recent tax cases (e.g., *Starker*), you can time buying, selling, and trading to the best effect.

---

[2]Other portions of the Revenue Code permit homeowners to sell their residences, to delay purchase of another for up to 24 months, and to defer taxes. Thus a low-risk approach similar to Starker is, and has been, available to homeowners.

Best Uses of Low-Risk Investing

*It requires a strong
constitution to withstand
repeated attacks
of prosperity.*

J. L. Basford

We've come a long way. We've progressed from an explanation of what money truly is to the practical use of risk for winning in the stock market and to tips for beating taxes. The following pages will remind you of what we've discussed and provide a series of specific steps low-risk investors can use to maximize profit potential.

A Recap

- Investors should focus on the value of money in terms of units of goods and services it buys, not on rising prices during an inflationary era. This leads to a correct view of how to beat inflation through *total* investment return, not just by price appreciation.
- This view also leads directly to a focus on the total return from multiple investments, not each investment singly. The latter often creates

309

an "investment stew" of mismatched or partially contradictory investment holdings. Organized multiple investments compose a *portfolio*.

- Many factors bear on portfolio creation. Among them are your age, temperament and risk tolerance, goals and specific needs, plus asset diversification requirements, and identification of those investments that optimize results on the road to less dependence on working income.

- In order to effectively organize these diverse factors and to bring to bear such concepts as the return you can reasonably expect to achieve and the adequacy of capital, the need for financial planning was addressed and a test for the degree of planning needed was given in Chapter 4.

- The points that must be considered in proper portfolio design include risk control through identification of types of risks and weighting of cash and growth investments. Proper cash management is important. We explained ways to accomplish it and a set out series of practical rules for establishing a proper portfolio, including organizing the various segments and assessing actual risk in your present portfolio.

- Cycles in the investment world range from business cycles to election cycles to the most useful of all, the money cycle. We saw how the money cycle can identify the most significant high- and low-risk periods in the stock market.

- Regarding insurance, protection against loss of one's earning power is one consideration, and protection against loss of money's earning power is a second. Targeting for investment returns on funds utilized for protection is essentially a misdirected concept, and effective use of capital will separate the two.

- Gold is both a protection and an investment asset. It has responded to several identifiable trends, and timing of purchases and sales on a sequence of those trends has caught all the major ups and downs of the gold market since the mid-1960s.

- The stock market came under close scrutiny both for the realistic rate of return investors can expect from it over time and for its interaction with the money cycle. The critical high-risk and low-risk periods in stocks, including the 1983–84 market, can be used to determine which types of stocks to buy and sell at each progressive stage of market development. How and when to use different categories of mutual funds in this risk-stage analysis was described. A glance at a current money cycle chart and a fresh chart of a stock market average at any time will show what degree of portfolio commitment to make to stocks and which type of stocks or funds to be buying or selling.

- The balance of the book dealt with specialized areas of investment knowledge on tax shelters, hedging concepts, opportunities in foreign markets and real estate investing, in addition to tips for beating taxes in our convoluted tax system.

To apply the preceding information, take the following action steps. (All investors, regardless of age or wealth, can apply these action steps with minimal modification.)

1. Recognize the high-risk nature of these financial times, and remember that regularly making high-risk investments can raise your total level of risk to dangerous levels. Low-risk investing, on the other hand, can produce high returns when market conditions are right, and it can protect the investor when they aren't. It can get you off the "win big, lose big" roller coaster.

2. After becoming familiar with the common ground described in the first three chapters, decide how much preinvestment planning you should do right now. Take any action necessary to set your goals clearly. Check Chapters 8 and 9 to make certain that your earning and asset-protection levels are adequate.

3. Determine from Chapter 4 exactly where you fit in the wealth stage sequence, which investments you should be emphasizing, and to what degree. Make a short list of those investment types you should be stressing now.

a. Since such retirement plans as IRAs and Keoghs can do some of the work in your portfolio, take those assets into account.

b. True tax shelters in the form of at-risk limited partnerships should be considered outside the portfolio. Other tax-related assets, such as municipal securities, are part of either cash-equivalent or growth portfolio segments.

4. Check Chapter 7 on portfolio design, and plan to invest funds now available, or when they become available, into the segments noted. The protection segment will be "filled" with gold when the market is right, per Chapter 9. The growth segment will be composed of those types of net worth growth and/or tax-related assets noted in point 3 above. The cash-equivalent segment will be made up of any cash assets you're accumulating plus cash equivalents you're using to balance the rest of the portfolio. (This is a good segment for IRA/Keogh plan assistance).

5. Next, write out the elements of your portfolio on paper. Use the financial plan you've developed and the percentages of assets recommended there to mesh with this portfolio design. It will perhaps take a

little rethinking, especially if you have already accumulated substantial assets, but it can be done.

One question that usually arises at this point is where to place any income real estate owned or contemplated. Such property is properly a tax-advantaged, growth and income asset and therefore cuts across the categories suggested here, which were designed primarily to cover securities. I suggest considering income property to be exportfolio and managing it outside the securities portfolio criteria. Take the property's tax, growth, and income qualities into account, however, when setting percentages in your portfolio. You might be able to reduce the percentage invested in one segment or another as a result.

6. Now you're ready to look at the current markets for new purchases or realignment of old ones. Chapters 5 and 6 on cycles, Chapter 9 on gold (its timing section), Chapter 10 on notes and bonds, Chapter 11 on equities are critical. It will also be worthwhile to recall the concepts in the hedging and foreign trades chapters, 13 and 14 respectively.

7. Decide the amount of capital to commit to the appropriate markets. Then list the current risk stage of each market (high risk or low risk) and begin the search for appropriate notes, stocks, or mutual funds to which to commit capital. Note which securities are immediately ready for purchase. Don't be concerned about those not ready; but put them on a watch list, and draw up a timetable for acquiring them.

8. If your investment stage requires tax planning, reread Chapter 12 and Chapter 15 before making any tax-related investments. Naturally, Chapter 16, on property, is recommended for investors invested in or considering this important investment area.

9. Now you're ready to work your plan.

This book has offered no formula to get rich quick. That's not because it's a bad idea—there's just no practical way to accomplish it. Over two decades of advising people about money, I've discovered that if investors are sensible enough to protect assets first, they can take smart risks when times are ripe for them and take smaller risks when times aren't. That's exactly what low-risk investing in these high-risk times is all about. If you'll follow the preceding ideas, you'll have enough time available to enjoy more meaningful things. Enjoying life and the pursuit of happiness is the best payoff from low-risk investing.

Index

M

McCracken, Paul, 58
Market cycles
  cycle inadequacies, 53–55
  and gold, 62
  Kondratieff Wave and, 49–50, 51–52, 54
  long and short cycles, 49–50, 51–52
  political influence on, 55–59, 61–63
  and reliability improvement, 49
  sample size and, 54
  types of, 47–49
Modified life insurance, 108
M1, M2, and M3, definitions of money,
    11–12
Monetary De-Control Act of 1980, 14
Money
  creation of, 13–16
  defined, 11–12, 14
  destruction of, 16–17
  and Federal Reserve Board, 11–12, 13–16
  and monetary seesaw, 17–19
  M1, M2, and M3, 11–12
  purchasing power of, 21–22
Money cycle; see Interest rate cycle
Money Cycle Index
  anticipating returns, 153–55
  and bonds, 142
  buying stocks, 161–64
  choosing stocks, 168–69
  delay in recognizing interest-rate trend
    changes, 156–58
  dividend yield, 182
  detailed applications, 158–68
  and equities, 151–90
  growth funds, 174–79
  high-risk signals, 159, 160, 162, 164–65
  *Individual Investor's Guide to No-Load
    Mutual Funds*, 178
  load versus no-load funds, 178–79
  low-risk signals, 159, 161, 162, 164–65
  and moving averages (MAs), 78–79,
    158–59
  overlooked stocks, 180–81
  quality versus speculative stocks, 179–80
  relationship to interest rates, 78
  risk adjustments, 187–90
  risk comparisons, 188–90
  signals during 1969–84, 81
  stages of investment, 170–74
  track record and financial ratios, 183–87
  and timing, 171–74
  two-tier market of 1970–73, 181
  use of, 75–78
Money inflation, 5
Money supply, and gold and inflation, 131,
    132
Moon, and market cycles, 48

Moore, Geoffrey, 132
Moving average (MA), 78–80, 158–59, 160,
    164, 165, 168, 171, 172, 173
Multiparty exchanges, in real estate, 303–4
Murphy, J. D., 130
Mutual and growth funds, and Money
    Cycle Index, 174–79

N

Naked option, 223
Net real rate of return, 42–44
Net worth growth, and financial planning,
    39–40, 44–46
Nixon, Richard M., 172–73

O

Oil and gas tax shelters, 207–12
Options
  on futures, 237–38
  gold, 123
  stock, 222–30
Overlooked stocks, 180–81

P

"Parable of the Rolls-Royce," 268
Portfolio balance, and risk, 92–93
Prices, and interest rates, 66–67
Puts, and stock options, 230

Q–R

Quality versus speculative stocks, 179–80
Reagan administration
  and money supply, 131
  and tax cut, 196
Real estate investment
  and Accelerated Cost Recovery System
    (ACRS), 307, 308
  buying, holding, and selling, 284–87
  changing aspects of, 275–76
  cycles in, 279–81
  and Economic Recovery Tax Act of 1981,
    307
  enhancing property value, 288–89
  and goals, 278–79
  and herd mentality, 281
  importance of knowing profits, 294
  importance of knowing property, 281–82
  importance of property location, 282–84
  multiparty property exchanges, 303–4
  options in investment, 298–301
  personal considerations, 277–78
  negotiating, tips on, 289–91
  and return on equity, 296–97
  and return on investment, 296, 297
  risk involved, 291–94
  and Section 1031, Internal Revenue
    Code, 301–2, 304, 306, 307